Comparative Employment Relations

Comparative Employment Relations

An Introduction

Jack Eaton

Polity

First published in 2000 by Polity Press in association with Blackwell Publishers Ltd

Reprinted 2000

Editorial office:
Polity Press
65 Bridge Street
Cambridge CB2 1UR, UK

Marketing and production:
Blackwell Publishers Ltd
108 Cowley Road
Oxford OX4 1JF, UK

Published in the USA by
Blackwell Publishers Inc.
350 Main Street
Malden, MA 02148, USA

A catalogue record for this book is available from the British Library.

Library of Congress Cataloging-in-Publication Data

Eaton, Jack.
    Comparative employment relations : an introduction / Jack Eaton.
        p.   cm.
    Includes bibliographical references and index.
    ISBN 0-7456-2292-5 — ISBN 0-7456-2293-3 (pbk.)
    1. Comparative industrial relations.   2. Industrial relations—Japan.
    3. International business enterprises—Employees—Legal status, laws, etc.
    I. Title.
    HD6971.E28 2000
    331—dc21
                                                                                    00-029127

Typeset in 10.5 on 12 pt Palatino
by Ace Filmsetting Ltd, Frome, Somerset
Printed in Great Britain by T.J. International, Padstow, Cornwall

This book is printed on acid-free paper.

Contents

Acknowledgements   vii

1   Overview: Convergence or Continuing Diversity of Industrial Relations Systems?   1

2   From the Fabulous East: The Japanese Origins of Human Resource Management and the Convergence Hypothesis   23

3   Japanese-style Employment Practices outside Japan   34

4   Trade Unions – in need of some International Solidarity?   45

5   Comparative Collective Bargaining   62

6   Training: Comparative Routes to Skill Formation   80

7   The Rules Governing Employment: A Comparative View   94

8   Comparative Labour Law – Individual Employment Rights   108

9   Collective Labour Law   124

10   Transnational Companies, Globalization and Industrial Relations   142

11   Minimum Standards in International Trade   164

12   Participation: Partnership or Teamworking for
     Productivity?   181

13   Conclusion: Prospects for Comparative Industrial
     Relations   197

References   209
Index   227

Acknowledgements

One author's name appears on the cover. However, in many ways this book has been a collective enterprise. I would like to express my appreciation to all those people who have taught me about employment relations over the past thirty years. In particular Colin Gill, from whose idea for a previous enterprise this book in a sense derives.

At Polity Press, Lynn Dunlop and Gill Motley have been most closely concerned with the project and have helped me to improve it; their *kaizen* was supportive.

Academic staff at the School of Management and Business Aberystwyth, though pressed to meet their own publishing targets, have been comradely. Jackie Carroll has borne the huge burden of trying to decipher my handwriting and improve my word-processed documents with a smile and a joke. She was well assisted by Linda Jones.

For permission to reproduce illustrative material thanks are due to Blackwell Publishers; Walter de Gruyter publishers; the *Akron Beacon Journal*; the *Guardian Media Group* and the *Observer*; the *Financial Times* and *Independent* newspapers. Every effort has been made to contact all copyright holders but if any have been inadvertently omitted, corrective action will be taken.

Finally, *errare est humanum*, so may the reader aspire to divinity where mistakes occur!

1

Overview: Convergence or Continuing Diversity of Industrial Relations Systems ?

Too many books on comparative industrial relations become overextended splurges, especially if they are multi-authored editions. It might be helpful to take a leaf out of the typical comparative law textbook and state that comparative industrial relations does not mean a comparison of different industrial relations systems *per se*. Rather, we are talking about the comparative method of analysis. Formerly, it could be said that the aim of comparative analysis was to promote wider understanding of industrial relations by demonstrating what was special about one type of national system or by qualifying what appeared to be special or distinctive national characteristics by showing that they also arose elsewhere.

This approach is probably untenable now on account of globalization. What would you say is the most vital theoretical concept in economics and one of its most discussed topics in practice? Competition, it is fair to say, is the lifeblood of economics. What would you say is the practical effect of competition on different national economies?

At its simplest, there are winners and losers. The mobility of finance capital and technological transfer will have outcomes. The losers will tend to copy the winners or lose even more heavily. There are international agencies that will advocate similar economic policies of flexible adjustment. Or, to the extent that there are self-equilibriating mechanisms in the world economy, correcting tendencies will emerge in the poorer economies that will make them resemble the more successful economies, although not in average living standards.

The conventional wisdom of the last few years has been that the more intense international competition for markets will inevitably lead to increased homogeneity of economies around the world. There is now clearly competition among organizations and among countries based on quality and especially cost of labour.

Most economists and policy makers have argued that, to contain labour costs, labour markets must be deregulated. Crudely, if labour costs are cut, the rate of profit will rise and that will attract firms to invest and employ more labour. However, such arguments depend on *ceteris paribus* and other things are usually very unequal. Nevertheless, the consequence of growing intensification of international competition is a pervasive decentralization of industrial relations from the national and industrial (industry-wide) level towards company- or organization-based arrangements.

Economic growth and labour

The message of the 1995 World Development Report: *Workers in an Integrating World* was clear. Economic growth is good for labour. Growth is good for labour because the evidence shows that in wealthier industrialized countries (and, in recent years in particular, also in east Asia) labour productivity and real wages rose. However, we have to ask at an early stage in our exploration of comparative industrial relations, which sorts of labour are able to benefit from economic growth?

It is fairly evident that not all categories of labour, even in the wealthier countries, were able to benefit. The work of Adrian Wood (1995) shows rather conclusively that unskilled workers in the wealthier countries would be hit by lower wages, more exacting working conditions and, frequently, unemployment, as their industries were threatened by imports from newly industrializing economies. Not only that but some labour markets are truly global in that services such as data-processing operations can be located by transnational companies anywhere that they can find suitable labour and stable social and political conditions. India is currently a favoured location as programmers are well trained and paid about a quarter of what they would have to be paid in Britain.

The World Development Report (WDR) authors were determined to be upbeat, putting the best possible gloss on the consequences of increasing international integration of trade, migration and capital flows. Though migration remains constrained, the labour market for many skills is now essentially global. Competition is fiercer because of greater opportunities to compete on world markets as a result of new technology and increasing mobility of capital. As Hazel Henderson (1993:34) has remarked, 'information has become money and money has become information'. Whoever enjoys or creates the right conditions will attract capital and have a rocky but prosperous ride on the roller coaster of global competition. It is unavoidable. We have to make the best of it. However, the WDR had to concede that the beneficial effects of globalization do not mean convergence in living standards. Globalization is not about catching up.

The 'industrial' view of industrial relations

Industrial relations is about the rules governing employment. Management is about control. Managers perceive employees in the first instance as a commodity to expand production. They purchase the presence of people and their declared willingness to work that must then be converted into effort. Control is either by compliance with the rules governing employment – that could be codified 'works rules' or company rules or management authority – or by enthusiastic commitment that renders the rules unnecessary.

Rules may be set unilaterally by management (see chapter 7), jointly by collective bargaining (chapter 5) or by co-determination (chapter 12), or, by legislation (chapters 8 and 9). There are other bases for rule, such as custom and practice and joint consultation but the latter is essentially a weak form of participation.

Industrial relations has traditionally been a nationally based subject of study. A seminal influence was the concept of industrial relations systems, generally attributed to John T. Dunlop (1958). An industrial relations system was essentially a sub-system of the national economy with its main protagonists – employers, unions and government – on the industrial relations stage and its own national web or framework of employment or industrial relations rules.

Dunlop was a labour economist and his approach (which continues to be influential) also considered the pressures and constraints from the wider economy via technology and competition in product markets on the industrial relations system. Such an approach can facilitate consideration of different national economic and political features. To what extent, for example, does a particular country utilize economic planning, intervention in the economy or, by contrast, deregulation of markets? There may be variations among countries that are apparently deregulationist; the UK, for example, was deregulationist from 1980 but that deregulation included tough intervention to weaken the trade unions. Other countries deregulated product markets but were unwilling or unable to act against trade unions.

In figure 1.1, *Deregulated* does not mean the complete absence of rules. Rather, that those rules derive from unilateral employer decision-making and prerogative and complete contract sovereignty. Collective bargaining would contain varying degrees of regulation, depending on the level at which it was exercised. There would, for instance, prima facie, be more regulation with industry-wide or multi-employer collective bargaining but relatively little where trade unions were denied recognition except insofar as they could represent employees in disciplinary and grievance procedures at the workplace level. *Regulated* includes collective bargaining but, at its most extreme, moves towards administered pay and conditions, as under centrally planned economies – the antithesis of liberal market economies. There are few examples among industrialized countries; even the People's Republic of China purports to be moving towards a social market economy.

Globalization: comparative industrial relations as a misnomer?

In comparative analyses of economies, the extent to which the practices of different countries converge or diverge over time has always been a focal point of study. Kerr et al. (1962) theorized that there was a universal drive towards industrialization and, consequently, convergence in employment practices. Their thesis maintains that, as technology – seen as the driving force of change – and industrialization become more uniformly applied, the countries involved will tend, over an extended period, to develop similar industrial features, including their industrial relations arrangements, practices and 'web of rules'. The more or less explicit technological determinism of the hypothesis left it vulnerable to attack and for twenty years it took a pounding. Some schools of thought, such as the Aix (France) school, were able to show that countries with similar industrial structures could have very different personnel management and industrial relations institutions at the workplace level. Comparative studies by Sorge and Warner (1980) on Britain and the then West Germany suggested that, although factories in different countries might be similar in terms of their size, technology and products, they could

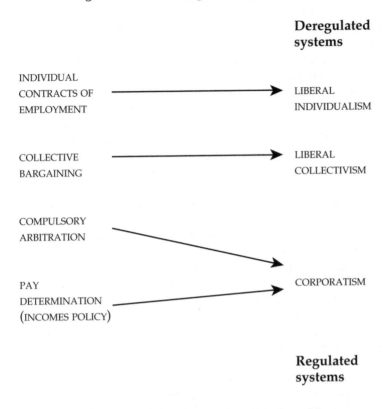

Figure 1.1 Industrial relations as a rule-making system

nevertheless come up with distinctly dissimilar forms of organization. It appeared that economic and technological change produced
divergent outcomes in different countries, either corporatist or free
market models. (Sorge & Streeck, 1988)

In any case, national policies involving labour and labour markets
were very different. Some countries operated incomes policies relatively successfully, others persisted with them despite disappoint-
ing results. Other countries avoided such interventionism. The
persistence of national policy differences form a big component of
comparative industrial relations. The national systems approach is
an important feature of such studies. Hypotheses are drawn from
peculiar conditions in one country that can be compared with and
tested against other bodies of experience. Therefore, one important
aim of comparative analysis is to promote wider understanding of,

and foster insights into, industrial relations, either by showing what is unique about one set of national arrangements or by reducing what might well appear to be specific and distinctive national characteristics by simply demonstrating their occurrence elsewhere.

At the turn of the century, there cannot be much doubt that this old-style comparative approach is obsolete, so much so that, strictly speaking, *comparative* industrial relations is a misnomer. Nevertheless, even in 1998, researchers were using the systems model to explore industrial relations transformations in Sweden, South Africa, New Zealand and the USA (Erickson and Kuruvilla, 1998:3). There are obviously continuing national differences in industrial relations but these mainly reflect economic development – or industrialization. In short, it seems that the authors of *Industrialism and Industrial Man* were right or would have been so if able to foresee globalizing capital and rapid international financial flows.

The industrial relations systems approach now looks the quaint province of those who envisage union-management relations as a pendulum. They see the present period of industrial relations – a period characterized by lessening union power in bargaining and in organizing – as similar to previous eras. They see current bargaining outcomes as not new and imply that they will be reversed. This cyclical point of view treats union–management relations as operating in a world of its own by classic power principles, played out by experienced practitioners of labour relations. If some of these old-time labour relations experts think about Human Resource Management (HRM) at all, it is as a union avoidance strategy. Some even interpret every move towards worker participation as motivated by a management desire to weaken and supplant unions – everything is part of the closed system power struggle between the two sides of industry. This view is no longer feasible. It is much better nowadays to think in terms of *international* industrial relations. Yet there remain powerful redoubts of national industrial relations practices, as was pointed out by Muller (1997) in a spirited corrective to the convergence idea.

The dominant paradigm for the study of industrial relations

There is scope for comparative analysis but the dominant paradigm nowadays is much more diffuse. It focuses on the pressures external to industrial relations. It perceives the management of human resources as driven by incentives that arise in the strategic choices facing the firm or organization. So, the management of HR is always propelled towards adaptation to new business conditions. This approach views the last twenty years as a period of major structural change in which the parties (employers and employees) have had to adapt in a far more competitive business environment.

Main types of structural change

As outlined by Van Liemt (1992), these are generally agreed to be:

- increasing internationalization of economic activity
- availability of more flexible production techniques, growing out of information technology
- shorter product cycles/ faster innovation
- increased importance of competitive advantage from quality
- a shift from manufacturing to service; blue collar to white
- changes in the composition, attitudes and education levels of the workforce.

Flexibility in Japan

'The flexibility of production and labour in Japan are frequently highlighted as essential components of that country's competitive advantage. Workers in the large Japanese companies display a great deal of flexibility in combination with employment security.' (Van Liemt, 1992) In the more open world environment, Van Liemt argued, workers and managers will find it difficult to resist the pressure to align their ways of organizing production (and the corresponding labour practices) with those of the most efficient producers – whoever and wherever they might be. Of course, Japan and the fast-growing Asian economies are now facing economic recession, partly because of their previous rapid growth. But, this does not change the fact that many changes in human resource management practices emanated from Japan's perceived competitive advantage in incremental process improvement.

Flexible specialization

Organization theorists have tried to depict these changes by referring to the pre-1980s paradigm (model) as mass production or

Fordism and have distinguished more recent approaches as 'flexible specialization' and, even more recently, 'lean production'. Sabel (1982) coined the term but most representations of flexible specialization drew on the Japanese flexible mass production system – called the 'Kanban' or 'Just-In-Time' production system. (Urabe, 1988) It was a product of incremental process improvement in which technical innovation was minor. At the time, this new integrated model of a flexible mass production management system guaranteed Japanese manufacturers an entrenched competitive advantage in terms of cost reductions and productivity improvement. The Japanese producers' competitive advantage may have been eroded by a rising exchange rate for yen but the methods that produced operational effectiveness continue to dominate.

In setting out his flexible specialization model, Urabe (1988) specifically criticized the cultural approach to comparative industrial relations. In this approach, a unique management system for each country is treated as a mixture of common technology and the unique culture of the country. For example, Morishima (1982) emphasized the Japanese version of Confucianism and group-oriented values as vital factors in Japan's economic performance.

Does flexible specialization exist?

Some industrial relations researchers, such as Anna Pollert (1988), doubted the actual existence of flexible specialization and pointed out that employers have always been interested in flexibility – on their terms. Williams et al. (1987) remarked that if flexible, it was nonetheless mass production and thereby contained similar authority relations.

Lean production

In the 1980s, in the UK in particular, the view gained ground that manufacturing did not matter and that an economy could exist on provision of service industries. The revival of interest in manufacturing in the USA and western Europe in the 1990s was everywhere accompanied by a search for international 'best practice'. This global convergence was partly a result of the internationalization of manufacturing, resulting in a global tendency to organizational similarity. For nearly all participants in this crusade, 'best practice' was synonymous with Japanese practice. The authors of *The Machine that Changed the World* (Womack et al., 1990) presented a study of Japanese superiority – in car production, at least. From this study of car manufacturing, they formulated the 'best practice' perspective in its extreme form. According to Womack and his co-authors, we had reached a virtual 'end of history' in industrial organization. Lean production is not only the most efficient way of designing and making cars, it will be the *only* way of producing in every manufacturing field.

Lean production – myth or reality?

Williams et al. (1992) argued that lean production is a myth. The difference between lean production and mass production is not empirically sustainable: Japanese motor firms are less vertically integrated; some Japanese companies (e.g. Honda) have a mediocre work-in-progress (Just-In-Time) turnround; and the value-added gap between Japanese motor firms and US motor firms is narrow. Moreover, the claim that lean producers build cars with 'half the human effort in the factory' is exaggerated. It is necessary to analyse how the Japanese take labour out and control labour costs. There is considerable evidence that the Japanese make cars by way of ever-more intense exploitation of working time, filling the gaps in the working day and eliminating slack.

Opinions about lean production

There is a wide variety of opinions about lean production and it could be said that this demonstrates the importance of comparative analysis in industrial relations. The system is based on 'trust and feelings of reciprocity' (Womack et al., 1990:112). However, Berggren (1993) has also contested the claims of the MIT researchers:

(a) lean production remains volume production;
(b) transplanting these productivity levels to other economies necessitates important deviations from the Japanese model in personnel management;
(c) job security and an egalitarian profile are required;
(d) lean production may also be 'mean' production in relentlessly eliminating slack, unlimited working hours and a rigorous factory regime.

Corroborating Berggren's second point, Wickens (1993), formerly the human resources manager at Nissan, Sunderland, has interpreted the process of *kaizen* [a Japanese concept, referring to changes in the production process and signifying continuous improvement in quality or reduction of inefficiency] as 'satisfying and constructive . . . if properly implemented'. His interpretation underlines the importance of comparative analysis when he remarks that 'the Germans are right when they say it should not simply be about efficiency or quality or be solely short-term results-oriented. The process is as important as the results. It must begin with the workforce and allow expressions of creativity and must also be concerned with safety and the working environment. Under no circumstances should any *kaizen* activity threaten employment.'

Wickens's view is a managerial one and sophisticated at that. However, it does not reflect reality in many companies where 'under the *kaizen* system, each operator or crew is responsible for an increasing number of machines: that is the inexorable logic of demanning with unchanged capital equipment. And, if assembly line work was more relaxed at Toyota Motors, that was not obviously so in the company's press shop which had to meet tough targets for manpower reduction' (Williams et al., 1992). A Toyota manager observed to Williams during his field research, 'if a manager cannot take labour costs out, what can he do?' (Williams et al., 1989:297).

By 1993, it was claimed that lean production methods had been adopted by virtually every leading industry in the USA, including motor vehicles, vehicle parts, steel, computers, consumer electronics and machine tools (Florida and Kenney, 1991).

Universality, convergence and comparative industrial relations

Critiques of universal prescriptions for best practice, such as lean production, show the continuing relevance of comparative analysis in industrial relations. Comparative analysis rubs against the possible universality or alignment of 'best practice':

> With the increase in global competition for jobs, first from China, now from Russia, Americans (and others) are hard pressed. Automation has cut jobs in banking and construction and all companies are being 'down-sized', 'right-sized' or 're-engineered'. In today's America, bosses boast about how many people they have fired, laid off, retired in advance of vested pensions, and how they have turned full-time staff into contract employees with no benefits at all.
>
> The blue collar workers and their unions are big losers. Trade

unions used to have countervailing power to get a fair deal, or more, for their members. The United Automobile Workers was rarely defeated or even forced to compromise. But no longer. President Clinton and others urged workers to keep competing: competition is the way forward in a world of low tariffs. Americans must grab the hi-tech jobs. But it's not happening. Edith Holleman, counsel for the House of Representatives' committee on science, space and technology, told a meeting of American technicians that, 'as international corporations move their facilities to cheaper locations, jobs in the field, such as product design, process engineering and software development are moving with them'. The key to protecting your job during downsizing is to keep your income low, refuse all raises and other forms of additional compensation. Also, if you are over 40, lie about it . . . the Cold War is over and the bosses won (Pringle, 1995).

What emerged in the USA during the 1990s was a new ruthless economy, a fiercer marketplace for labour that is ultimately turning every worker into a contractor, assessed and rewarded in the stark terms of what he or she adds to production and at what cost. When competition is intensified, individual employers who provide benefits when competitors don't are – *ceteris paribus* – operating at a competitive disadvantage. The labour market is a global one with real price competition in certain quarters. Nobody's job is safe. Labour standards, benefits packages and union agreements cover fewer workers each year. Lay-offs and contract employment also mean huge transfers of social cost from businesses to the taxpayer, as governments are left not only with higher social security and health costs but also rising payments for welfare and crime control.

Arguments against convergence of lean production

One argument may be derived from human resource management itself. In its 'hard' aspect of redundancies and downsizing, it does not look very attractive. So an important part of its discourse has to be about empowerment and participation – a possible source of comparisons. Rationalization and downsizing lead to a depressed and demoralized workforce. However, 'management does not seem especially worried about the decline in worker attitudes' (Cappelli, 1995:588) and why should managers worry when performance does not seem to be adversely affected?

One possible reason is that, in the long run, drastic moves to cut full-time employees contradict the human resource and human capital rhetoric that the only viable strategy for future prosperity is through a quality workforce. In a world where capital and production is increasingly portable, the only way to create and maintain high-paying jobs is through investment in and empowerment of the worker, through education, training and technology. A 'disposable workforce' suggests disinvestment in human capital and the breaking down of loyalty to companies – and therefore of incentives to 'work smart', innovate and compete (Black, 1993).

Industrial relations writers have long argued that human resources should be valued (by nations and by companies) as assets, rather than being conceptualized solely as costs. In a study published in September 1995, the World Bank proposed a method for valuing the wealth of nations that substantiated that proposition. According to this method of calculation, the fifteen richest countries in the world are: (1) Australia; (2) Canada; (3) Luxembourg; (4) Switzerland; (5) Japan; (6) Sweden; (7) Iceland; (8) Qatar; (9) United Arab Emirates; (10) Denmark; (11) Norway; (12) USA; (13) France; (14) Kuwait; (15) Germany.

Table 1.1 World Bank's 10 richest countries by latest measure (September 1995) ($ per capita)

| | | Sources of wealth (% of total) | | |
Global wealth	Est. wealth	Human	Produced	Natural
1. Australia	835,000	21	7	71
2. Canada	704,000	22	9	69
3. Luxembourg	658,000	83	12	4
4. Switzerland	647,000	78	19	3
5. Japan	565,000	81	18	2
6. Sweden	496,000	56	16	29
7. Iceland	486,000	23	16	61
8. Qatar	473,000	51	11	39
9. UAE	471,000	65	14	21
10. Denmark	463,000	76	17	7

Australia and Canada did so well in part because they are very rich in physical resources. However, Switzerland and Japan 'have modest natural capital but rank near the top because they invest more in human resources'. Most economists think of wealth mainly in terms of produced assets. Ismail Serageldin, vice-president for environmentally sustainable development and director of the World Bank wealth project, said that he was surprised to discover that such assets 'constitute only 20 per cent or less of the real wealth of most nations'. By contrast, human resources on average accounted for about two thirds of total wealth. The inference drawn by Serageldin is that investing in human resources is the most efficient way to promote development.

This viewpoint can be applied to companies. It accepts that intensified international competition necessitates restructuring: 'The aim of restructuring is to secure strong and defensible positions in the markets open to the enterprise in the face of changes in economic circumstances that have threatened its survival. The emphasis in new strategic theories is on the human factor as a durable source of development. Human resources are seen as the principal lever of economic success. They are less exposed than clients, products or technology to the pressures of competition. All this has resulted in a new approach based on the notion of the core activity.' (Piganiol, 1989).

However, the labour market *is* open to global competition. Enterprises may not wish to relocate in search of less expensive labour and they may not have to. Electronic technology allows many data processing tasks to be done at a distance. Non-core activities may be extensively sub-contracted locally. To the extent that numerical flexibility through short-term contracts, sub-contracting and distancing are practised, the much harder model of human resource management emerges.

Scope for policy differences

It follows that, given the severe constraint of intensified international competition and pressure from international financial markets, there remains scope for policy differences at national government and organization/company level. At the most basic, in practice complete labour market flexibility is difficult to achieve and implementation remains uneven.

As Jonathan Eyal (1996) has put it, 'while everyone extols the virtues of free trade, few are prepared to accept that this means losing a job because someone in China or Korea can produce the same goods cheaper; economic theories about comparative advantage may be fine for erudite academics but they are useless as a political platform'. Getting away with substituting part-time, short-term contracts for permanent jobs can only be done by stealth. This crucial problem has been avoided, rather than addressed, in the European Union 'and the start of monetary union will make matters worse. What would be the purpose of electing a national government if it could not decide on most financial matters? And how would, for example, Spanish workers react when they are dismissed from work because someone whose name they cannot even pronounce has decided in Frankfurt that their country's deficit is too large for their own good? No answer is provided.' (Eyal, 1996)

Flexibility arguments suggest that those countries with the highest growth of productivity will do better in increasing employment. However, internationally, there has been no correlation between the rate of economic growth and either the growth in employment or the average level of unemployment. Paul Ormerod (1994:149) pursued this issue:

> Existing macro-economic models, of whatever theoretical nuance and of whatever developed economy, contain a link between the level of output in an economy and the level of employment. According to these models, the faster output grows, the more rapidly employment grows. The more jobs that are created, the lower is unemployment. But, for any path of economic growth, on the basis of international experience over the past twenty years, the rate of unemployment is indeterminate. In other words, a wide range of unemployment rates appears to be compatible with any particular average rate of economic growth over time.

Perhaps this is the main reason for the demise of macro-economics, replaced by concentration on the labour market as the exclusive area for macro-economic analysis and policy response. In Britain all such problems have been seen through the prism of their effects on the incentive to individual performance and competitiveness. This view of the 'labour problem' was the main justification for the radical transformation of collective labour law that took place, step by step, in the years after 1980. By this means, and severe deflation, trade union power was curbed and workers' employment rights reduced. The comparison between Britain – as 'leader of the pack' on deregulation – and other European countries (especially France and Germany) is further elaborated in chapters 5 and 8.

Are comparative industrial relations still valid?

Deregulation and individualism in the UK contrasts starkly with economic policy in Germany. The German social market economy is a coherent whole, into which each of the parts – social policy (including vocational education and training), competition policy and labour law – fit. These parts cannot be easily separated, a lesson that is hard to swallow for current German liberals on the right who would like Germany to be subjected to a dose of Thatcherite deregulation. 'Attempts to deregulate the German system of employment protection resulted in the Employment Promotion Act 1985. Its main objective was to create ways of circumventing the unfair dismissal law [see chapter 8] by easing the use of fixed term contracts' (Rogowski, 1997:157). Yet, despite extensive hype by the government, over 90 per cent of private sector firms ignored the legislation, preferring internal workforce adjustment.

Similarly, Kathleen Thelen (1991) has argued that centralized collective bargaining in Germany had been resilient in the face of employer demands for flexibility precisely because of the two-tier system complemented by works councils (see chapter 5). Nevertheless, unions in Germany have been on the defensive and calls for deregulation and flexibility are incessant. According to research, increasing decentralization pressures within collective bargaining will undermine the fine-tuning of works councils and the process of collective bargaining.

Despite the latest recession having cost Germany some one million manufacturing jobs, it remains exceptional in that 25 per cent of employment continues to be in manufacturing. Even so, calls for deregulation have increased as – exacerbated by unification – unit wage cost increases accelerated beyond those of other western European countries, resulting in reduced competitiveness and a migration of German production to lower cost economies. A report of 1998 revealed that staff employed by German companies outside Germany rose by 13.5 per cent but troubles in the domestic economy and political uncertainties led to a 1.2 per cent drop in employees based in Germany by the same big companies.

Nevertheless, the deregulation arguments can be countered :

1   Real wage increases in many countries have fallen behind productivity growth since the mid-1980s and labour's share of value added has fallen but the labour market has been sluggish in clearing;
2   flexibility of wages is compatible with a variety of industrial relations systems and co-ordinated bargaining seems to be at least as effective as decentralization. The performance of the UK labour market has not been marvellous, despite the decline in union density and the decline of collective bargaining;

3   minimum wage laws appear to have only a slight negative employment effect, even where they are relatively high, as in France;

4   relatively high levels of unemployment benefit have only a modest impact on the duration of unemployment spells and cannot explain high levels of European unemployment;

5   employment security rules also have a modest effect and the main consequence of relaxing such rules in recent years has been to shift the structure of employment towards temporary and short-term contract jobs, rather than boosting overall employment.

Strategic choices in human resource management and industrial relations

As a subject of study, industrial relations has traditionally been considered at the national level. Necessarily so, since it is about the rules governing employment and, as Dunlop (1958) put it, that 'web of rules' was determined by national labour law, employer prerogatives and collective bargaining.

Rapid, almost instantaneous information transfer and financial flows unleashed globalization. Deregulation and incessant pressure for flexibility have not only weakened trade unions and collective bargaining but emasculated the nation state as an effective force in economic policy. Increased usage of the term 'human resource management' partly reflects the growing internationalism of economics and politics. The intensification of competitive pressures has resulted in 'a widespread, if uneven, decentralization as companies shift the locus of industrial relations regulation away from sector-level towards organization-based arrangements (Marginson, in Hyman and Ferner, 1994:17)

There does seem to be consensus that a new paradigm has emerged – one that is quite distinct from the old national systems of industrial relations. Not surprisingly, the precise parameters of this new paradigm are more difficult to delineate. Convergence, as ever, is a germane issue for comparative industrial relations, even though some writers think that it is played out. However, whether convergence seems to be heading towards flexible human resource management originating in the idea of lean production in Japan (Taira: 1996) seems worth debating.

The defining characteristic of human resource management is a perceived link with business strategy. Put simply, HRM is seen as

proactive and integrative, by contrast with older models of personnel management that were reactive and overly concerned with trade
unions and collective bargaining.

In the strongest form of the integrationist model of HRM, specialist personnel management is disarmed or merely advisory with responsibility for human resources integrated into line management.
Ultimately, there is little or no scope for trade unions because managers are proactively dealing with employee concerns and employees are normally working with enthusiasm and commitment. It is a
very unitary frame of reference that skates over the fundamental
problem of industrial relations 'under any economic system that separates those who perform work from those who control its performance. On the one hand, employers need pure contract in their relations
with labour, so that its effort and reward can be bound more closely
together; but they also want workers to co-operate like willing partners. For their part, workers do not want to give any more than they
are paid for but also want to be treated like reasonable human be-
ings' (Crouch, 1994:28).

Analysing strategy – as in business strategy – is far from straightforward. There are at least four perspectives, each of which has
implications for comparative industrial relations: planning, evolutionary, processual, and national or systemic. The most obvious is
associated with 'strategy as planning': 'Strategies are presented as
emerging from a conscious, rationalistic decision making process,
fully formulated, explicit and articulated, a set of orders for others
lower down the organization to carry out' (Legge, 1995:98). It does
not seem to be in keeping with the turbulence of current economics
but there may be sheltered sectors where it survives.

By contrast, the evolutionary perspective concentrates on the competitive processes of natural selection. 'The only real competitive
advantage is relative efficiency and close control of the transaction
costs of organising and co-ordinating' (Legge, 1995:99). It is the 'one
best way' or universal approach of exponents of lean production.
Enterprises that do not adopt lean production methods will not survive. It is all rather ex-post facto; we do not know the efficient enterprises until we survey those that have survived or flourished at the
end of a phase of economic activity.

The processual perspective on strategy rejects both rational strat-
egy-as-planning and market efficiency. Rather, enterprises are seen
as 'sticky, messy phenomena, from which strategies emerge with
much confusion and in small steps' (Whittington, 1993:22). In industrial relations terms, due attention is given to different interest groups

and power relationships in the enterprise, dissolving the unitary frame of reference of human resource management.

A fourth perspective on strategy relevant to the human resource management model is the systemic perspective – similar to the national system perspective. 'Embeddedness' is important. Strategy does not emerge *ex nihilo* but is shaped by the social system where it is embedded, by factors such as class and national culture. (Morishima, 1995:617) National culture is a broad term and usually requires further explanation. Indeed, Max Weber thought that explanations in terms of national culture were 'but an expression of ignorance'. In general, economists tend to believe that culture cannot be important when similar cultures perform differently in response to different incentives, as in North and South Korea and the former East and West Germany.

Nevertheless, culture can be an important starting point for discussing reasons for continuing differences in employment practices amid intensified competition and globalization. Human resources strategies involving international corporate mergers often stumble over divergences in national culture.

In short, the human resources model is acceptable in implying international exposure and the importance of attempted (not necessarily successful) management strategy. It leaves open the question of whether the human resources strategy is 'hard' (e.g. maximum numerical flexibility) or 'soft' (e.g. a psychological contract of commitment to employee development). This necessarily leads to further questions about power relations and how far human resource management is embedded in existing institutions, laws and, yes, culture. A model proposed by Goddard (1997) can be adapted to show the systemic factors that affect human resource strategy choices.

It seems that as industrial relations becomes more international, national economic policies and the nation state may have declined but strategic choices in HRM are not unconstrained. For example, Kuruvilla's analysis (1996) hypothesizes a close link between industrialization strategies and industrial relations systems. Import substitution strategies are accompanied by passive, pluralistic, paternalistic HRM/IR policies. However, export-oriented industrialization is accompanied by flexible and dynamic IR/HRM policies. In his recent edited study, *Globalization and Third World Trade Unions*, Henk Thomas treats this as palpably obvious. The oppression of labour organization was indeed an important part of the export-oriented industrialization strategy. Yet Third World labour and trade union studies 'need no longer be defended as a separate field of inquiry' (Thomas, 1995:20). Rather, the study of industrial relations in various countries remains important. 'The diversity of conditioning factors, whether of an economic, political or social nature, is so large that divergent labour systems, rather than convergence, are to be expected in the foreseeable future.' He says this, despite being very pessimistic about the considerable risk that organized labour may lose its historical national stature. Even in very intimidating conditions, workers continue to form unions – one indication, among many, of the continuing relevance of comparative industrial relations.

How this book is organized

In chapter 2, discussion of globalization is spearheaded by its effect on the changing patterns of the management of employment *inside* Japan. The convergence model is defended as a reasonable basis for beginning to analyse globalization. This and the following chapter show how the Japanese Human Resource Management model provided a Trojan horse for the rapid invasion of customary IR practices in other countries, beginning with the USA and facilitating a rapid recasting of their employment relations on lean production lines. There was, of course, no single clear-cut model of 'Japanese' management practices and any heuristic or archetypal model became even harder to delineate as Japanese inwardly investing enterprises adapted to local practices (as learning organizations must) and local firms emulated some 'Japanese' practices. There have been critical, as well as favourable studies of Japanese management overseas and this debate is introduced.

In chapter 4 the falling numbers of those unionized is discussed in relation to the intensification of international competition. A conceptual background of functions and structure is provided (and) it is submitted that previous attempts at international co-operation by unions in more propitious circumstances have failed; they are essentially local organizations rooted in the workplace. For broader focus, they need the oxygen of governmental and legal support for collective bargaining.

Collective bargaining's focus is rarely above the national level. Consequently, it continues to have distinctive contours, justifying a switch to a country-by-country approach, as seen in chapter 5. In Britain, the decentralization of employee relations proceeded faster,

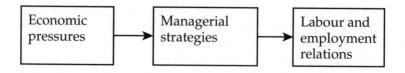

Model I : The conventional model

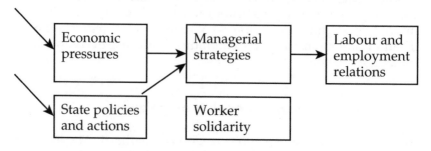

Model II (a) : An alternative model

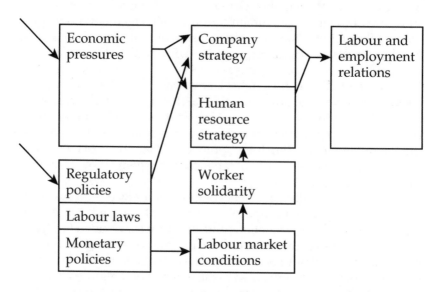

Model II(b) : An elaborated alternative model

Figure 1.2   Alternative Models (*adapted from Goddard, 1997*)

partly because trade unions had unwittingly helped to start the job with an emphasis on plant bargaining long before human resource management was invented.

The growing influence of corporate international management over employment relations is strongly proclaimed through the alleged human resource management emphasis on learning and staff development. In chapter 6 this claim is examined and found to be exaggerated. Sovereign governments, unsurprisingly, continue to want to exercise the main control over skill formation, though they may be influenced by 'corporate' views of how to promote enterprise and lifelong learning. Contrary to commercial organizations' current dislike of collective bargaining, collective organization of employees seems to help them carry out training and have a coherent view about education for work.

The second half of the book is mainly devoted to the continuing tension between globalization and competition that seeks out lowest unit costs and the institutions that are designed to maintain minimum standards of employment. They are, in a sense, protectionist and chapter 7 discusses industrial relations in terms of the rules governing employment that repudiate the treatment of labour as a commodity.

Despite the power of multinational corporations, strategic choices of human resource management are substantially embedded in national institutions, especially employment law. Discussion of employment law is divided into chapters in this book on individual and collective employment law. However, it is accepted that this is an artificial separation, as the individualization of employment can be effected by an attack on the institutions of collective bargaining, as has occurred in the UK.

Employment law is perhaps the main constraint on the international diffusion of employment practices by transnational companies. Despite its ubiquitousness in management parlance, strategy is problematic and never as straightforward as the rational, purposive model assumes. How much more likely, then, that international human resource management strategies may encounter dysfunctional decision-making and labour recalcitrance at the local level.

In countries with high living standards, this resistance may be supported by politically mandated social standards such as the EU social dimension, as is explored in chapter 11. Moreover, the information revolution cuts more than one way, informing articulate consumers about poor conditions in supplier countries and workers about exploitative conditions that may be termed unfair competition.

In chapter 12 the aim is to provide a consolidation of the main themes of globalization in tandem with the maintenance of acceptable local standards and conditions of work. It is sometimes claimed that, properly done, human resource management could become a substitute for unions and collective representation by means of empowerment and direct participation of workers. This is discussed in relation to traditional legislated and collectively bargained participation mechanisms, such as co-determination.

Question for discussion

'In every country, North and South, workers, employers and governments have both common and divergent interests, short term and long term. The divergent interests must be accommodated and reconciled. The way in which such interests are expressed and reconciled is the subject of industrial relations. It will of necessity vary from country to country. International comparisons must bring out and explain the differences and similarities of national industrial relations systems.'

Discuss in order to demonstrate convergence and divergence.

2

From the Fabulous East: The Japanese Origins of Human Resource Management and the Convergence Hypothesis

The convergence hypothesis that is pertinent to an introductory comparative book such as this one concerns institutional convergence in human resource management, as originally proposed by Kerr, Dunlop, Harbison and Myers (1962). They suggested that, as a result of worldwide industrialization, employment institutions and practices would become increasingly similar throughout the world. A decade later, Dore (1973) broke with convention when he examined reasons for the differences to be found in the employment systems of Britain and Japan. He did not follow the conventional interpretation suggested by Kerr and his colleagues – a move from backwardness to industrialization. Rather, he envisaged a different sort of convergence – towards the Japanese model.

Nevertheless, Dore's was still primarily an industrial relations systems approach to comparative industrial relations. In the previous chapter it was suggested that a new paradigm had emerged, associated with human resource management. In many ways, this human resource management model may be said to have been derived from Japanese management practices. As Japan developed into the most successful industrial economy during the 1980s, managers and national policy-makers in other countries were influenced to recommend emulation of the management practices of successful Japanese enterprises. There was so much discussion about the scope for repli-

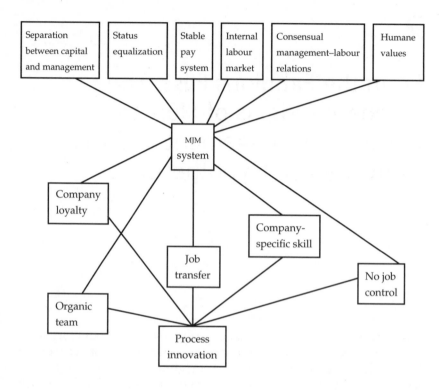

Figure 2.1   Modernized Japanese Management (MJM) System and Innovation – the basis for Lean Production (*Source*: Urabe, 1988)

cation of Japanese management practices that the word 'Japanization' began to be used.

The approach to comparative industrial relations analysis used in this book is resolutely thematic, rather than country by country. To have a second chapter on industrial relations in Japan does not contradict this approach. It is fair to say that the human resource management model, into which industrial relations has been transformed, is itself derived from a generalized model of Japanese human resource practices.

From flexible mass production to lean production

First, 'Japanese manufacturers attempted – successfully – to create flexibility within the mass production process . . . They built a flexible mass production system – called the Kanban or Just-In-Time production system' (Urabe, 1988). As this ensured Japanese manufacturers of a competitive advantage in cost reduction and product improvement, other manufacturers, including Ford, determined to emulate it. Later, the Japanese HRM/IR system 'evolved in parallel with technical change towards lean production and exhibits many features that may be taken as norms of HRM/IR systems compatible with lean production' (Taira, 1996:112). So this chapter is really about human resource management, as well as being about Japan. In the following chapter, discussion is broadened to human resource policies and practices in Japanese companies located outside Japan in order to explore their association with national culture or whether they can be successfully adapted.

In the opening chapter, it was suggested that the human resource management model needed to be refined by reference to four strategic perspectives. Concentrating on Japan enables us to refer to these perspectives at an early stage. The classical perspective of maximum profits is represented by Hiroyuki Odagiri's (1991) view that Japanese managers treat the firm as a collection of human resources. This does not mean that they are 'caring' managers, rather that the enterprise is best seen as maximizing the employees' interests, subject to a certain minimum level of the owners' (shareholders') interests.

Utilizing the evolutionary perspective on human resource strategy, with the rise of lean production in Japan, the direction and process of convergence in industrial relations practices have apparently been reversed towards the Japanese model. Womack et al. (1990) postulated that the lean production model of HRM would have to evolve in other countries as a result of international competition. According to Taira (1996:104), the American system of HRM and IR that used to be tightly integrated with mass production has been changing into a system compatible with lean production: 'What has now become very clear is the importance of a steady, benign (as against unpredictable, adversarial) climate of labour–management relations in which both sides strive to keep *kaizen*-ing. There is considerable evidence that this kind of HRM/IR system is possible in the United States.'

Taira also believes that Europe is endowed with the organizational and institutional infrastructure that can facilitate its change in the direction of lean production. Whilst not having countenanced lean production, Dore (1973) had long before tended to support a view of convergence towards Japan by other economies adopting similar human resource management practices.

Arguments against convergence – culture and the systemic perspective

The most obvious, if rather facile, argument against convergence or homogenization as a result of globalization is from national culture. The idea is that values and beliefs developed in particular countries are peculiar and inhibit transmission of management practices across countries. Michio Morishima, himself Japanese, proposed an entire hypothesis to this effect in his book *Why has Japan Succeeded?*(1982). Unusually for an economist, he stressed Japanese culture, particularly its specific form of Confucianism. In a claim that looks rather extreme now, Sethi et al. (1984) reckoned that the Japanese management system was essentially a response to Japanese culture. However, most Japanese economists and writers on management do not like the culture argument. Urabe (1988) points out that the cultural approach adheres to traditional, non-changing aspects of management, despite continuous change in management systems.

Viewed properly, the culture argument is only one facet of the systemic perspective on human resource management strategy. That is to say that human resource management is shaped by the social system – including culture – but also by law, institutional and sectional interest groups. A 'traditional' view of Japanese firms was pioneered by Abegglen (1958) who noted lifetime employment and seniority pay as features peculiar to Japan. The third of the 'sacred treasures' or pillars of Japanese industrial relations was enterprise unionism. Of course, it was recognized, even by Western writers, that the Japanese industrial relations system was not devised according to some abstract plan and then imposed on a compliant workforce. 'Rather, the main features of the system were introduced in response to specific problems' (Riddell, 1986).

Enterprise unionism

Comparative collective labour organization in trade unions will be discussed in chapter 4. Japanese trade unionism was legitimized in the labour law imposed by allied occupational forces in 1946. Unions were encouraged as a countervailing power to the *zaibatsu* or monopoly Japanese enterprises that had helped to promote military expansionism. However, the political climate changed with the start of the Cold War and in the early 1950s the US occupying forces helped Japanese companies such as Nissan to break strikes and the communist-influenced industrial unions (Cusumano,1985). The *zaibatsu* were modified into looser networks of producers, known as *keiretsu*.

Enterprise unions survived. Controversy continues about their independence. They are often depicted as weak and dominated by management. Local officials are often from management ranks (Kamata, 1984). To many observers it does seem very much as though the bargaining that does take place is hedged about with statistics upholding productivity and results in 'sweetheart contracts'. (A 'sweetheart contract' is a term of derision for an agreement about working conditions entered into by a company union and the employer.) There is certainly a very detailed information-sharing process linked to collective bargaining. According to Morishima (1991), this is a quid pro quo for union co-operation. The formerly ritualized bargaining round or *shunto* (spring offensive) seems to have been moribund for many years.

Lifetime employment

In the mid-1980s, British Steel sent a study group to Sumitomo Metal of Japan. In an unpublished report, 'Now for Something Completely Different', S. H. Best (1984) reckoned that the lifetime employment bond, although not sanctioned by statute or collective bargaining, was nevertheless a cornerstone of Sumitomo's and other companies' employment arrangements. Others had noted that, although applicable to only about 25 per cent of employees, it was sufficiently pervasive among larger enterprises to be counted as a norm of the system.

The whole approach was sophisticated and geared towards fully utilizing and improving the permanent labour force, from whom a corresponding commitment was expected. Consequently, the British Steel group noted how few holidays were actually taken by Sumitomo employees. Recruitment and selection were of critical importance (see also Bronfenbrenner, 1988) with firms normally drawing almost their entire regular workforce directly from schools and universities. The workers were therefore seen as a collection of human resources much like other high-cost capital items. To make the most of these resources, large Japanese firms provided continuous training and job rotation to endow employees with comprehensive knowledge and experience.

Seniority-based wages

The career commitment practice was coupled with the *nenko*, or seniority-based pay system, so that pay rose with the multiple skills and experience that could be expected to be acquired. Koike (1988) was among the first to point out to Western readers that seniority curves for wages are not applicable to the majority of Japanese workers; a persistently rising profile is confined to a minority. He believed that it is what he termed 'the white-collarization' of large companies' blue-collar males that should be seen as the special feature of Japanese workers. He further argued that the essence of white-collarization was the acquisition of wide-ranging skills and this, in turn, was the foundation of high labour morale in Japan. There was also an effect on the enterprise unions: the wide internal promotion system had spread to large companies' regular workers 'who had consequently taken on characteristics that basically resemble those of white collar workers and it is large companies' regular workers who have an important role in Japanese labour unions' (Koike, 1988:284).

Consultation to soothe bargaining tension

Some writers on Japanese companies used to propose the *ringi-sei* or consultation process as a fourth 'sacred treasure'. However, this idea is hard to accept. The *ringi* system implied that almost everyone in the organization has a part to play and all decisions must be the result of consensus. In reality, the decision had usually already been made at the top but top management initiated the *ringi-sei* to make employees feel that they had contributed. Nevertheless, Whyte (1987) argued that Japanese managers in the 1950s, looking for new ideas to help them rebuild industry, assumed that the participative styles advocated by American Human Relations theorists were actually being implemented by US companies and they therefore set out to reshape industrial relations along these lines.

Labour market segmentation

Norma Chalmers (1989) and Gill Palmer (1983) questioned the other sacred treasures, even while they were being proclaimed as the way to go. They asked how employers in large Japanese firms, operating with a fixed (lifetime) and increasingly costly labour force, could respond to market fluctuations and the need to cut labour costs. They concluded that labour market segmentation enabled superior conditions in the larger companies that sub-contracted component work to two tiers of supplier firms. The peripheral workforce in the sub-contractor firms performed a buffer role. This system of dual employment, supported by related subsidiaries, was an integral part of the 'lifetime employment' system.

One researcher had reported a similar approach in Italy (Paci, 1981:206). The proliferation of small enterprises was a specific feature of the Italian economy and true of no other advanced economy, except Japan. In subsequent years, however, as Western organizations began to copy Japan's management practices, many other economies developed segmented labour markets. As a result, Atkinson (1984) proposed a core-periphery model that 'clearly has some similarities to the Japanese employment system of permanent and temporary workers'. This started a debate about whether 'the search for increased flexibility in the use of human resources (was) a reflection of the adoption of Japanese methods of management, or Japanization' (Rollinson, 1993:25).

Unfavourable features of the Japanese employment system

Other writers and researchers began to report on less admirable features of employment in Japan. These included:

1   Significant limitations in Japan's Labour Standards Law (see chapters 7 and 8) in that it offered little preparation for part-time and temporary workers and did not properly regulate working hours and other working conditions for part-timers or temporary workers.

2   Considerable discrimination against female workers who comprised some 40 per cent of the workforce but were largely excluded from jobs that required in-house training and were crowded into

specific low-skill jobs. A limited Equal Opportunities Act had been established in 1985, requiring companies to make some effort towards fair employment practices but, in general, women's working lives remained restricted.

3   Growing complaints about dirty (*kitanai*), hard (*kitsui*) and dangerous (*kiken*) jobs (Berggren, 1993). Working hours were extremely long. It was reported in 1991 that 10,000 Japanese died annually of *karoshi* or overwork – a mixture of stress, long hours, obligatory team bonding with other workers and long commuting hours. In a landmark case that year, the Tokyo High Court ruled that workers could be victims of *karoshi*, even if the illness that eventually killed them was only partly the result of harsh working conditions. In general, however, the courts are rather hostile to individuals who try to sue companies for damages and the procedure for obtaining government compensation is cumbersome, long-winded and unlikely to succeed.

4   Training and lifetime employment opportunities in top firms depended on rigorous selection beginning in the fierce competition often referred to as examination hell – *shiken shigoku* – permeating down even to primary school and kindergarten level.

The end of Japanese-style employment?

During the 1990s, as the exchange rate of the yen appreciated, there were increasing reports of tensions in the Japanese employment system. Whittaker (1990) believed that the system now faced serious challenges in the form of a rapidly ageing workforce, the changing attitudes of young workers, rising numbers of female employees and technological change. It seemed possible that two of the three 'sacred treasures' or 'pillars' of Japanese employment – lifetime employment and *nenko* wages and promotion – were in for a period of reform. There was more multitrack employment; there was more group employment in the sense of workers being 'loaned' to other companies, such as subsidiaries; and there was increased job changing. Finally, adapting wage systems to better reflect ability and performance now featured strongly in human resource management in Japan.

Western admirers of Japanese manufacturing efficiency had tended to overlook inadequacies in company office bureaucracy. A significant number of office workers and managers were *madogiwa-zuko* (literally, window-side employees who had been sidelined), who must hang around trying to look busy, in return for job security under the lifetime employment practice. Japanese consumers thus indirectly subsidized low white-collar productivity through higher prices for goods and services – the concept of white-collar workers adding value to products had been absent. The high yen exchange rate now caused a restructuring and hollowing-out of the Japanese industrial base. Restructuring had to extend to management grades that some companies had allowed to spiral out of control during the 1980s. Methods chosen were necessarily rather different from those used by Western companies. While some Japanese companies announced sackings and early retirements, the public outcry was so voluble that other companies had to try to retain their existing white-collar staff while increasing efficiency.

By 1995 the situation could be summarized by a quotation from Toyoo Gyoten, chairman of the Bank of Japan and previously a respected civil servant: 'Definitely, the so-called lifetime employment system will not disappear immediately but it will become very weak. When I talk to business people, they all complain about introducing drastic measures, particularly in personnel policy, so it is difficult to bring about real substantive restructuring' (Rafferty, 22 April 1995).

Yet, in a profile of 'Mitsubishi's Company Man' in the same year, *The Economist* (9 December, 1995) remarked that 'Mitsubishi man has every reason to believe that, in his company at least, jobs for life will survive'.

Conclusion – industrial relations inside Japan

Japan is the only country that will be focused on in such depth in this book. The new human resource management model has been largely derived from a generalized model of Japanese human resource practices. There was convergence towards the Japanese model in the 1980s and Koike (1988) implies that Japanese industrial relations might have been in the vanguard at that stage.

Since then, the idea of Japan as a model for economic policy generally has collapsed because of the huge debt problems that have threatened Japanese banks and other financial institutions. During the 1990s, 'the effectiveness of many of the unique Japanese institutions that captivated social scientists and struck a mixture of fear and awe into the hearts and heads of people in industry, labour and government throughout the world declined precipitously'

(Asher, 1996:232). However, a discrepancy existed between Japanese industrial productivity and that of its competitors, mainly due to ease of production and the integrated work teams of Japanese manufacturing, developed in a system that valued loyalty and labour discipline.

To appreciate this properly we need to return to the systemic perspective on human resource management, taking account of the social system, law and institutions. Motohiro Morishima has examined this very effectively in an article entitled 'Embedding Human Resource Management in a social context' (1995). He argues that strategic choices made by employers in changing the system of human resource management are not of an unconstrained kind. Rather, they are choices made in historical context with constraints imposed by existing institutional factors. 'Japanese companies will need to find ways and means to restructure themselves in accordance with their past and present managerial and organizational idiosyncrasies. In other words, Japanese firms need Japanese-style *risutora* instead of a full-scale transfer of (reorganization) practices in use elsewhere' (Dirks, 1998: 90).

It was true that the four-factor model of Japanese employment practices based on (a) long term employment; (b) concomitant training; (c) employee involvement; and (d) seniority advancement had been affected by structural change. Japanese employers had introduced performance-related pay more directly. Nevertheless, Japanese employment security, according to Morishima, is firmly grounded in legal precedents set by the Japanese courts. Hence it was nearly impossible for employers to terminate or lay off their regular status employees without the employees' (or their union's) consent. In any case, employment security for regular employees is strongly supported by management norms, whilst employment security has been an explicit government policy. For Japanese unions, wage issues have always been secondary to employment security. 'In short, the traditional system values performance but such valuations are made in a social context of credentialism, consensual decision-making, distrust of individualism and veneration of loyalty' (Jacoby, 1995:646). It is impossible as yet to say how this will stand up to the increase in unemployment since 1997.

That Japanese human resource practices are embedded in a particular social system does not mean that some of them cannot be transplanted to other countries. At the start of this chapter, the point was made that the lean production model developed in Japan had figured strongly in a revised form of convergence – from Japan to the USA and Europe. The feasibility of transplanting Japanese human resource management practices – that was briefly called 'Japanization' – is examined in the next chapter.

Question for discussion

'The Japanese HRM/IR system has evolved in parallel with technical change towards lean production and exhibits many features that may be taken as norms of HRM/IR systems compatible with lean production' (Taira, 1996).

'To carry out *risutora* (restructuring), Japanese firms are experimenting with new HRM tools.'

Is it possible to reconcile these statements?

3

Japanese-style Employment Practices outside Japan

The feasibility of transplanting Japanese-style employment practices by Japanese companies investing directly in plant and establishments in other countries provides a fulcrum for evaluating the whole idea of convergence or divergence in comparative industrial relations. As discussed in the opening chapters, the Japanese model has been the main impulse behind the transformation of the approach of industrial relations towards human resource management. Essentially, the focus has shifted from scrutiny of national systems to investigation of company-level human resource management strategies that take place globally (Clark, 1995). In contrast with the model of Japanese-style employment inside Japan based on the 'sacred treasures', the main feature of Japanese management that has influenced human resource management, initially in Japanese overseas subsidiaries, and then in other companies, is quality and continuous improvement (*kaizen*).

The idea of mutual commitment by management and employees to organizational success has been gradually reinterpreted in a unitary frame of reference as pushing responsibility for quality down the line to employees at the point of production or point of contact with customers. Although HRM may still lack a genuinely strategic approach, there are few human resource managers or personnel managers who have not attempted to activate the empowerment of employees, at least as far as involvement in problem-solving, fault-finding and zero defects goes (Wickens, 1993). The argument of one very influential book was that Japanese lean production methods provided a new best practice that competitors would have to follow

(Berggren, 1993). It did not take long for lean production methods to be adopted by virtually every leading industry in the USA: autos, auto parts, steel, computers, consumer electronics and machine tools among them (Head, 1996).

A model of Japanese-style employment outside Japan

At the beginning of the 1990s, Wood (1991) claimed that terms to describe the Japanese model of management and its diffusion to other countries had proliferated. He concentrated on two – Toyotaism and Japanization. These, he argued, should be distinguished by restricting Toyotaism to the just-in-time (JIT) method of production management. The term 'Japanization' could then be used to refer to the evolution and diffusion of Japanese-style employment. He further argued that there was little evidence, with the exception of the Japanese Nissan (UK), of serious attempts to change systems of supervision, training, assessment and payment along the lines central to Japanese systems. It seemed premature, he concluded, to talk of Japanization of work systems and the concept of Toyotaism was limited.

Actually, Japanization is now obsolescent in application to work systems. The paradigm model contained so much that was derived from the old human relations school – trust, motivation, the importance of work groups and participation – that it always overlapped the ideal type of human resource management. Essentially, as previously expounded, so much of Japanese-style management is now conveyed by the HRM approach that Toyotaism (at any rate, as defined by Wood) is the only residue of distinctive Japanese style.

It can readily be agreed that many customs and practices are, necessarily, context-specific. It is not possible to further analysis, however, by recoiling just because 'everything is different' from one workplace to another. There is sufficient in common to proceed by noting dissimilarities and contrasts. Taylorism was often not carried out as F. W. Taylor might have recommended but sufficient was retained for a definite approach to be generalized.

Similarly, there is sufficient of Toyotaism in most Japanese production management styles for it to be a useful benchmark in comparative analysis. Almost invariably, case studies start with some implicit or explicit Japanese management model. The analysis then considers how local management practices have been modified and to what extent an intensified labour process has resulted. The overwhelming balance of the evidence shows that management practices have changed and work has intensified.

A good example is the work of Laurie Graham (1995). In a participant observation study of the Subaru-Isuzu Automotive (SIA) plant in the USA, she sets out what she calls the 'seven dimensions of control' that underscore 'the Japanese model'. They are (a) pre-employment selection; (b) orientation and training for new workers; (c) team concept; (d) *kaizen*; (e) top-down manipulation of organizational culture; (f) computerized production; (g) just-in-time (that Wood reckoned distinctive to Toyota).

A study of Japanese production management by Fisher (1994) shares at least five of these dimensions, though in somewhat different phraseology. He has (a) the team concept; (b) elimination of slack (*kaizen*, in effect); (c) work standardization (that would go hand-in-hand with computerized assembly; (d) ideology – or commitment to managerial goals – that parallels top-down shaping of culture; (e) flexibility that would encompass orientation and training.

Studies of Japanese management in Britain

Facetiously it may be said that, in general, recent studies of Japanese-style management in Britain boil down to three points of view – good, bad and indifferent. The 'good' or favourable studies tended to focus on Japanese revivals of under-performing British plant. The earliest example was Hitachi in south Wales. A second example, Rover's resuscitation by partnership with Honda, was no longer current after Rover's takeover by BMW. Previously, however, Rover management did learn a great deal from Honda. Re-engineered from top to bottom, the company transformed its design and production of cars and process management. HRM was fundamentally different as under the Rover 'New Deal': shop-floor workers received job security and career development opportunities in return for flexibility. A third positive example is ICL, owned 80 per cent by Fujitsu since 1990 and where the emphasis was on long-term human resource development and quality that might not have enabled an independent ICL to survive. ICL called itself 'an autonomous company within the Fujitsu federation of companies' (Caulkin, 1993). Nevertheless, Fujitsu's image as a 'flexible international family' took a knock when it announced closure of a semi-conductor plant in Durham due to over-capacity in global semiconductor manufacture in September 1998. Some UK-based Japanese companies have been hit by the failures of parent companies, themselves victims of the Asian financial crisis of 1998. For example, Showpla (UK), an injection-moulding company supplying components to the car industry, was forced into receivership following the failure of the Japanese parent company.

Japanese inward investment and management has been credited with reviving British performance in car manufacturing. Nissan's Sunderland plant is the most productive in Europe. The guiding principles of its human resource management were claimed to be 'quality, flexibility and teamwork' by its former human resource manager who commended the 'human' or participative aspect of *kaizen*. Even so, he had some reservations about it that are important for comparative industrial relations: 'The Germans are right when they say it should not simply be about efficiency or quality or be solely short term results-oriented. Under no circumstances should *kaizen* activity threaten employment' (Wickens, 1993:75).

Unfavourable studies of Japanese-style management

'Bad' or unfavourable studies envisage the Japanese companies as utilizing a socio-technical systems approach that enables a high degree of compliance with managerial control, rather than a high level of commitment from a willing workforce. They started with single union and 'no-strike' agreements to marginalize the trade unions and then instituted teamworking. The team concept attempted – often successfully – to use issues such as product quality, productivity and job rotation as a basis for integrating otherwise conflicting management-union objectives.

Garrahan and Stewart (1992) claimed to have cracked what they called the 'Nissan Enigma' by asserting that a process of incorporation through subordination was instituted by teamworking that stifled dissent. Just-in-Time and Total Quality Management regimes do devolve responsibilities to workers and team leaders but this was achieved by a discourse that masked coercive autonomy or responsibility without rights (Delbridge, Turnbull and Wilkinson, 1992:100). Teamworking became a 'neighbourhood watch' or peer group surveillance method. Electronic technology harnessed to such supervision enabled individual workers' productivity to be continually monitored and the shaming of below target performers by overt presentation of output and defect figures.

At a Japanese-owned plant making consumer electronic goods all assembly operators were made responsible for quality. A final electronic test on the completed product instantly identified any defect and traced it back to the individual responsible. An identifying mark was then positioned above the work station of that individual who would be taken to the final test area to check and rectify the whole batch if more than three mistakes were found. 'Quality and productivity performance information were sent to head office in Japan, with any improvements over current standards and norms incorporated in new standard times in updated assembly manuals' (Sewell and Wilkinson, 1992:285).

Moderate or indifferent studies of Japanese-style employment

'Moderate' or indifferent is used here to apply to studies where supposedly superior or more efficient Japanese management practices had encountered resistance or were found to be inappropriate to the local economy. There was, in other words, no 'goodness of fit' in the human resource management strategy.

Management at one Japanese company's British subsidiary, manufacturing automotive components, decided to experiment with U-shaped production lines. The Japanese philosophy was that the communication link among operators was better in the event of quality problems. However, it had the opposite effect by increasing gossiping. At an electronic office machine producers, the Japanese policy of recruiting school leavers foundered when the young workers' dislike of tight work discipline led to absenteeism and high turnover. At another company, the reluctance of workers to participate in zero defects groups presented challenges to the management (Palmer, 1996:135).

In general, however, it is hard to avoid the impression that Japanese management techniques have made competent performers of British managers and workers, once thought to be 'bad at manufacturing'. A film in the Channel 4 series *The Thatcher Audit* in the late 1980s dramatized this. It opened with footage of Wrexham women assembling Japanese electrical goods as the soundtrack by Mary Goldring commented: 'Simple operations. Simple factory. Basically very simple technology – even if it did cost £50 million. But things we don't make, never have made, gave up making, could not make cheaply enough – photocopiers, video-recorders, not to mention microwaves and televisions.' The camera then moved to a single shot of the local Lord Lieutenant in all his regalia bestowing the

Queen's Award for Industry on a delighted Sharp manager, high-lighting the discrepancy between the outdated pomp and ceremony of the UK and the fruits of Japan's progressive modern management practices.

Studies of Japanese-style management in the USA

Team-working as a pathway to management by stress in Japanese plants in the USA was noted by Parker and Slaughter (1988) who demonstrated that even minimal benefits attributed to teamworking, such as consultation and concern for employee welfare, vanished once initial production difficulties had been overcome. Although one reviewer reckoned that 'the practices reported by Graham at SIA are quite context-specific and do not appear in Japanese–US electrical companies' (Smith, 1996), Graham's description reminded another reviewer immediately of NUMMI, the joint GM–Toyota plant. 'The two plants have much in common: careful, time-consuming selection and training, a heavy emphasis on teamwork and cooperation, team organization, team meetings, just-in-time production, *kaizen*. In both plants a strenuous effort is made to indoctrinate employees to create a cooperative workforce willing to conform to company demands' (Strauss, 1996:183).

Graham made clear that Japanese companies use very thorough recruitment and selection techniques to ensure that they only take people who will fit in. Saltzman (1995) examined efforts by managers of a Japanese autoparts plant to avoid hiring potential labour union members but found only weak evidence that management overtly favoured anti-union job applicants in their selection procedures. However, the majority of Japanese supplier plant managers visited by Florida and Kenney (1991) stated that they were opposed to unionization and would 'vigorously combat organizing drives'.

In a section of a commentary on lean production where he acknowledged the high productivity of Japanese plants located in the USA, Berggren (1993) also counted meticulous screening and selection of personnel among the prerequisites. He referred to IQ tests, tests of manual dexterity and tests of ambition, initiative and adaptability. A fiercely achievement-oriented workforce resulted. This was also the case at the US Mazda plant where employees exulted in its high quality workforce.

Berggren also agrees with Graham about indoctrination or 'top-down manipulation of organizational culture'. The problem of production management is part way solved by insistence on the involvement of the total organization with everybody contributing. In fact there is much to admire in the methodical and systematic approach of Japanese-style management; at its best, it has a very methodical and systematic approach to finding defects and problems. In the case of Toyota/NUMMI, the term 'learning bureaucracy' has been used, to indicate how the predictability of the bureaucratic, formalized and proceduralized work process helped to facilitate organizational learning. Standardized work, for example, captured learning by codifying best practice and workers were encouraged to continuously improve on this best practice (Adler, 1993:111).

Comparative studies of Japanese-style management in other countries

The extent to which eight Japanese parent companies transferred HRM practices to their subsidiaries in Canada has been researched by Jain (1990). Three of them tried to introduce quality control circles but gave up in the face of worker antipathy. A possible explanation was that quality control circles are best suited to factory work, whereas, at the time, most Japanese subsidiaries in Canada were service firms.

More recently, Rinehart, Huxley and Robertson (1997) researched industrial relations in the context of lean production at CAMI, a joint venture between General Motors and Suzuki that manufactures cars at Ingersoll, Ontario. Their findings were very similar to those of Graham at Subaru. Both Graham and Rinehart and his co-authors emphasize the rigorous standardization of human time and motion that is a feature of lean production. Standardized operation processes show the best ways of performing every operation so that potential waste can be identified and *kaizen* facilitated. Most jobs are fragmented, standardized, short-cycled and repetitive, multi-tasked, not multi-skilled. Recruitment and selection procedures at Subaru and at CAMI were lengthy and meticulous. CAMI reported that it processed 43,000 applications to hire 1,200 employees. Much of the training in both plant had a definite ideological purpose of fostering worker commitment to the firm and its objectives; teamworking was of crucial importance. However, an important difference was that the workers at CAMI are members of Canadian Auto Workers Local 88, making it the only unionized auto transplant in Canada. Rinehart et al. show how union organization used health and safety issues and the contradictions inherent in *kaizen* to negotiate modifications of the lean staffing formula. They also point out that union organization reduced gendering of sub-cultures and issues, in contrast with Graham's study.

Jain's study of Japanese transplants (1990) also collected industrial relations data from subsidiaries of the same eight Japanese companies in Singapore, Malaysia and India. There were more similarities with parent company practices in Singapore than in Malaysia or India. Japanization of Singaporean management had been encouraged by government and supported by the National Trade Union Congress. Enterprise unionism and quality control circles had also been encouraged. In Malaysia and India, there were significant differences in training and industrial relations with Japanese-style practices. For quality improvement and participation, there was one exceptional case: Lakhanpal National Ltd., an Indian–Japanese joint venture. Here employees were willing to participate in early morning meetings and sing the Matsushita company song. They were grateful to Japanese managers who had helped to save the company from collapse by working long hours, re-equipping plant, providing on-the-job training and employee involvement. Otherwise, quality control circles were not popular and achieved scant success in Malaysia and India, according to Jain. From the limited evidence of Jain's survey, it might be concluded that workers' motivation for participating in quality control circles is mainly socio-cultural. However, Watanabe (1991: 57) reckoned that *kaizen* was difficult to transplant but that this may be due to misconceptions about workers' motivation for participation in quality circles – which he believed were economic, rather than socio-cultural.

The issue seems to be one of control, as in Palmer's research at 'Communico', where some operators participated willingly but others resisted involvement. 'The response of management (was) to re-educate, cajole or motivate reluctant staff into participation' (Palmer, 1996:138). Whatever spin you put on it, the practice of *kaizen*, or continuous improvement, seems to necessitate a dominated workforce offering its consent under duress. Labour discipline is tight – which is fine if you are not among those subjected to it. Even if you are, it may be better than being under-utilized and bored, as long as you are fit enough to take the strain of management-by-stress. In the past, however, a higher incidence of carpal tunnel syndrome (damage to nerves and hand and wrist tendons) appears to have occurred in such manufacturing plants. In her study of Subaru-Isuzu, Laurie

Graham thought that the workplace was unsafe, not because of hazards, but because of the work process itself.

Conclusion – Japanese human resource management outside Japan

In the mid-1950s, W. Edwards Deming gave a series of lectures in Japan that subsequently revolutionized the global economy. Deming insisted that the monotonous routine of the deskilled assembly line that garnered economies of scale by standardized production had to be reformed. Japanese managers learned from Deming that the future of the competitive firm lay in the full use of the workers' mental capacity. There were various routes but they usually necessitated multi-tasking, flexibility and teamworking.

Kanban and Deming transformed the Japanese production process, assisted by inter-firm networks *(keiretsu)*. Japanese firms subsequently developed a formidable competitive advantage in their ability to manage the acquisition and utilization of learning. Their superiority benefited Japan whose share of world exports doubled between 1965 and 1990. The rising exchange rate led to investment overseas and by 1989, 400 Japanese subsidiaries in Europe employed 50,000 workers.

There is now an extensive research literature on Japanese transplants. This is of great assistance to comparative industrial relations. Comparing similar plant and similar technologies may enable distinctive industrial relations practices to be identified. For instance, Rinehart et al.'s (1997) study of CAMI is very similar to Graham's study of Subaru-Isuzu. Both emphasize the rigorous standardization of human time and motion that is a feature of lean production. Despite Deming's undeniable influence, standardized operation shows the best methods of continuous improvement, perhaps because it fits in best with the idea of the 'learning bureaucracy'.

Converging on the Japanese model?

Dore (1973), Koike (1988) and Taira (1996) each wrote about human resource management practices in other countries converging on the Japanese model. Their theories can now be considered in relation to the numerous studies of Japanese-style management outside Japan. Despite constant rejoinders by reviewers that such practices are context-specific, they seem to have sufficient in common to signify some convergence. What they share is what some have called Toyotaism, though others rightly caution against the assumption that 'Toyota tenets' will be installed even in Toyota plants within and beyond Japan in a uniform fashion (Smith and Elger, 1994:89). The *sacred treasures* of industrial relations are hardly transplanted in their entirety. Indeed, study after study confirms that the Japanese subsidiaries tend to abide by local industrial relations law and practice. John Lie (1990:113) made a straightforward study of South Korea where it might be thought that management practice would be similar to that in Japan. He found no evidence of the sacred treasures.

It is not that the sacred treasures are lost in transplantation, rather that they become secularized treasures. There might be a certain commitment to job security but only for those who put their heart and soul (and sometimes their bodies too) into the company. Human resources management, if realistically defined in its performance management and total quality aspect, was 'made' in Japan. It means the effective utilization of human resources – and no waste. And why should we disagree with Yasuhiro Monden's description of the Toyota production system:

'It would probably not be overstating our case to say that this is another revolutionary production management system. It follows the Taylor system (scientific management) and the Ford system (mass assembly line) . . . more than likely another gigantic advance in production methods will not appear for some time to come' (Fisher, 1994:20).

Smith and Elger (1994) have cautioned against the assumption that 'Toyota tenets' will be installed in Toyota plants within and beyond Japan in uniform fashion. Of course, this is fair comment, particularly with respect to assuming similarities of approach in human resource management in other Japanese companies or in services, rather than manufacturing. For all that, there are similarities. A study of two Japanese bank subsidiaries located in London found that they utilized at least some aspects of the 'Japanese management system', if defined in terms of selection procedures, training and corporate culture (Evans, 1993).

Moreover, there are similarities across countries in the problems that arise from flaws in Japanese management practice. As the shine of the Japanese miracle began to be wiped after 1997, Japanese companies cut staff in their subsidiaries. In January 1997, a tribunal ruled that three men sacked by a Japanese financial information company were victims of racial discrimination. One had apparently been excluded from meetings held by Japanese executives and sacked without warning. Many such cases involve complaints about 'corporate culture'. Although often construed as positive, culture can conceal discrimination, such as the harassment cases that were brought against the company by female factory-floor workers at a Mitsubishi plant in Normal, Illinois, in 1994. Union organization might have compelled the management to mend its ways, as in the case of CAMI where gendering of industrial relations issues was definitely reduced. In the following chapter, the comparative approach is applied to unions and whether they have a continuing role in partnership with human resource management.

Question for discussion

'The Japanese human resource management system is successful but it is only possible in an industrial relations environment where there are hardly any limits on managerial prerogatives.' Discuss.

4

Trade Unions – in need of some International Solidarity?

Trade unions or labour unions are everywhere in decline (or, if not, finding it very difficult to grow). The reason for this is the intensification of international competition, especially in industries where trade unionism has traditionally been strong: textiles, steel, metalworking, shipbuilding, transport. If competition was perfect, trade unionism would not exist. As competition is very far from perfect, even if only theoretically, there is a place for unions. Furthermore, although economic theory predicts that competition and globalization will select more rigorously than ever the various economic institutions according to their efficiency (survival of the fittest), historical studies and international comparisons continue to indicate a more restrained perspective.

What is the nature of trade unions in industrialized societies? What functions do they perform in macro and micro perspectives? One possible answer would be to say that 'industrial relations is a social construction, exhibiting a strong historicity and a clear national flavour. Therefore unions differ drastically in their objectives and organization through time and space. Thus, it is possible to contemplate highly internationalized economies, along with contrasting traditions and trajectories for industrial relations and unions' (Boyer, 1995:555).

In this chapter we consider some of the differences in trade union objectives and organization. In addition, there are sections on union structure and government. Structure and government are also considered separately in relation to international trade unionism. Since trade unions in developing countries usually face even more severe difficulties in just surviving and securing basic legitimacy, they are also considered separately.

Generally speaking, 'trade unions do have the capacity to create a system of industrial jurisprudence at the workplace – enabling employees' rights to be enforced' (Deery, 1995). There is no avoiding the fact, however, that this capacity may, by its very nature, impose additional costs. Usually, therefore, it follows that trade unions need a minimum of governmental support, or, at least, the absence of governmental or state opposition.

Trade union objectives and methods

Back in 1894, Sidney and Beatrice Webb defined trade unions as continuous associations of wage earners with the purpose of maintaining or improving the conditions of their members' working lives. The original function of unions in the context of industrial relations was to improve wages and working conditions through workers' concerted action. Owing to the lack of bargaining power of individual workers in their relationship with employers, there was a need for combined action. The main difference now is that the term 'wage earners' sounds a bit archaic and many workers are employed by transnational companies.

We can therefore generalize about trade union objectives up to a point. Unions need some legitimacy and support in order to exercise their functions. If unions are outside the law of the land (i.e. the law of any sovereign state) and/or not recognized by employers for collective bargaining or representative purposes, they will be weak. They may perform an associational role of solidarity but their bargaining power will be, at best, fleeting. So continuity and stability will be hard to achieve.

Unions in developing countries are in this position. Even when national governments are sympathetic, they fear that economic costs will result from supporting trade unions who might exacerbate inflationary tendencies or assist opposition factions. When governments are dictatorial, unions face repression. Their leaders risk imprisonment, torture, perhaps murder. Their members may suffer similar fates or discrimination.

So, in general, unions need a minimum of legitimacy in order to gain bargaining rights or friendly society functions and maintain them. They need the same protection of the law for their finances and property that is afforded to other organizations. At this stage, however, unions may be purely voluntary bodies. It is if and when they acquire bargaining rights and the potential to impose costs on employers and society at large that the government, legislature and courts may seek to regulate their activities.

More than thirty years ago, Allan Flanders, a professor of Industrial Relations, seeking an answer to the question 'What are trade unions for?', suggested that their aims could be inferred from their daily activity. Then that was collective bargaining – which is hardly the case now, even in countries where unions remain relatively strong. It may well be that the absence of what Flanders perceived as the essence of collective bargaining – rule-making, regulation and job control – is the cause of their demise. Managers are not necessarily willing to cede control of decisions affecting productivity to trade unions or their representatives.

The union voice effect

It can be argued that, the greater the extent of trade union control, the greater is the incentive for management to oppose unionism. It has been claimed that US labour unions have bargained a bigger wage premium (compared to wages of similar non-union workers) and that this gave management a bigger profit incentive to oppose them (Blanchflower and Freeman, 1992). Unions provide a 'voice' effect in representing their members in pursuit of improved pay and conditions but, at the same time, management wants to 'shut up' the union (sometimes by shutting down the workplace).

This is a dilemma for supporters of trade unionism as a legitimate means of representing and defending workers' living standards. One answer is to say that raising the voice of employees forces management to make improvements in efficiency (Freeman and Medoff, 1984). However, some research casts doubt on this (Fitzroy and Kraft, 1985), even in its most favourable context – the German works council. A real problem in such research is controlling for quality, as one would expect the efficiency effect to be greater where there was more value added. One attempt to get round this by studying a fairly homogeneous commodity – timber production – estimated that union mills were 12–20 per cent less productive (Mitchell & Stone, 1992). A British study found no support for the 'voice' idea that unions cause a higher level of expenditure on research and development but nor was there much indication that unions retarded innovative activity (Addison and Wagner, 1994).

The social or welfare role of unions

In the absence of a 'voice' effect, the argument for trade unionism has to rely on the wider social role of unions. Even if unions can be shown to have negative labour market effects, there would still be reasons for promoting an environment where they would operate as instruments of democracy: 'Unions have many potential roles, not the least being to provide a sense of collective identity and labour security, as well as working class consciousness that can be translated into political agendas' (Standing, 1992:349).

A fairly crude initial sort of comparison can be made of 'business unionism' and welfare unionism. From one perspective, US unions have been primarily concerned with the narrow economic interests of their members, while Canadian unions have adopted a philosophy of social unionism, emphasizing political action to advance broader working-class interests. Among other things, Canadian unions tended to pursue social democratic political objectives and to follow strategies such as encouraging greater union participation by women and minority groups that resulted in greater union membership than in the USA (Kumar, 1993).

This sort of contrast may be broadened: 'Central to this view of social-movement unionism are union democracy and leadership accountability, membership activation and involvement, a commitment to union growth and recruitment, a vision and practice that reach beyond even an expanding union membership to other sectors and organizations of the working class. This view sees unions as taking an active role in the struggles against international and domestic capital and their neo-liberal political allies. It is not an attempt to shape national labour relations systems or make all unions have the same structure. While an industrial strategic approach is important, social-movement unionism can guide the actions of today's typical merged unions, as the case of the Canadian Auto Workers indicates' (Moody, 1997).

Traditionally, union behaviour in France appeared to be far more influenced by ideology than by factors such as economics, employer objectives and government policy (Bridgford, 1994). Workers' decisions to join the Israeli Federation of Labour – the Histadrut – can be partly explained by non-work benefits provided by the Histadrut (health insurance and legal aid, for example) and by the workers' social values (Haberfeld, 1995). In Denmark and the Netherlands, trade unions developed a role in administering unemployment benefit. This provides a secure support and legitimacy for their continuation. The collapse of union membership in Israel (table 4.1) can be mainly explained by the transfer of responsibility for the provision of health insurance to the state in January 1995. Union membership declined immediately.

Unions at turning point, says UN

Union membership has dropped sharply over the past decade in most countries, but the spread of democracy presents historic opportunities, according to the International Labour Office, an arm of the United Nations.

And despite an estimated 10 per cent drop in the number of trade unionists over the past decade, there has been no corresponding reduction in union influence, says the ILO's latest annual World Labour Report.

Duncan Campbell, a senior author of the report and adviser on industrial relations to 10 east Asian countries, argues that the 'globalisation' of trade and the increasing independence of individual enterprises, does not necessarily mean the destruction of trade unionism.

Mr Campbell says that while it is likely that some countries will continue to 'bid down' the wages and conditions of workers and unions would lose influence, most economies even in the Third World are realizing there is a limit to economic expansion fuelled by low costs and unsophisticated products.

There is also evidence that the so-called tiger economies in the Pacific Basin are contemplating some form of labour market regulation in order to cope with growing industrial unrest. That presented unions with a role, he believes.

Part of the explanation for a decline in unions – there are now 337 million members out of a non-agricultural workforce of 1.3 billion – was the removal of Communist governments in central and Eastern Europe where membership of 'unions' was compulsory.

Presenting the study in Geneva yesterday, Michel Hansenne, director-general of the ILO, said the results pointed to a 'turning point' in global industrial relations and that a decline in union membership told only part of the story.

He said: 'Where many observers . . . see only decline, I see increased democracy, greater pragmatism and freedom for millions of workers to form representative organizations to engage in collective bargaining with their employers.'

Barrie Clement,
Independent, 4 November 1997

Table 4.1   Trade union density in European countries, 1985–95

The ILO's 1997–98 World Labour Report contains statistics on trade union density (the percentage of wage and salary earners who are trade union members) in European countries. The figures for trade union density relate to 1995 and the percentage change figures relate to changes in trade union density in the ten-year period 1985–95.

Country	Density	Change
Austria	41.2%	-19.2%
Czech Republic	n/a	-44.3%
Denmark	80.1%	+2.3%
Finland	79.3%	+16.1%
France	9.1%	-37.2%
Germany	28.9%	-17.6%
Greece	24.3%	-33.8%
Hungary	60.0%	-25.3%
Iceland	83.3%	+6.3%
Israel	23.0%	-77.0%
Italy	44.1%	-7.4%
Malta	65.1%	+35.8%
Netherlands	25.6%	-11.0%
Norway	n/a	+3.6%
Poland	33.8%	-42.5%
Portugal	25.6%	-50.2%
Spain	18.6%	+62.1%
Sweden	91.1%	+8.7%
Switzerland	22.5%	-21.7%
UK	32.9%	-27.7%

Source: ILO; Geneva

Economic effects of trade unions

Many studies have confirmed that workers in unionized establishments in the USA earn substantially more than their non-union counterparts with similar skill and experience. American trade unions have achieved a relatively high wage premium in the short run. In the long run, however, this has given employers and managers a bigger profit incentive to oppose unions and drive them out to increase profits by reducing real wages (Blanchflower and Freeman, 1992, cited by Deery, 1995). There was an effect from union weakness – the male median wage fell every year in the 1990s until 1996.

It is rather hard to speak of a union/non-union differential in Israel where one union federation, the Histadrut, formerly negotiated pay for 80 per cent of the labour force – a unique occurrence.

Despite the fact that unions in Japan are mainly enterprise-based, they also operate at industry, sectoral, regional and national levels and perform most of the functions of industrial unions in other countries. However, the direct effects of unions on wages and benefits in Japan are currently very small; there was no difference in the cost of union labour relative to non-union labour. The *shunto* seems to be a thing of the past. Consequently, the enterprise union model that is typical of Japan has little impact. Unions tend to be servants of management power (Tsuru and Rebitzer, 1995).

Nevertheless, in a study of Japanese manufacturing enterprises (Benson, 1994), enterprise unions were found to be associated with significantly lower levels of profit and productivity and higher levels of capital intensity. These results challenge the conventional model of a dependent trade union movement of subservient company unions in Japan. Although incorporation in management affects some enterprise unions, other Japanese unions do appear to bargain successfully for higher pay from company profits. Nor did an earlier study (Brunello, 1992) support the view that unions in Japan are weak company unions that co-operate as willing slaves of management.

Do unions impede structural adjustment? A test case

The process of German unification and economic integration provides a test bed for the proposition that unions impede structural adjustment. In April 1991, I G Metall announced a collective agreement that wages in the former East Germany were to be raised to West German levels by 1994, with holidays and hours to be equalized from 1996. The employers' federation later announced that it would unilaterally abrogate the 1991 agreement – 'an unprecedented act that flouted the legally binding status of collective agreements' (Hyman, 1996:612).

However, after a perilous strike by I G Metall, the employers withdrew abrogation of the agreement. Nevertheless, the union conceded a delay in full wage equalization. 'This could be judged a success for the union – which was able to confirm the formal sanctity of agreements – but a failure for members since the employers' substantive demands were at least partly accepted' (Hyman, 1996).

In recent years, the rhetorical and political opposition to unions in many countries has rested largely on claims that they constitute obstructions to efficiency, impeding economic growth and structural adjustment, while being inflationary and job destructive, directly or indirectly (Standing, 1992:327). As might be expected in a historical period when real wages have been falling in most regions, the evidence does not support those who wish to oppose unions on economic grounds. Between 1973 and 1995, productivity of all non-farm workers in the USA rose by 25 per cent but real hourly earnings of production and non-supervisory workers fell by 12 per cent.

Anxieties of Third World governments about the impact of trade unions on fragile economies are understandable. However, economic studies about their impact are inconclusive. Some conclude that a union wage differential provides a profit incentive for managers to oppose unions. Others reckon that the slightness of this differential provides little incentive for workers to join unions. Taken together, such hypotheses suggest that unions just can't win. Yet, what other defence has the individual worker when the law and works rules favour the employer ?

Trade union structure

Structure in relation to unions has a special usage, meaning the coverage of unions in terms of general, industrial or occupational categories of worker. The most general national example may be the Israeli Histadrut trade union federation that formerly represented 80 per cent of the workforce. By contrast, unions in Japan are mostly enterprise-based, even though they also operate at industry, sectoral, regional and national levels.

General unions tended to originate with the need to provide as wide a coverage as possible of workers in transport and mass production who could be easily substituted. The British Transport and General Workers' Union, the Australian Workers' Union and the American Teamsters developed in this way. Mergers of unions in an attempt to increase collective strength and economize on resources resulted in even more 'general' unions, more akin to federations. For example, the Teamsters Union became more wide-ranging after merging with the United Auto Workers and the Machinists Union. In Britain, the AEEU (Amalgamated Engineering and Electrical Union) was created by a merger of the engineering workers union and the electrical union, themselves already hybrids. In some countries, for example, France, general unions are federations based on ideological or religious affiliations.

Apparently declining in importance as a classificatory basis for trade unions is the industrial union model where there is a union for all workers of the same sector of the economy. Germany, where sixteen industrial unions were set up in West Germany during post-Second World War reconstruction, probably remains the best example. In some countries there is one union for most public sector workers, a function provided in Britain by Unison and in France by Force Ouvriere.

Historically, craft and occupational unions are important in the development of trade union activity. Nowadays this category is most prominent for certain groups of professional or white-collar employees, such as teachers. The only comprehensive study of union mergers that transcends national borders has been produced by Gary Chaison (1996). Britain, Australia and New Zealand were reported as having experienced an increase in merger frequency that had not, at the time of writing, been seen in North America. However, the book tended to over-simplify by failing to distinguish between the absorption of small trade unions by larger unions (implying limited autonomy and representation in the larger union) and amalgamations of unions of roughly equal size.

Trade union government

How unions are organized and governed is of course closely related to their structure. Roughly speaking, smaller occupational unions may tend to be closer to members and to models of popular democracy. The larger the union, the more likely that representative democracy must be established to take account of dispersed and heterogenous membership. There may be a strong tendency to oligarchy, especially in relation to business unionism or where unions become an arm of the state.

The question of union government is bedevilled by terminology. Unionism is rooted in the workplace but the vitality of local and workplace representation varies. The relationship between the industrial unions and works councils in Germany seems to have been highly significant. Pressures for the decentralization of collective bargaining have been deflected onto the works council. The works council system and its linkage with industry-wide bargaining has endowed the German economy with a unique capacity for what

Thelen (1993) called 'negotiated adjustment'. Far from weakening unions, co-determination provides an institutional underpinning for a wide variety of union policies intervening in the organization and operation of the economy. Although works councils are formally autonomous and separate from unions, over 80 per cent of works councillors in Germany are members of DGB unions. Union dominance in works councils provides a crucial link between these legally supported bodies and the wider system of voluntary unionism in which they are embedded. This means that unions participate in adjustment in virtually all sectors of the economy. Even where union membership in a particular workplace is low, the works council is often composed of mainly union members. The works council system can offset low membership levels and encourages direct participation (see chapter 12).

Repression and tolerance of trade union activities

Is it better for the health and survival of unions that they are self-reliant, achieving recognition by recruitment, campaigning and bargaining power? Or, is some degree of public and/or legal support and tolerance from governments and employers necessary for their proper functioning? In general, it seems fair to say that the form and methods of trade unions will be influenced by the favourability of the legal framework that governs their activities. Trade unionism can and does exist despite repression and persecution but it is a shadowy and often transient activity with no way to protect funds and suffering from discontinuities in learning and education. At the other extreme, extensive legal support and legitimacy may provide excessive bargaining power and invite a reaction from government and employers.

Comparative analysis shows that union activity among and within independent nations varies considerably. It may be true that intensified international competition has weakened trade unionism generally. Within this, there are national variations depending on development, industry structure and, of course, the legal framework, among other things. Union decline is obviously linked with institutional variables. From a comparative study of the USA, UK, Germany and Sweden, Lowell Turner (1991) concluded that in some countries, for example Germany and Sweden, unions have retained importance despite pressure from economic competition and the introduction of new technology. However, union organization declined in those countries where the institutional environment allowed management to circumvent or radically amend the existing industrial relations system. The important influence of the legal framework as a factor in a systemic perspective on human resource management strategy is considered in chapters 8 and 9.

Anti-union activity by employers

The Commission on the Future of Worker–Management Relations in the USA showed that, in general, American employers are willing to engage in almost any form of legal or illegal action to create or maintain a union-free environment. Evidence shows that a majority of employees believes that companies are willing to harass, intimidate or fire employees who openly stand up for a union. There are also more clandestine schemes to defeat unions. In a case reported in 1997, union-busting managers at a Florida subsidiary of Coca-Cola were accused of recruiting *agents provocateurs* to break a union-organizing campaign.

US companies have developed a sophisticated array of techniques to browbeat low-paid insecure workforces in recognition ballots. In theory, many of such tactics are an unfair industrial practice and the unions could formerly call upon the National Labor Relations Board to assist them in securing recognition. Corporate lawyers and consultants devised tactics that used the same body of labour law to tangle unions in a mesh of rules, regulations and procedures. American unions have tried several times without success to obtain reforms in the law to gain more protection for organizing campaigns. The conservatives in the Senate are in a strong position to frustrate such moves.

The question arises then, whether unions benefit or not from state support. Despite strong arguments that unions ultimately pay for state support (Goldfield, 1987), in general it would appear that continuous trade unionism needs a degree of state support (Deery, 1995), if only to restrain the more rapacious employers.

Public sector v. private sector

An important source of support for trade union membership is the public sector. Public sector and private sector unionism are subject to different forces and have separate origins and life cycles. Market

The Coke driver and the Ruby Tuesday bribe

Union-busting executives at a Florida subsidiary of Coca-Cola Enterprises have been accused of recruiting *agents provocateurs* to break a trade union organization campaign.

According to federal prosecutors, the vice-president of the Atlanta bottling operation, James Wardlaw, secretly met a truck driver at Ruby Tuesday's, a downmarket suburban restaurant, and agreed to pay him $10,000 to persuade fellow workers to vote against union representation in 1994. The Bakers, Confectionery and Tobacco workers' union lost the subsequent poll but the driver confessed to the authorities.

Mr Wardlaw and branch manager Eric Turpin have each been charged on five counts of conspiracy and bribery, after passing the cash to Jeffrey Wright at shops and bars.

Police claim that on one occasion, after a clandestine transfer of cash in a grocery store, Mr Wright realized the episode had been videotaped and bribed the manager to hand over the cassette. With the Labour Party committed to US-style ballots for a legal right to union recognition, such dirty tricks campaigns by anti-union managements could become common in Britain.

The American labour movement is conducting an aggressive campaign, using young politically-committed activists to recruit in the workplace to stem declining union membership. Only one in seven US workers is in a union, compared to a third in the UK.

Coca-Cola Enterprises, the worldwide bottling operation in which the drinks manufacturer has a majority holding and which owns the Atlanta Coca-Cola Bottling Company, is 'extremely disappointed and deeply distressed' at the indictments. The two men have been given paid leave to mount their defence. If found guilty, the pair face fines of up to $300,000 and up to 25 years behind bars.

But the scheme to foment opposition to trade unions – which also involved promoting Mr Wright from driver to sales representative and giving him a $2,500 pay rise – is simply a high-profile version of everyday attempts by managers in the US to subvert laws allowing collective representation if the majority of workers want it, according to union activists.

Richard Thomas, *Guardian*,
17 March 1997

forces that have undermined private sector unionism across countries are virtually inconspicuous as a determinant of trends in the public sector. Public industrial relations policy has been neutralized by markets in the private sector but it continues to have an effect in the growth and stability of public sector unionism. For those who perceive elements of monopoly in public sector unionism, therefore, privatization appears the best remedy.

Hence, although falling by 75 per cent in density since 1985, unionism remains important in Israel on account of the Histadrut that has more than 2.5 million members in its forty-two affiliated unions, representing 80 per cent of the labour force. There is evidence that Israeli workers' decision to join the Histadrut can be explained in part by non-work benefits of the Histadrut (health insurance and legal aid, for example) and by the workers' social values (Haberfeld, 1995:656). Denmark and Sweden have maintained high levels of trade union membership. This is on account of public sector employment but also because unions in Denmark and Sweden form part of the apparatus for administering unemployment insurance and labour exchanges.

Recorded union membership in France is low and 'the picture of overall union decline in the face of a growing labour force is unmistakeable' (Jeffreys, 1996:515). Nevertheless, in France, 'non-unionism should not be confused with anti-unionism and the greater the presence the unions have, the larger the audience for election slates and calls to action is likely to be' (Jeffreys:516). Furthermore, it is impossible to overlook the observation that union influence and presence has been sustained most strongly in the public sector in France:

> The fact that the nationalized industries and public transport are both counted statistically within the market sector, and, that these two groups make up a high proportion of market sector strikes, means that the strike propensity of the publicly-funded sector is even greater than the figures suggest. If strike action were likely to recur in France on any scale, it should therefore surprise no-one that it would do so in the publicly-funded sector. (Jeffreys, 1996:521)

Industrial conflict and unions

Governmental policy towards industrial conflict is a vital signifier of tolerance of union activity. Unions hold in reserve, as an ultimate resource in collective bargaining, the ability to call upon their members to withdraw their labour. In situations such as the Israeli Histadrut this is problematic. There is a very delicate issue of how to manage workers when a Histadrut workplace is suffering a strike as the union is really on strike against itself. Strike action is also contentious for public sector unionism. This is not only because such strikes may be in essential services – transport, health, education, policing and prisons. It is also because the union is using coercion to try to increase the public resources expended in a particular part of the public sector. This may lead to animosity from other workers and claims that certain public sector staff are overpaid and underworked, as was the case, for instance, with Iberia Airways in 1996 (Eaton, 1996:45).

National governments are usually in a position to amend the framework of law governing trade union activity. They may choose to do so, particularly in order to control trade union bargaining power and ability to engage in overt industrial conflict, especially through strikes. During the 1980s, successive UK governments legislated to change what had been largely a voluntary system of industrial relations into one where the ability of unions and workers to mobilize a lawful strike was tightly circumscribed.

Legislators may seek justification for such changes in notions of the balance of power. Explicit or implied, the idea of the balance of power seems to be an important one (see chapter 9). If trade unions have a modicum of power, they may be able to mobilize support and action to defend against repressive legislation. In South Korea in January 1997, tens of thousands of workers went on strike to protest against a new labour law passed in a secret early morning vote by ruling party MPs when no opposition MPs were present. The law would have made it easier to lay off employees (job protection had been fairly strong) and banned the formation of trade unions at any workplace until 2002. Confederations of trade unions were already banned and the legislation was designed to strengthen this ban. However, the Hyundai company differed from the government in their handling of employee relations and proposed legalization of the Korean Confederation of Trade Unions. Lee Hyoung-ken, a senior Hyundai director, said that it was realistic to authorize the federation as firms were already dealing with it. His company was more worried about having too many trade unions within the group than it was about dealing with the confederation (Barrie, 1997).

In general, government economic policy in newly industrializing countries, such as the so-called 'Pacific tiger' economies, has not encouraged trade union activity. Policy has been to deregulate markets but to strictly regulate trade union formation and growth. For example, in 1993 a report by the US trade representative's office concluded that Indonesian law and practice effectively prohibited the

formation of organizations alternative to the SPSI (the officially sanctioned trade union). Such prohibitions tend to apply even more
strongly to trade unions in developing countries.

Conclusion – Third World trade unions and international unionism

Henk Thomas (1995) edited a collection of studies of Third World
trade unionism under the impact of globalization. He observed that
'while, for more than a century, the trade union movement has been
an important actor in defending the interests of workers and in struggling for independence and democracy, it now faces in large parts of
the world, almost total elimination as a significant social institution'.
As in advanced industrialized countries, industrial development
depended on national policies that also governed labour under industrial relations laws. An obvious example was the history of the
labour movement in India which was 'intimately linked with the
protectionist economic policies followed by the government for fifty
years' (Ramaswamy, 1995).

Rapid technological change, intensified international competition
and footloose finance capital undermined protectionist policies and
structural adjustment policies accentuated the process. In east Asia,
rapid industrialization was often accompanied by trade union repression. In Africa, relatively strong trade union formations were
unprepared for the rigours of structural adjustment policies.

Consequently, the conclusion was that 'today and in the foreseeable future, it appears that a new rationale needs to be defined in
which key labour market issues, such as segmentation, unemployment, household work and poverty are taken as direct challenges.
The trade union movement otherwise risks being reduced to a mar-
ginal phenomenon' (Thomas, 1995).

The problems and threats faced by trade unions in developing
countries were so acute as to make them analytically separate from
trade unions in the richest nations. Consequently, it may well be
that Third World trade union studies need no longer be defended
as a separate field of inquiry. Rather, the study of unions, just like
that of other issues of labour, work and employment, begins to form
an important chapter on global and comparative labour. Third World
trade unions cannot be compared in a simple way with those in
richer countries. The conditioning factors are so diverse, whether
of an economic, social or political character, that divergent labour

systems, rather than convergence, are to be expected for the time being.

While the contours of international production and services may be well known in trade union circles, very few unions have actually acted on this basis. The problem is not simply that today's leaders for the most part do not do enough on the international level. Most of the struggle against globalization occurs on a national level: 'Although it is believed that workers can often exert quite considerable local or even national power, there is little faith that they can do so globally – witness, for instance, the admonition, now so popular among many on the left, to "think globally" yet to "act locally"' (Herod, 1995:347). They do – though not in the way the maxim intends. In January 1997, the British Amalgamated and Electrical Union combined with industrial bosses to publish a joint appeal to Far Eastern and German firms to invest in Britain (Milne, 1997). The AEEU brochure, translated into Korean, Japanese, Chinese and German, aimed at encouraging foreign investors to sign single union deals with the union which the executives describe as 'pragmatic'.

The International Trade Secretariats are a logical forum for international co-ordination but tend to be dominated by partnership-minded union leaders from the US, Japan, Germany and Britain. They are bureaucracies, 'yet there is no reason to believe that the proliferation of fax machines, electronic mail and other high-tech telecommunications devices which corporations use to co-ordinate their operations internationally cannot also make it easier for workers to communicate more effectively across national frontiers. Indeed, one trade secretariat – the International Federation of Chemical, Energy and General Workers' Unions (ICEF) – has already established an electronic mail computer system to track and disseminate information concerning corporations' current operations and proposed investments, information which has been used successfully on several contract negotiations and disputes' (Herod, 1995:347). In the EU, it may be that trade unions will be helped by the European Works Councils. However, union hopes to use the Social Charter to create regulations for multinational collective bargaining have been disappointed. These issues are discussed in the chapters on minimum standards and participation.

Questions for discussion

1 What are the most important roles that unions perform today? Are they the same as they were twenty years ago? Why or why not?

2 Have unions outlived their usefulness? Make a case for and against this issue with comparative examples from different countries.

3 What is your forecast for union–management relations for the year 2005?

5

Comparative Collective Bargaining

Before the 1990s there was still a vigorous debate in the area of industrial relations. Was there then a fundamental change – the end of consensus and free collective bargaining? Or, is collective bargaining continuing, even if not at present flourishing? Those who envision union–management relations as a pendulum perceived the present period of industrial relations – a period characterized by subdued union power in bargaining – as similar to those in previous eras of slump. They perceived prevalent bargaining outcomes as nothing new and suggested that they would be reversed when employment conditions recovered.

However, by 1998 this diagnosis did not seem to fit the facts. The salient facts making for change in industrial relations were mainly exogenous to the union–management bargaining relationship. Those facts are exemplified by Daimler/Chrysler, Ford, ABB (Asea-Brown Boveri), Canon, Daewoo and steel producers and manufacturers in newly industrialized countries. In a more deregulated world economy there are also many new telecommunications companies, new airlines and new services that are continually realigning previous business arrangements through joint ventures and networks. At the end of 1997, Union Bank of Switzerland merged with Credit Suisse to create the world's second largest bank. Finance sector mergers, such as Travelers/Citicorp, continued to be floated through 1998 and 1999.

There is still some bargaining and occasionally it is very tough but overall, it is a shadow of its former self. In the USA in 1996, the United Auto Workers (UAW) was struggling to contain the new manifestation of an old fashion in corporate strategy – outsourcing and sub-contracting of work that had been done in-house. Ford and Chrysler had re-engineered production operations and cut workforces. A significant feature had been contracting out some production and pre-assembly work to suppliers – often non-union firms paying wages below UAW-negotiated rates. In an attempt to stabilize working conditions, the UAW reached three-year agreements with Ford and Chrysler that contain job security clauses. The Ford agreement showed the union's weakness as Ford secured a two-tier pay structure that allowed lower pay to new recruits than to existing workers – contrary to union principles. However, unions can still defend work practices, as in the eight-week strike of 1998. What began as a local dispute about productivity and investment at a metal-stamping plant in Flint, Michigan, spiralled into a showdown between GM and the United Auto Workers union.

How can we apply comparative analysis to collective bargaining?

There seems little alternative to a country-by-country study as, despite fitful efforts by unions, collective bargaining rarely extends beyond the national level. Consequently, bargaining is very weak in relation to globalization and can be fairly easily circumvented (for provoking anxieties about 'social dumping', see chapter 11). A pathfinder in discussing the 'decentralization of the structure of collective bargaining in six countries: Sweden; Australia; Germany; Italy; the United Kingdom, and the USA' was Katz (1993:3). He examined similarities of trend across the six countries, finding that the intensity of local bargaining had increased – an example of convergence, perhaps. He found that a common feature of industrial relations change in Sweden, Australia, Germany, Italy, the UK and the USA was significant employer-initiated decentralization of bargaining.

It makes sense to follow in these footsteps but there seems no need to do so slavishly, as countries other than those discussed by Katz can also be considered. Sweden, as formerly the model of the centralized neo-corporatist collective bargaining system, has to be included. A brief commentary on Denmark is added in terms of a 'Nordic' collective bargaining model. France is an interesting case where bargaining has never been strongly formalized, yet, paradoxically, proves hard to uproot. Germany's unification was a unique test case in loading even greater strains on a centralized bargaining system that, nonetheless, refuses to buckle. There are quite a few recent studies of bargaining in Italy and of USA–Canada bargaining comparisons. In view of its central role in the discussion of convergence in the second and third chapters, Japan can hardly be overlooked. Finally, it is impossible to ignore the dramatic decline of collective bargaining in the UK. From still being assumed to be 'the best way of conducting industrial relations' in the mid-1980s, collective bargaining in the UK covered a much-reduced portion of the economy and dealt with far fewer issues.

Sweden – decline of the centralized model

Few countries came as close as Sweden to attaining the ideal-type neo-corporatist economy. The key features of the model were: (a) a functional market economy; (b) independent competitive enterprises and export-led growth; (c) centrally powerful and fully independent employer and union organizations; (d) workers' participation at company level; (e) atmosphere of co-operation and consensus; (f) centralized solidaristic bargaining between LO, the union organization, and SAF, the employers' confederation – the social partners. The basic central agreement included a peace obligation – no strikes for the duration of a collective agreement. Disputes of interest and disputes of right were legally distinct. There was to be no industrial action in the case of disputes of right. Such disputes – about interpretation of labour law or collective agreements – must be referred to the National Labour Court as the final arbitration of all labour disputes (see chapter 9).

From the beginnings of the 1980s, employers and managers began to attack the centralized bargaining model. They had repudiated the socialized investment programme of wage-earner investment funds that had been foisted on company profits by the Social Democratic government and LO in 1983 (Pontusson and Kuruvilla, 1992) and became more combative as a result. Emboldened by success in overturning the wage-earner funds, they espoused strategies of flexibility, technological change and upskilling.

'The demise of the Swedish model was made more certain by the simultaneous need to restructure industry in line with world trade developments. As in many countries, older industries such as steel and shipbuilding have contracted, while others, more technologically advanced, have expanded.' The SAF hardened their policy on pay. It was not to be considered as an element in macro-economic planning but as an important incentive. 'Pay policy should be determined at the company level, in line with the firm's profits and ability to pay' (Ahlen, 1989:336). For a while the unions believed that changes in the nature of work simply provided new opportunities for solidaristic pay bargaining. Jobs were becoming more specialized and knowledge-based, blurring the division of white collar and blue collar. This professionalization of work was significant in the white-collar workers' strike of 1988. The dependence of large industrial companies on new technology made them temporarily vulnerable to strikes by computer and administrative staff.

The Danish centralized industrial relations system proved more unyielding than that of Sweden. A process of adaptation that some writers (Due et al., 1994) have called 'centralized decentralization' began to take shape in the 1990s. To increase flexibility in an increasingly global economy, bargaining has moved from central to sectoral and enterprise levels. However, there remains strong employer and union organization with sectoral framework agreements setting at least basic requirements:

> In a comparative perspective this is a very important characteristic of the Nordic labour relations model. In the USA, it is, for example, quite normal for employers to compete with each other on personnel costs which very often are fixed within the sphere of control of the individual (big) employer. When multinational enterprises with American parent companies operate in Scandinavia through subsidiaries, American executives coming to Scandinavia are quite often surprised to find that their level of personnel costs is fixed by collective agreements between trade unions and employers' organizations of which they are not and do not want to be members. They are forced, by means of sympathetic actions which block all supplies, to choose between entering into a collective agreement or leaving Scandinavia. If they provide services they need to stay if they want the Scandinavian customers. As an example of the coercive power of the Danish trade unions, McDonald's in Copenhagen which in 1989 was forced to accept a collective agreement may be mentioned. The Danish Labour Court found very extensive and compelling sympathetic actions lawful under Danish law (Nielsen, 1996:63).

The Danish system might decline if centralized decentralization degenerated into deregulation but it has been resilient (Due et al., 1994). Social partnership models (regulated in part by collective bargaining) remain viable in the contemporary global economy, as is promulgated, officially at least, by the European Union Commission. Nevertheless, it has been shown that collective bargaining is much lower than union density in Denmark as salaried employees have lower collective bargaining coverage (Scheuer, 1997:65).

France – a special case?

In a 1995 article, Jean-François Amadieu posed just the sort of question that we need to consider for comparative analysis of industrial relations – is France a special case? (Amadieu, 1995:345). Although he reckoned that the peculiarity of the French system of industrial relations has been exaggerated, he still believed that there were distinct features. Does France remain 'abnormal' because of important national and sectoral centralized collective bargaining, or is it converging by either the structured downward shift in collective bargaining, as in Germany, or the unstructured downward shift, as in Sweden and the UK? (Jeffreys, 1996:511).

Traditionally, important bargaining was industry-wide and collective agreements were signed by a branch of the union. The emergence of company or plant bargaining ran counter to the principles of unions that had constantly endeavoured to keep workers from being too company-oriented. Consequently, in 1982, Jean Auroux, then Minister of Labour, proposed legislation that purported to transform industrial relations 'and create a real rupture with the existing model' (Gallie, 1985:205). The five laws that constituted the *lois Auroux* were intended to transform part of the *Code du Travail* (see chapter 7). Auroux depicted the development of collective bargaining as the keystone of this reform programme. There was to be an obligation for employers and unions to hold regular negotiations at both industry and firm level. Secondly, the reform aimed to make it more difficult for employers to try to reach a quick and facile agreement with a union that represented only a minority of the workforce. Would this presage a move from state-inspired regulation to joint regulation? In fact, the state has continued to play a leading role in the laying down or rescinding of rules (Amadieu, 1995:348). At the national level, collective bargaining between CNPF (Conseil National du Patronat Français) and all the unions led to a framework agreement on the recruitment of young unemployed.

The main function of sectoral collective agreements has been to set out or amend sectoral job classification hierarchies or job evaluations. However, such industry-wide grading systems are being challenged by the concept of job competence. Unilateral employer decisions and individual bargaining are 'preferred to the criteria laid down in collective agreements' (Amadieu: 348). Local agreements do not usually reflect formal bargaining, rather a 'take it or leave it' process of consultation with workplace union delegates. The intention of the Auroux laws to formalize this level of bargaining seems to have been disappointed. 'Nor is there any evidence that managements are making use of this level of employee representation to discuss training or working conditions, two of the specific intentions of the original legislation' (Jeffreys, 1996:513). There seems to be an unstructured decentralization but not of bargaining as such, unless the view of Sisson (1987:35) remains true that much of the workplace bargaining that takes place is informal and between first line supervisors and delegates. In fact, in one case study of a company mass producing consumer goods (Lawrence and Barsoux, 1990:199), the boss perceived in the Auroux participative management legislation 'an excellent means of keeping people informed and allowing them to vent their grievances in an informal setting – thereby outflanking the unions by depriving them of ammunition'.

Germany – centralized system depends on works councils

From a British perspective, the most striking aspect of the system of collective bargaining in the former West Germany was its high degree of centralization. After the Second World War, sixteen industrial unions were set up and an exceedingly tidy structure of industry-wide and regional collective bargaining developed.

At company and workplace level, there is a formally separate and tightly legally regulated works council (*Betriebsrat*). However, in almost all industries, the candidates of the Deutscher Gewerkschaftsbund (German Trades Union Federation) industrial unions regularly gained 80 per cent of works council seats. 'The complex relationship between works council and unions is one of the most crucial and typical features of the German industrial relations system' (Streeck, 1982).

By the mid-1990s the *Betriebsrat* had largely taken over the bargaining task. A symbiosis had occurred between trade union activities at company level and the activities of the *Betriebsrat*. Consequently, works councils became similar to company unions. What had happened? The economic base, as ever, is the key. The German economy entered a severe crisis in the 1990s. Transformation after German unification was tortuous. The West German economy had moved into recession with heavy unemployment. The Eastern European economies beckoned with low labour costs and acceptable productivity levels – but they needed massive investment in updated plant and machinery.

German unification caused huge organizational problems for trade unions and employers' associations (Sadowski et al., 1994:532). During unification, the West German employers' associations had been adamant that they wanted the basic structure of the West German system to be transferred to the East. They favoured industry-level agreements and wanted to minimize the use of company-level agreements. The vast disparity in living standards made collective bargaining on pay very difficult. Average monthly wages in 1990 were 1184 GDR marks in East Germany, compared with 3809 in West Germany. Yet, for political reasons, the conversion ratio had been set at 1:1. Furthermore, the unions had negotiated reductions in standard hours and industry-wide pay increases of 7 per cent in metals and engineering, 7 per cent in construction and 6 per cent for public service workers.

In 1993, German engineering employers moved to abandon the agreement to bring Eastern wages up to the level of their West German counterparts by 1994. The union I G Metall resisted, fearing that the tradition of industry-wide collective bargaining was at stake in the West too. A compromise agreement, mediated by Kurt Biedenkopf, premier of Saxony, maintained the pay increase but in three separate stages. But the system remained under pressure and the industrial dispute in the spring of 1994 – in which the Gesamtmetall (employers) initially called for a reduction in labour costs by as much as 10 per cent – was widely considered to be decisive for the future of German industrial relations (Sadowski et al., 1994:533).

The social market economy remained in place in 1997 even though the wider political climate had become much less favourable for collective bargaining. However, even conservative politicians were obliged to publicly support it. Apart from legislation affecting strike action, the legal framework regulating collective bargaining at industry level and workplace negotiations by the works council was unchanged.

An influential explanation has been attempted by Kathleen Thelen (1993). In a deeply researched study, she treated Germany as a special case of neo-corporatism. As a result of the works council, pressures for decentralization of collective bargaining were less of a threat to Germany than to other corporatist countries. The works council provided the German economy with a unique capacity for what she called 'negotiated adjustment' without national level 'political exchange'. The German unions have met the perceived rigidities of centralized bargaining by adroitly exploiting the close linkage with the works councils that can bargain about quality, training and flexibility. Muller (1997) tended to confirm this view. He examined twenty-five case studies of employment practices in German and foreign-owned banks and chemical firms, finding that companies still complied generally with multi-employer bargaining and that those firms covered by centralized collective bargaining could achieve flexibility similar to that of a non-collective bargaining firm. However, McElvoy (1998) brusquely dismissed such ideas: 'The corporatism of post-war Germany is under attack and will not survive the next five years in its present form. In the East, employees regularly vote to bypass collective bargaining in order to maximize jobs.'

The percentage of employees in West Germany who are covered by collective agreements decreased from 83 per cent in 1995 to 75 per cent in 1998, leading one researcher to forecast that 'the German model of industrial relations will more and more lose its exclusivity and distinctiveness' (Hassel, 1999:503).

Italy – legislated workplace representations

Until fairly recently, there had not been much written in English on industrial relations in Italy. Perhaps Chalmers (1987) awoke some interest when she referred to Italy as possibly the closest example at the time to the segmented labour market (and extensive subcontracting) that characterized employment relations in Japan. Recent interest owes much to the work of Locke (1994). Through an analysis of recent changes in Italian industrial relations, he advocated a new approach to comparative industrial relations theory. Instead of treating national systems as the benchmark for analysing and searching for macro-institutional features, Locke's approach is to scrutinize micro-level developments and strategic choices by decision-makers to explain variations *within* countries. Some might say that this is not comparative at all and Locke is simply changing the terms of reference of a subject of study. However, he has studied bargaining levels, finding that union experiences with industrial adjustment at FIAT and Alfa Romeo had been very different.

Italian law does not require trade union recognition. However, there is a workers' statute (*Statuto Dei Lavoratori*, 1970) that guarantees and protects employee 'representation even in workplaces where the level of unionization may be very low' (Terry, 1993:142). Article 19 of the statute enables workers – whether unionized or not – to take the initiative to establish a *rappresentanza sindicale aziendale* (unionized presence in the workplace), irrespective of the views of the employer. Its usual form is a works council. The law also provides a strong incentive to bargain by allowing employers to vary legal minimum standards but only by collective bargaining. There are further legal supports for collective bargaining, including the right to time off (for union representatives), the right to attend a specified number of meetings in working time and the right to promote unions. Trade union representatives have enhanced protection against dismissal. Various laws and collective agreements maintain the rights of unions and workplace bargainers to extensive disclosure of information.

The adaptability of the 1970 legal framework at the workplace level has to some extent compensated for the trade union concessions at the national level. In 1992 the *scala mobile*, Italy's forty-seven-year-old system of automatic wage indexation, was abolished. After this, the employers' main aim was to simplify the bargaining system, ideally by reducing it to one level of industry-wide negotiations, with companies free to opt out in favour of agreements at plant and company level.

Locke reckoned that the unwillingness of national unions to adapt to changes such as new technology and intensified international competition had obliged individual firms to pursue various alternative labour arrangements. He analysed collective bargaining rearrangements at Fiat and Alfa Romeo. Union experiences with structural change at these two firms had been radically different. Whereas Fiat Auto reorganized by asserting managerial prerogatives and repressing the unions, Alfa Romeo experienced a more negotiated process. Alfa's unions managed to maintain their strength but Fiat's unions lost membership and practically all influence on the shop floor. This divergence was remarkable since both firms have the same ownership, their workforces are represented by the same unions, their plants possess similar technology and they operate within the same national setting.

The USA – a comparative analysis with Canada

In 1988 the famous industrial relations professor, John Dunlop, believed that 'it is difficult to conclude that the events of the 1970s and 1980s have altered in any fundamental way' the main features of the industrial relations arrangements of the USA (Dunlop, 1988). He was 'aware that workplaces under collective bargaining constitute a minority of all workplaces' but supposed that 'collective bargaining provides leadership to a much larger group in the labour force'.

By 1997, this point of view was no longer tenable. Even Dunlop had admitted that concession bargaining, whereby unions conceded two-tier pay structures, lump sum payments and cost-of-living adjustment clauses, was pervasive. In this section of the book, the decline in collective bargaining in the USA is assessed by comparison with collective bargaining in Canada, with reference to articles by Roy Adams and Leo Troy. Adams, a doyen of comparative industrial relations research, believed that there were divergent trends in Canada and in the USA: an example of the institutional or 'national systems' approach. Troy accepted that there are significant differences between the Canadian and US systems of industrial relations. However, he opposed Adams's view that they continue to diverge; rather, there was a tendency to convergence.

Adams rested much of his case on the collective bargaining relationship. In both Canada and the USA there was a long-established convention of 'bargaining in good faith'. In the USA, a statutory union recognition procedure enabling a majority of employees to vote for union certification, the establishment of a bargaining unit and the requirement for the employer to bargain in good faith was enshrined in the National Labour Relations (Wagner) Act of 1935. These procedures also refuse a petition for an election in the bargaining units where there is existing union representation – at least for the first three years of a collective agreement (Townley, 1987).

In both countries, there was traditionally no question of management's even contemplating union participation in strategic decisions. In general, unions accepted managerial prerogatives on product design, pricing and investment, in return for collective agreements providing some assurance that real wages would rise if the company prospered and protection against arbitrary dismissals by management. Adams (1991) argued for continuing divergence because such mutuality continued to underpin Canadian industrial relations but had been eroded in the USA. 'Bargaining in good faith' had been undermined by decertification, union-busting and the 'runaway shop' (relocation of employment in states where unions were weak). The legislative framework had been attacked. Increasing numbers of non-union employers in the USA had been avoiding the Wagner Act in order to stop collective bargaining, often by firing union members or being careful not to recruit people who might join unions.

Adams highlighted the divergence by pointing to the split in the

United Auto Workers. In 1984, the UAW in the USA gave up its COLA (cost of living agreement) and annual increase in return for profit-sharing. However, the Canadian UAW resisted profit-sharing and struck at General Motors, as dramatized in the documentary film *Final Offer*. As a result, the Canadian UAW seceded to form an autonomous union. Adams also contrasted management initiatives to transform bargaining in line with Japanese management practice characterized by teamworking but individualized wages.

Leo Troy (1992) was sceptical about the view that collective bargaining was flourishing in Canada but dying in the USA. He reckoned that public sector unionism, which exceeds private sector unionism by a wide margin in Canada, obscured a similar decline. Another bias in the Canadian figures came from Quebec where three of the four provincial federations had no link with the Canadian Labour Congress.

That the convergence/divergence argument should remain unresolved between the USA and Canada confirms the continuing relevance of comparative analysis of bargaining and industrial relations. Perhaps the balance of the argument is with Troy but the debate is not over. The formation of the North America Free Trade Agreement (NAFTA) has accentuated the competitive strains on trade unionism and bargaining in Canada. It does look as if bargaining there will go the way of the wrenching changes that swept through long-established collective bargaining relationships in the USA over little more than a decade. Signposts for this are contained in a detailed study of collective bargaining events, trends and outcomes in key American industries edited by Paula B. Voos (1994). A brilliant chapter by Charles Craypo presents an overview of the near-collapse of collective bargaining in the meat-packing industry. In an integrated North American trading area, doubtless there are lessons here for the future of bargaining in Canada. However, the economics argument can be turned on its head. Goddard (1997) maintained that high unemployment (generated by harsh monetary policies) substantially lowered worker expectations and labour militancy, thereby reducing the problem of control at the level of the firm and lessening the need for Canadian employers to adopt various workplace innovations associated with the transformation/'convergence' thesis. In 1996, again unlike the UAW in the USA that year, the Canadian Auto Workers proposed an aggressive bargaining programme, including shorter work time, restrictions on outsourcing and guaranteed job levels for the communities in which each plant was located. The CAW reached agreements with Ford and Chrysler but as General Motors was intent on increasing its level of outsourced production, dis-

Bridgestone/Firestone and United Rubber Workers Agreement

Akron, Ohio – Nov.6

For 27 months, the ground-level headquarters of the former United Rubber workers Local 7 in Akron, Ohio, had the look and feel of a bunker under attack. Bridgestone/Firestone Inc. – which the union saw as its labour-gutting enemy – seemed to be winning in its record-setting industry strike. But posters bearing rifle-toting 'scab hunters' decorated the local's office walls. A black flag, which union members handed out at auto races and rallies in protest, was draped above a desk. But yesterday, as members of the union – now merged with the United Steelworkers of America – heard word a tentative agreement had been reached, the mood was shifting. 'We were under siege. We called it the "War of 94",' said Bob Rocco, vice president of the local. 'And now it looks like it's over. If I were a betting man, I would have bet everything I'd never see this day.' But just who won and how it came about remained a mystery to union leaders and members yesterday. Employees learned of the agreement from a brief memo posted at the plants. 'We've heard rumors of a settlement for so long now, we didn't know what to believe,' said Herman Rushin, a 37-year Firestone employee who lost his job in the company's shipping depart-

ment and then got one back building tires. 'This has been a whole cloaked thing.' Jim Eubank, a member of Local 7 and a tread maker at Bridgestone/Firestone said most employees yesterday had a 'wait and see' attitude about the agreement. 'We're glad to hear something finally happened,' Eubank said. 'But it was a surprise.' In fact, the recent negotiations were conducted in such secrecy, even Rocco didn't know they were going on. 'I knew all of the officers were down in Pittsburgh for the hearing (with the National Labour Relations Board)' said Rocco. 'I thought this thing would drag on and on.' Clark Lantz, Local 7's president from 1976 until his retirement from Bridgestone/Firestone in 1992, was surprised when a reporter told him of the tentative agreement. 'It's good news, but I just hope and pray they didn't sell some of us out,' said Lantz, referring to Bridgestone/Firestone retirees.

The message from the Bridgestone/Firestone dispute was clear to some workers and retirees: The union doesn't have the power it once enjoyed. Companies have little reason to bargain – if there's a strike there are plenty of replacement workers to fill the ranks. The companies, they say, call the shots.

M. Ethridge, *Akron Beacon Journal*, 6 November 1996
Source: Reprinted with the permission of the *Akron Beacon Journal*.

agreement led to a three-week strike (Moody, 1997:61). The merger of Chrysler and Daimler-Benz, announced in 1998, appeared to offer advantages to the US Union of Automotive Workers that had a mediocre record when trying to organize at foreign-owned plant in the USA (see chapter 12).

Collective bargaining – Japanese-style

Decrescendo, rather than decentralization, may be said to have characterized collective bargaining in Japan in the last fifteen years. Its centrepiece since 1995 used to be the *shunto* or Spring Offensive, virtually an annual pay round. However, it always was talk rather than action, sound designed to allay fury. So when two visiting Japanese professors of industrial relations stated during an Economics Society seminar at Aberystwyth in 1990 that the *shunto* was 'almost dead', there was no doubting that it had gone quiet as the grave.

According to Dore (1986), the synchronized spring offensive method of pay bargaining provided a 'fine example of the quality of data available for discussion towards consensus'. The consensus has a powerful influence on collective bargaining. After a couple of weeks of serious bargaining, a norm is established that has a strong and restraining influence on all other settlements.

It could be said that bargaining has been sterilized by statistics. A handbook of statistics was produced every January – in time for the preliminaries of the *shunto* – by the Japan Productivity Centre, a tripartite body representing government, employers and unions. It provided quick reference to percentage growth of real and nominal GDP; employment figures and real GNP per person employed; consumer prices; manufacturing output, real wages and average remuneration per employee, and, of course, labour productivity. But the whole theme was strategically business-oriented, emphasizing that statistics are at the heart of all planning and rational discourse in business and government.

While economic growth rates were high, unions could at least sound belligerent in bargaining, whilst always being concerned to protect employment. When Japan's growth declined and the rising exchange rate affected competitiveness, causing job losses, the *shunto* game was up. Nevertheless, in 1994 Japan's unions were reported (Rafferty, *Guardian* , 1994) as demanding 6 per cent pay increases, although employers' organizations were insisting on zero.

Moreover, there is an argument that the information-sharing process of synchronized bargaining has helped the emergence of joint consultative committees at enterprise level. Motohiro Morishima (1991) reckoned that 'management's strategic information-sharing was associated with significantly reduced union militancy'. He concluded that this supported the finding that information sharing and prior consultation are a quid pro quo for union co-operation. Also, information-sharing through joint consultative committees has been instrumental in Japanese firms' ability to secure labour–management co-operation. If unions are weak to begin with, then this argument somewhat loses its force.

Australia – from compulsory arbitration to flexibility

It is no longer possible to treat Australia's industrial relations as a special case in which compulsory arbitration is central. Hancock and Rawson (1993) are among many writers who have analysed the metamorphosis. At one stage, Australia's industrial relations *did* provide a special reference point as a centralized industry-wide system. Edwards (1986:173) noted that the state arbitration system in Australia had performed many of the regulatory and industrial relations functions carried out by collective bargaining in Britain. But no longer. However, it may be said that the path of change was determined centrally by the Australian Congress of Trade Unions, employers' confederations and federal (Labour Party) governments.

The proposals of the Labour government in 1993 encouraged companies and unions to negotiate pay and conditions at plant or workplace level. National or state-wide agreements were relegated to providing a safety net (Rees, 1993). The powerful federal and state arbitration tribunals that formerly approved collective agreements and arbitrated disputes adopted a lower profile. It may not be that compulsory arbitration is 'all gone', but it is vestigial. According to Professor Judith Sloan, director in 1993 of the National Institute of Labour Studies at the Flinders University of South Australia, 'what we now have is a hybrid system of enterprise bargaining for a fraction of the workforce, large numbers left out of the process altogether and an unclear future for national wages cases' (John, 1993).

Although the arbitrated awards system is evidently vestigial, some researchers still find enough there to 'provide an interesting benchmark for comparative analysis'. One is Janet Walsh (1997:2) who noted that the state in Australia has regulated employment and industrial relations more extensively than its counterpart in Britain.

Most national wage agreements since the late 1980s have been linked to restructuring and productivity at the individual firm level. However, 'although enterprise agreements represent a significant decentralization of the Australian industrial relations system, they have in practice supplemented the provisions of awards without fundamentally altering the overall principles of the wages system' (Walsh, 1997:21).

British collective bargaining – from riches to rags

The 1980s were a watershed for British industrial relations. Successive Conservative governments set out deliberately to weaken the collective bargaining model. 'This Thatcherite policy of market orientation and deregulation in order to weaken the trade unions also included the abolition in 1983 of the Fair Wages Resolution which had safeguarded public employees from being rewarded at levels below those prevalent in the private sector' (Nagelkerke and Nijs, 1999:752). The policy of privatization and 'rolling back' the public sector was vigorously applied, gradually undermining industry-wide and pattern bargaining as a redoubt of trade unionism.

Another main thrust of this assault on the names and institutions of collective bargaining came via legislative changes. Eventually, trade unions lost their immunities from liabilities in tort for actions taken in the context of secondary and unofficial action and their abilities to indemnify members against fines imposed for offences or for contempt of court, as well as their power to discipline members who refused to take part in industrial action, even if that action complied with complex balloting requirements. Under a late amendment, the Trade Union Reform and Employment Relations Act of 1993 allowed employers to deny pay rises or other benefits to employees who refused to sign personal contracts – a clear blow at collective bargaining.

Small wonder then, that the Conservative government chafed at provisions imposed on it by UK membership of the EU with its much more regulationist approach. For instance, in 1995 the British government was obliged to set up regulations concerning extended information and consultation rights for employees in the event of collective redundancies and company transfers. 'This quite un-British act was a consequence of a European Court of Justice condemnation in 1994: the UK did not sufficiently comply with EU directives dating back to the 1970s' (Nagelkerke and Nijs:752).

The governmental policy of deregulation was widespread internationally but 'the comparatively harsh and extended de-institution-alization policy was typically British and in accordance with the British tradition of *laissez faire* liberalism' (Nagelkerke and Nijs: 753). Consequently, within the bargaining structure, multi-employer bargaining decreased rapidly with the growing emphasis on enterprise-specific employment relations and human resource management. More importantly, collective bargaining as a whole declined – even in its decentralized form. By 1990, key elements of the system of collective representation had faded and the reality of declining union presence was undesirable. The proportion of employees covered by collective bargaining agreements fell from over 70 per cent in 1984 to 54 per cent in 1990. The 1992 workplace industrial relations survey demonstrated how dramatically collective bargaining had contracted but also how much worse off were employees who did not enjoy its protection (Brown, 1993).

The findings of the 1998 Workplace Employee Relations Survey (Cully et al., 1998) confirmed the continuing decline of collective bargaining; there are no unions at all in 47 per cent of workplaces, compared with 36 per cent in 1990. Union recognition for collective bargaining purposes is even more strongly associated with establishments employing large numbers than in 1990. The latest workplace survey reported a very strong link between union membership and managerial attitudes towards unionism. Management hostility towards unionism is closely associated with low trade union membership; nearly two thirds of employees are union members in the 29 per cent of workplace where management is in favour of union membership; in the 17 per cent where management is not in favour, union membership is very low indeed. The implication is that – on the reasonable assumption that at least some of the employees in these workplaces would be willing to join unions – the statutory recognition procedure introduced by the Labour government in 1999 might have considerable impact.

Collective bargaining – a comparatively spent force?

The deregulatory climate of globalizing competition is hostile to collective bargaining. In theory, collective bargaining has to take pay and/or working conditions out of competition. If this is disturbed by import competition or even by just one significant domestic producer avoiding collective bargaining, the relatively higher cost of the bargaining firms makes them uncompetitive. The classic way to take pay and employment conditions out of competition is by industry-wide bargaining or by the union's reaching a key settlement with a leading firm that then provides a pattern for settlements with other firms in the industry. Many years ago Lloyd Ulman (1974:105) suggested a distinction between connective and competitive bargaining that is still useful. Connective bargaining referred to industry-wide or pattern bargaining. However, competitive bargaining occurred when companies began to perceive advantages in bargaining individually at the enterprise or establishment level. If they go further and decline to collectively bargain at all, the other firms are faced with a problem. The union may offer – and some of the employers may accept – a co-operative, rather than an adversarial bargaining relationship (Savoie, 1994:529). Instead of being a zero-sum game, bargaining is seen as an integrative process with both managers and worker representatives seeking productivity gains.

There may be quite a lot of scope for this sort of partnership under oligopolistic conditions. If, however, competition intensifies so that output and value-added decline, there may be little or nothing to share with the union in bargaining. If the union cannot even demonstrate health and safety protection or fairness of treatment and due process, then the collective bargain begins to resemble a 'sweetheart contract' between union and employer. US management has created a variety of non-union innovations aimed at fostering worker involvement and loyalty but has been unable – as a result of a self-interested wish to retain 'flexibility' – to satisfy vague employee desires for participation and decision-making. GM's strategy was clear since the hi-tech, non-unionized Japanese came into the American market in the 1980s: to close inefficient plants, especially in unionized centres like Flint, and open new ones with non-union labour. Its bargaining relationship with the UAW lengthened the transformation. Instead of closing plants outright and risking confrontation, GM tended to promise new investment in return for better productivity. In many cases the workers then achieved the new targets, despite outmoded machinery, but the investment was not forthcoming. The 1998 strike was born of such divergent viewpoints in bargaining.

Under what conditions does significant decentralization of industrial relations processes and outcomes indicate a change in basic assumptions about the system? In this chapter and in a recent article by Erickson and Kuruvilla (1998), mainly country-specific indicators are identified. They highlighted two types of transformation : incremental (or gradually adoptive) and discontinuous (or punctuated equilibrium). Clearly, change in collective bargaining is a key criterion in evaluating industrial relations transformation – and comparing systems, if it is still valid to talk of industrial relations systems. Union organizations, such as the European Trade Union Institute, advocate stronger co-ordination of bargaining at European level but it seems more likely that decentralization will continue.

Questions for discussion

1   'Unions are too aligned to an outdated collective bargaining approach.'

    Discuss and consider alternatives, using international comparisons.

2   'Apart from a few notable victories, transnational labour resistance to global capital has generally been a failure. In contrast, local initiatives in resistance are less ineffective.'

    Discuss the implications for human resource management in transnational companies.

6

Training: Comparative Routes to Skill Formation

There is a demonstrable link between training and the wider issues of industrial relations, as explored by Christel Lane (1990). She demonstrates how the vocational and educational training system in Germany played a pivotal role in the virtuous circle of high investment in training, effective utilization of advanced technology, high levels of skill, high wages – but low unit costs – and high levels of competitiveness, at the quality end of the market. These in turn are linked with functional flexibility and low levels of labour conflict.

By contrast, while it is increasingly accepted that training and development are critical in any high-value-added competitive strategy, the UK does not have the infrastructure at national level that other countries do in order to deliver the needed competences. It was reported in 1991 that the cash value of training by UK employers was 40 per cent below the figures quoted by the government and CBI. At the CBI conference in February 1996, Alf Gooding of the Welsh CBI, who introduced himself as a lifelong Conservative, declared that the UK was 'going down the tubes. We're not investing and not training people. It's frightening' (Beavis and Ryle, 1996).

As a result, 'probably more than any other country, Britain has shown an abiding interest in international comparisons of VET [Vocational Education and Training]' (Noble, 1997). However, to state the obvious, education and training policy is a sensitive topic for national governments who do not welcome being seen as weak in these areas. For example, an unpublished report by the OECD in 1995 concluded that the UK had a skills deficit compared with many other developed nations. It was felt that Britain was overemphasizing the importance of labour market flexibility and that the improvement in education and training came from a relatively low base. The OECD argues that National Vocational Qualifications have scant appeal because they lack credibility with employers and are even considered 'a bit of a joke'. The report was also highly sceptical about Training and Enterprise Councils, saying that the idea of handing responsibility for training over to private industry simply has not worked. However, the report also condemned the much more interventionist policy of the French government (Elliott, 1995).

Market forces v. government intervention

In comparative studies and analyses of training programmes in different countries, the market v. government intervention comparison is fairly standard and just about unavoidable. It is therefore the approach taken in this chapter. Putting the debate at its most basic in the case of the UK, sceptical analyses of the level of training and education in the economy and the economic benefits that it can produce, tend to conclude that there is probably not a shortfall and that increased state expenditure would benefit only vested interests (Shackleton, 1992). Similarly, it has been claimed that much of the economy does not, and perhaps even *need* not, demand high skills – recalling Nigel Lawson's notorious 'not so much low tech as no tech' prognosis for British employment. By contrast, S. Harkel, a textiles entrepreneur, was quoted in the *Human Resource Management Journal* of 1991 as stating that 'training cannot really be left to the market. It is too long-term and there is no real financial pay-off for market provision.' Many experts doubt that training policy can be designed using market forces (Hyman, 1992).

So the chapter will begin using this framework and drawing on Noble's (1997) international comparison of training policies. Then it will seek to expand the debate by exploring institutional factors. (In terms of the human resource strategies delineated in the first chapter, this means reference to systemic factors: culture, values, law, social policy.)

One variation at least on the market v. government intervention debate is to observe that training policies may be very closely regulated and yet the forms of regulation may be distinct. There have been continuing attempts to imitate the German VET model which 'remains a benchmark for industry policies and practice' (Noble, 1997) but the extent to which it is of a piece with the German state constitution and the German idea of the social market economy makes imitation difficult. 'Considerable doubt developed about the ability to transfer training arrangements from one political system into a nationally distinct cultural and institutional environment' (King, 1997:405).

Employer-led or education-led training?

The evidence appears to point to the importance of institutions and in particular those that are capable of adaptation in line with the growing independence of corporate management. Some researchers perceive this as setting up a distinction between an 'employer-led' model of training and an 'educational' model. It may be more accurate to describe the British system as an 'employer-led' model where the predilection of employers is for firm-specific skills with less enthusiasm for skill accreditation (credentialism). The differences between the two models in terms of government intervention are not as strong as has normally been assumed (Felstead and Green, 1994). Followers of the divergent national systems school of thought tend to espouse the second type of model (educational) because 'in each country there is a tendency for a close relationship to develop between the organization of general education and occupational training and the behaviour of firms' (Maurice et al., 1986).

International comparisons of training policies

A serviceable overview of comparative training policies has been provided by Noble (1997). First he examines the importance of international comparisons which he views as part of 'a resurgence of interest in workforce skills and qualifications and a growing recognition of the importance of learning organizations'. He then issues a number of caveats about comparative analysis and its use in policy-making: 'Comparative analysis has many limitations. Research evidence points to the need to be critical of blind faith in training and development and to treat international comparisons with caution' (Noble, 1997:6).

   He usefully reminds us of the systemic approach to human resource management in pointing out the limitation of institutional differences: 'Attempts to transfer part of one VET system from country to country have no sound economic justification. Effective forms of economic organization vary considerably across European countries and they are deeply embedded in their particular institutional contexts.'

Skilled workforce 'is no economic panacea'

Improving the skills of the workforce might be at the top of the government's jobs agenda, but it is no panacea for improving Britain's economic performance. That will also depend on companies aiming to sell higher quality goods and services, according to a new report from the Employment Policy Institute.

Many British businesses opt for what the authors identify as the 'Gerald Ratner strategy' of competing on the basis of low price and low quality.

When the former head of the bargain jewellery chain described its products as 'crap', he might have been foolish but he was honest, according to Ewart Keep of Warwick Business School and Ken Mayhew of Pembroke College, Oxford.

Their research suggests that many British companies opt for this strategy rather than developing high-quality products that require skilled labour.

This can make sense for businesses that do not have a wealthy customer base or do not have the internal organization to move upmarket.

Given this pattern, improved workforce skills will not by itself guarantee a more competitive UK economy.

Mr Keep said: 'For many British companies, competitiveness lies not in upskilling workers to make quality products but through price. Providing companies with more highly skilled workers can only increase levels of dissatisfaction when those workers are employed in poor quality, low-paid jobs.'

The paper, 'Was Ratner Right?' recommends a dual policy of encouraging businesses to opt for the high-value strategy at the same time as improving standards of education and training.

Companies would also have to switch to patterns of work organization that allowed employees to use their skills, and improve employee relations to improve trust and motivation.

It concludes that this 'poses a major challenge to policy-makers for whom upskilling has for too long been a convenient "major bullet" solution'.

D. Coyle, *Independent*,
25 March 1998

However, the main body of the article is devoted to comparative analysis of attempts to increase employer involvement in training through training levies and other means by looking 'at the experience of countries with a similar socio-economic system, such as Australia, France and Germany'. Consequently, this is a variant on the market v. government intervention theme.

France's approach has considerable attraction for policy-makers who favour centralized decision-making. There are negotiations involving the social partners – trade unions and employers' federations – and statutory requirements that employers spend 1.5 per cent of payroll on training and paid training leave for employees. In fact, it has been claimed that 'the main objective of the training plan was to force companies to negotiate training matters with employees' representatives, usually the unions. Views on the importance of the training plan are conflicting. The larger the company, the more useful it is considered to be. To the smaller companies, it is an irksome bind. Observers in training organizations hold the view that often the plan is purely a collection of disparate needs, a mish-mash put together to comply with the legal obligation. The issue of a strategic policy over the next five years is rarely broached and training adds up to nothing more than a response to short-term requirements, e.g. computerization. Often the whole question depends very much on the personality of the human resources manager and whether he can push a cohesive plan at board level' (Handy, Gordon, Gow and Randlesome, 1988:115).

'France was a partial model for the training levy operating in Australia from June 1990 until its suspension for two years from July 1994' (Noble, 1997:11). There is evidence that the levy played a valuable role in making many Australian companies devote resources to training, especially companies that had underinvested in human resources development. However, the levy was widely criticized by Australian business. It was held to be a burden on small and medium enterprises and a submission to a Senate Committee of inquiry reckoned that the levy made little difference to the amount spent and the training done in small business. Another submission doubted that it was the appropriate way of encouraging training in the longer term. As a result of such opposition, the government announced in its *Working Nation* White Paper that the levy scheme would be suspended 'in the light of the commitment by industry to meet its training obligations over the past few years' (Noble, 1997:10).

Australia and, in particular, Britain, 'where it has been difficult to get employers to increase their commitment to training', contrast strongly with the strong employer involvement of Germany whose VET system has been regarded by many industrialized countries as a source of competitive advantage. In the late 1980s, it was estimated that the German training system produced about seven times as many formally qualified supervisors as the British system (Prais and Wagner, 1988:34).

In Noble's discussion of the German system, the 'employer-led' v. 'education-led' distinction did not seem to help much. He noted 'an element of voluntarism, as no company is obliged to provide training and no young person is obliged to undergo training', yet 'government regulation plays a strong role' and 'the central government uses various instruments to influence the decisions of individual training enterprises, including the legally binding standard for major facets of training quality'.

German training system compared with South Korea

Jeong (1995:7) 'utilized the comparative study of industrial relations in an attempt to understand the malfunctions of the vocational training system in Korea', focusing on 'two major recent vocational training programmes in Korea' that 'failed to produce the desired industrial skills'. This is a matter of opinion, as others believe that the ambitious efforts 'to upgrade technical education in Korea were largely successful and helped the country overcome a skill deficit that might otherwise have resulted from its weak industrial relations system' (Turnham, 1996:570). However, Jeong perceived poor outcomes from Korean attempts to emulate the German model and believed that Korea's rigid, state-dominated bureaucratic vocational training system was mainly responsible. These poor outcomes did not mean that the German model had no relevance to the Korean economy. 'On the contrary, the German model still provides a crucial lesson for reforming the Korean vocational training system.' The problem was that transplantation of the German training models ignored the broad social context supporting them. Jeong observed that employers' associations and trade unions participate in the German vocational training system in five main areas: (1) the legislative process; (2) the provision of training services; (3) the formulation of training policy; (4) legal representation and participation in public regulation bodies at various levels; (5) the implementation of in-plant training. 'Hence, the German vocational training system may be called a corporatistically regulated market system' (Jeong, 1995:250).

Summing up the German training system

The German system appears to be more corporatist than interventionist, resting on written and unwritten agreements between employers and trade unions about how the German labour market, and training in particular, should be regulated. Taken as a whole, the evidence suggests that 'a degree of mutual interest and co-operation between employers and trade unions appears to oil the wheels of a number of successful training systems, including the German' (Steedman, 1993:292). In particular, centralized bargaining is significant in removing the incentives for non-training companies to poach ready-trained workers (Soskice, 1994). Despite the transferability of skills obtained through apprenticeship, there are effective internal labour markets which means that few trained workers seek employment on the external labour market. Mahnkopf (1992) tended to agree but thought that the attempt by collective bargaining to try to protect workers from rationalization and technical change was ineffective. The only way to counter it was a much clearer emphasis on skills and qualifications in German trade union policy.

The German model has been criticized for failing to respond to workplace changes. 'The system produces a surplus of skilled blue-collar workers but fails to provide workers with more sophisticated computer knowledge and the flexibility to switch from one kind of work to another' (*Economist*, 1994:26). One writer (James, 1985) observed that there is a large element of myth about the German apprenticeship system and that, far from being a purpose-built tool to handle the micro-chip, it is a rather odd relic of an odd past, and another pleaded for us to be 'saved from the credentialist fad' (Brittan, 1992).

If it is a fad, there are apparently many being misguided. The right to training is part of the German constitution. It may be training for skills in limited demand, e.g. goldsmiths, furriers, but it instils an attitude to skill and the idea of *Leistungbereitschaft* (professional community of work). It does not necessarily lead to over-supply of skilled manual workers. A broad-based pre-entry system of certified qualifications has provided the basis for German banks to develop a policy of functional flexibility amongst clerical personnel. The skills provided in Britain are considerably narrower than those available in the German system, so that, whilst in Germany there is evidence of task integration amongst clerical workers, in Britain there has been a polarization between career and non-career staff, the latter's work having been increasingly fragmented (Lane, 1987:67). Furthermore, 'whereas in Germany certification allowed employees to transfer their qualifications between companies and sectors, in France this training did not receive any qualification or certification, although 'the French have made limited developments to improve their provision of training along German lines' (O'Reilly, 1992:387).

The human resource management strategy (as planning) model and training

One of the original formulations of the human resource management idea – the 'commitment human resource management system', i.e., flexibility in return for job security – is very much associated with firms' commitment to training (Walton, 1985). In Japan, according to Dore and Sako (1989), the presumption of lifetime employment – at least for a firm's core labour force – still provides a strong justification for firms to invest in the training of their workers. The long-term perspective induced by the lifetime employment assumption has a number of consequences: (1) recruitment is for a career, not for a job; selection criteria concentrate on demonstrated ability to learn; (2) employers are more likely to be satisfied with graduates of any science, engineering, economics or business studies subject if they have a good general grounding in that subject as a basis for on-the-job training; (3) frequent retraining is seen as a necessary part of any career pattern; (4) diversification of the firm's business by way of hiving off divisions into subsidiaries becomes an essential way of coping with decline of established markets, structural change and technological change; (5) if people expect to be learners, they also expect frequently to have to be teachers. Many Japanese writers are specifically opposed to the cultural and/or 'group consciousness' hypothesis and take an individualist or economistic position (Koike, 1994). The strongest ground for regarding the Japanese firm's behaviour as 'groupist' has been the vagueness of job descriptions that apparently differentiates the Japanese from the foreign practice of specifying detailed job descriptions. However, Koike insisted that acceptance of responsibility overlaps with vagueness of job descriptions. He also discussed the late promotion system, arguing that delaying definitive selection of white-collar workers for the career tracks that lead to top managerial positions for ten or fifteen years stimulates long-term competition, motivates the acquisition of skills, and ensures fairness and objectivity in the selection process which is necessary for that motivation to be effective.

It may simply be a difference of emphasis in that, since employees have a strong lifetime stake in the firm and its success, they are also likely to identify with it and can be more easily motivated to improve existing skills and to acquire new ones. This will be partly for self-interest but willingness to learn is also why a worker is hired. The educational model is now more valid compared with the employer-led model. 'In Japan, the past success of large corporations was partly owing to the fact that they were able to hire the best from secondary school cohorts and train them in the internal labour market. The increasing quest for higher education among Japanese youth (also) calls into question the viability of the Japanese model' (Buechtemann and Soloff, 1994) i.e., as an employer-led model.

Lean production

Findings on lean production tend to suggest that skills, training and vocational qualifications – at least in the traditional sense – are less important to the extent that production can be streamlined. An exhaustive study by the McKinsey Global Institute (1993) found that in Japanese transnational companies, the need for skilled labour was in inverse proportion to rising productivity. What was more important was a different sort of 'skilling' (if indeed, it can be so called) where the integrated worker of Japanese lean production fits easily into a work team. According to Head (1996), integrated workers employed by Japanese industrial corporations need have few recognizable skills at all. Asked what importance they placed on the educational and vocational qualifications of most of their prospective shop-floor employees, personnel managers at Nissan and Honda plants in Europe said 'very little'. They were seeking dexterity, enthusiasm and ability to fit into a team.

There seems to be something of a contradiction here since Japanese companies are also noted for their training provision. The explanation may be that 'so much of their training is fully integrated into everyday practice' (Storey and Sisson, 1993:170). Certainly, the McKinsey study repeatedly criticized the much-vaunted German training model, saying that such reliance on craft labour can foster rigidity and compartmentalization on the line, reducing productivity.

Training and strategic human resource management

In UK organizations, neither the integration of the training function into other policy areas, nor the integration of employees through their involvement in training programmes had occurred to any great extent. Decentralization of decision-making to intermediate or business unit level seems to be associated with decentralization on training budgets and any strategic approach to HRM is weakest at these levels. First, the organization of the training function is not always well integrated with broader, personnel responsibilities. Secondly, business and HRM strategies may have conflicting rationales, with business strategies taking priority. Thirdly, the financial pressures introduced to account for training expenditure may make this kind of investment vulnerable to short term cost-cutting. Finally, line managers may be ill-prepared to take on the responsibilities for HR planning (Rainbird, 1995:87).

Question for discussion

According to Koike (1994), the development of intellectual skills can be thought of as a kind of software. Regarded in this way as technology, it can be transmitted to other countries given appropriate circumstances.

Discuss this view, with attention to 'appropriate circumstances'.

Integration of training through employee development programmes

A growing number of British organizations are establishing employee development programmes (EDPs) to provide employees with educational and training opportunities. Their establishment stemmed from the launch of Ford's employee development assistance programme. The US Ford programme, in common with those of the other two big US automobile companies, Chrysler and GM, is run jointly by management and union. This approach distinguishes them from many British EDPs. Even when joint union–management control is a feature of the British schemes, the degree of joint control is much less extensive. The national training centres established by the big three auto companies are undoubtedly costly to run. However, they do offer a way of avoiding the danger that it might come to be perceived that EDPs only subsidize the costs of training by getting employees to study on a voluntary basis in their own time. In the US schemes the *mutuality* of interest on which EDPs are premissed is protected. Jointism is also advantageous in providing the basis for mutually beneficial consultation about education, training and can therefore potentially be connected to HRM strategy (James, 1996). From a strategic human resource management perspective, jointness programmes are important. Any joint union–management training effort needs to include skills training in the specific areas necessary to meet the goals of the programme, as well as the usual component on motivation. Unions may have a useful role in promoting training but the question of what is meant by a social partnership approach to training is unclear (Heyes and Stuart, 1998).

Various routes to the formation of skilled labour

It might seem at first sight, accepting the main features of the HRM model, that general conclusions could be reached about training. However, researchers have struggled. They seem only to be able to make very broad classifications of training systems into 'interventionist v. market' or 'employer-led v. education-led' and even then they usually have to admit to mixtures and hybrids in practice. This is probably not too surprising if we recall the necessity to think of at least four perspectives on HRM strategy. Those researching training are therefore often thrown back on benchmarking with the German model, though this too has its critics. Thompson et al. (1995) researched training and skill acquisition in a cross-national study of the commercial vehicle industry in Sweden, Austria and the UK. They noted that 'debates about the formation and utilization of skills, particularly at an international level, have tended to follow two different paths. On the one hand, there are those theorists who proceed from general, 'universal' trends in markets, technologies and production systems, and, on the other, those who move directly from societal institutions to work organization' (Thompson et al., 1995:719).

They did identify similar tendencies within advanced manufacturing, especially a growth in cognitive and extra-functional coping abilities, normally within a teamworking context. However, there were marked national differences in managerial preferences for the type of labour (craft, professional or semi-skilled) perceived to be necessary for this more flexible work organization.

'As in Germany, in Austria the vocational training of a large number of workers is based on the dual system, combining in-plant training with education in part-time vocational schools (apprenticeship). The skilled workers' certificate is awarded by the industry's business association and is therefore a transferable qualification.

The wage system is based on job evaluation: most workers in cab production and in assembly are graded the same and only quality co-ordinators and relief workers earn more. According to the sectoral collective agreement, skilled workers may get paid at levels that are agreed for traditionally semi-skilled jobs, such as assembly operations, provided that the rate for semi-skilled work in a particular firm reaches the minimum wage for skilled workers laid down in the collective agreement. This means that the deployment of skilled, rather than semi-skilled workers, does not increase costs as it would in a pay-for-knowledge system. The wage system does not therefore provide incentives to learn additional jobs but, because of the high ratio of skilled employees, the workforce is already highly flexible' (Thompson et al., 1995:726).

However, in contrast with the claims of the new production paradigm, labour utilization in bus and truck production in the UK plant of Volvo has been based on non-apprenticed, semi-skilled labour. The decision to locate bus assembly at Workington, rather than Preston, reflected this: 'We were going to do away with skills, we had a lot of demarcation problems at Farrington (Preston) . . . ' The training manager at the plant therefore explicitly used the language of deskilling the operation. At the same time, he also referred to the conventional menu of shifting responsibility through teamworking, problem-solving, self-supervision and co-ordination. This sounds like the McKinsey recipe for streamlining production and reducing the *need* for skilled labour.

Conclusions on training and skill formation

It is fine to talk about varied routes to skill formation and, of course, human resource strategies are diverse at the establishment level. For comparative purposes, however, we have to try to bring the analysis of training and training policies into some sort of order. To this end, there still seems little alternative to classifying training policies as *employer-led* or *education-led* or as *market-based* or *state interventionist*. These dualities may well overlap.

Broadly, a free-market-based system of training may have some advantages in greater responsiveness and greater mobility between firms. Skill formation may become more relevant to the needs of firms and allocative efficiency may be encouraged. Nevertheless, market failure can occur through free riding (i.e. not investing in training but poaching trained workers from other organizations) and a shortsighted approach to training. In periods of economic upswing, this will entail skill shortages, poaching and bidding up of wages. According to a report on the UK in 1997 by Coopers and Lybrand, 'the shortage of skills is driving up wage bills at a time when companies are experiencing some difficulties in export markets. The combination of these factors is hampering growth amongst the very companies that are so keen to achieve it' (Ryle, 1997).

According to Gospel (1994:519), 'state intervention may overcome some of the problems of external and internal market failure'. State provision of training may improve access and may raise firms' awareness of the need for training. However, it does have disadvantages in that it often gives priority to job creation and the quality of training can be low. France, for example, moved in the direction of a state-based system. However, even with the investment of substantial resources and big changes in the educational system, it was not clear that there were gains by 1997.

The diverse and uneven nature of industrial development and institutional regulation across countries does make it difficult to identify transnational patterns and policy targets, except to say training is important. It may be that one clear point is 'that training and industrial relations interventions in technological and skill changes need increasingly to deal with management's growing independence at the enterprise level' (B. Jones, 1997).

Two opposed models of the development of national skills trajectories – a model of low-skill formation and a model of high-skills development – have been suggested (Ashton and Green, 1996). Britain and the USA are examples of the first category, with Germany and Japan as obvious representatives of the high-skill model. This still does not translate into the market v. state intervention duality, though. Low-skill formation in the USA and UK may be blamed on the state's voluntaristic delegation to employers. However, it is large firms, rather than state agencies, that are responsible for establishing Japan's high-skill system. A possible institutional explanation is that Japan's large manufacturing firms accepted 'lifetime employment' and seniority wages to settle their post-Second World War compromise with the unions. From this developed a pattern of skill-accumulating careers (see Koike (1994) on 'white collarization') that flourished without government intervention. It would appear that it is not so much a question of government intervention *versus* market forces as the disposition and attitudes of employers towards collective provision of training. Soskice (1994:102) has argued cogently that 'what is notable about all the advanced economies, such as the UK, in which business is weakly collectively organized is that none has an effective initial training system in which private companies play a major part'.

Earlier in the chapter a comment by Jeong was quoted about a rather desultory state attempt in South Korea to copy the German training system that many governments admire. In general, however, it seems that high-skill formation in the Asian tiger economies is associated with the use of training and vocational education as integral elements in state intervention and planning of successively higher levels of technological and industrial development. In Singapore, skill formation is integrated into industrial policy. So, it could be that there is scope for a third type of high-skill formation between the corporatist German model and 'internal labour market' Japanese model. The influence of macro-economics and deflationary economic policy on confidence, growth and expectations for trained workers who do not find requisite jobs in the Asian tiger economies may mean a decline in state interventionist policies, however. Nevertheless, despite the power of transnational corporations, they have not yet taken over the educational institutions of nation-states which continue to exercise the main influences over skill formation.

7

The Rules Governing Employment: A Comparative View

Industrial relations may be defined as being about the rules governing employment. In this chapter, the aim is to discuss the rules governing employment as a preliminary to discussing employment law – one of the main categories of those rules. For the most part, employment rules are set by employers and managers: they are work or works rules, such as starting and finishing times, rules about breaks and holidays, and about what is and is not allowed in the workplace. An example would be work clothes, uniform or dress codes. Employer freedom to vary such rules unilaterally may be limited by trade unions – if they become powerful enough to bargain collectively with employers. Until then, the only other limitation on employers will be through legislation. The simplest example from British history of such limitations were the Factories Acts.

Globalization, convergence and wages

In comparative industrial relations, the analysis is extended to comparing the rules governing employment among different countries. To the extent that globalization of economic activity is occurring, we might expect convergence of these rules. But there are many factors militating against this. To put it at its most basic, we would not expect the lowest level subsistence wages to be the same in Britain as in Haiti. Nevertheless, if we view labour purely as a commodity, as undifferentiated and unskilled, global supply and demand forces will tend to move wages to an equilibrium level. What stops this? The simple answer is other industrial relations rules, both at the micro (firm, workplace) and the macro (national/international) level. At the organizational level, the wages of the lowest paid will be affected by those of the highest paid, with or without trade union collective bargaining. However, senior managers of enterprises have shown an increasing ability to detach themselves and sections of the enterprise workforce from sub-contracted and part-time workers. As a result, real wages of those in the lowest decile of the US labour force have declined over the last two decades. US government statisticians lump the 80 per cent of working Americans whose jobs fall below the higher executive, managerial and technical levels under the heading 'production and non-supervisory workers'. The average real weekly earnings of these mostly rank-and-file workers fell by 18 per cent between 1973 and 1995, from $315 per week to $258 per week (Head, 1996). It is a remarkable fact that in 1999, when the USA was enjoying its longest business upswing in modern times, and Wall Street experienced one of the greatest bull markets in history, poverty in America was increasing. For the majority of people, real wages fell in the final quarter of the century. Economic globalization had undermined the trade unions that once gave workers a voice.

Equilibrium wages and minimum standards

At the macro level, the rationale underlying such devices as the Social Chapter and minimum standards clauses in international trade is to stop 'social dumping' and, therefore, to constrain the tendency toward equilibrium wages if this is at the cost of lowering living standards. It is argued that 'globalization is an important weapon for international capital because it keeps workers in their place and wages down'. As against this, the idea of global competition bearing down on Western living standards is a myth with only about 5 per cent of exports to Europe, North America and Japan coming from outside (Elliott, 1996).

However, such myths may be very powerful, especially backed up by the threat of enterprise closure or relocation to a cheaper wage economy. The issue of a competitive wage versus a living wage may be said to lie at the heart of industrial relations and its interface as a subject of study with economics. In policy terms, it dates back at least as far as the Labour Charter, established as part of the treaty that set out terms after the First World War. The Versailles Peace Treaty denounced treatment of labour as a commodity. Barbara (later

Baroness) Wootton considered the implications of this policy change in the 'Economic Journal' in 1920:

> Before the war we accepted in the main the view that labour was a commodity, fundamentally akin to merchandise and articles of commerce, that it was bought and sold and that the payment made for it, like the payment for other commodities, tended in the long run, to be equal to its value. Now we have the Peace Treaty denouncing the treatment of labour as an offence against both 'fact' and 'right'. Unless we are prepared to dismiss the Labour Charter of the Treaty off-hand as nothing but sound, designed to allay fury, it behoves us to inquire how far the facts already justify this new view of labour; what will be the ultimate results of carrying the new policy into effect; what are the conditions essential to its success and whether these can be permanently maintained (Wootton, 1920:46).

She went on to discuss the results of carrying this new policy into effect, accepting the possibility that the relatively more rapid progress of wages in less skilled occupations was partially due to the growth of a principle definitely designed to oust the commodity view of labour – the invention of the bonus. It was possible that the significance of this practice lay partly in that it was an attempt to give expression to the idea of a minimum standard of life and comfort. No one was to receive less payment than would enable him to reach this standard. If the value of his labour happened to be less than this minimum – well, the Peace Treaty had rendered obsolete this commodity view of labour. If this was true – and the short-run evidence seemed to support it – then Wootton believed that it was so momentous as to signify the end of economics as such:

> Wherever the policy of paying wages in excess of the value of the marginal net product of the labour which 'earns' them becomes actual, there the Paris Conference plants a flag of victory in the economist's grave. But many ghosts will rise after the slaughter of Paris and the economist is likely to be among them (Wootton, 1920:52).

The economist was likely to be among them, she thought, because she reckoned that the most important change in methods of remuneration had been the sliding scale that aimed at keeping real wages constant by eliminating the influence of fluctuations in the cost of living. However, she had already 'hinted that the economist will rise from his grave, in spite of the Peace Treaty's triumph; that the economic Humpty-Dumpty will not stay on the wall, in spite of the machinations of the sliding scale' (Wootton: 60). For mere regulation of wages could not do this without consequent unemployment and, consequently, regulation of numbers employed would also be necessary.

Ways in which rules are made and administered

There are essentially three ways in which the rules governing employment – the terms and conditions – are made and administered. First, and by far the most important, is where the pay and conditions are set by the employing organization or enterprise through the managers concerned. This may, therefore, be known as 'managerial prerogative' or 'management's right to manage'. Do note, though, that whenever these phrases are invoked by managers it is usually because there is some threat to management's unilateral decision-making. The ultimate incursion on management decision-making about employment rules or 'works rules' is through collective bargaining with trade unions or co-determination (co-decision-making) with workers' representatives. In the absence of union recognition and the willingness or obligation to 'bargain in good faith' – or of co-determination – there must be complete contract sovereignty or contract at will in the hands of the employer.

The contract at will

Writing about the evolution of collective bargaining in the USA, Selznick (1980:135) elaborated the importance of the modification of contract:

> The contract at will went hand in hand with absolute managerial discretion. If the contract is at will, no legal limits are set on the authority of the employer, especially on the key issue of dismissal. The employer is free to hire and fire unrestrained by the legal requirement that he have just cause for rescinding a contract not yet expired. Moreover, the contract at will is not a device for framing agreed-upon conditions to govern day-to-day activities. Since there is no definite duration, the terms of the contract are not binding for the future. The employer is free to modify them at any time, without notice.
>
> The main economic significance of the contract at will was the contribution it made to easy lay-off of employees in response to business fluctuations. But it also strengthened managerial authority. By the end

of the nineteenth century, the employment contract had become a very special kind of contract – in large part a legal device for guaranteeing to management the unilateral power to make rules and exercise discretion.

For this reason, Selznick called it the prerogative contract. Collective bargaining therefore must be an encroachment on managerial prerogative. As a manager quoted by Selznick put it:

> When we speak of management's rights in this context, we are referring to the residue of management's pre-existing functions which remains after the negotiation of a collective agreement. In the absence of such an agreement, management had absolute discretion in the hiring, firing and the organization and direction of the working forces, subject only to such limitations as may be imposed by law (Selznick: 178).

Statute law and works rules

This brings us to the third way in which industrial relations rules about the terms and conditions of employment may be made and administered – statute law or common law created through the courts. Writing in 1988, Toshiaki Ohta maintained that 'the role of works rules in different countries is closely related to the industrial relations systems in force. In general, it tends to be minor where collective bargaining is well developed, whilst in those where collective bargaining is still in its infancy, it can be very significant indeed' (Ohta, 1988).

This would apply, for instance, to developing countries where the government wanted to modernize by legislating a framework of labour law but at the same time to restrain trade union activity. Newly industrialized countries' governments face the problem of demands for trade union rights as they join the international competition for employment-creating investment funds. In February 1997, South Korea suffered a wave of strikes after controversial legislation that allowed firms greater flexibility to lay off workers who had expectations of lifetime employment.

Although Ohta mainly considered works rules as managerial prerogative – ' a social norm established by the employer for ensuring the smooth running of the enterprise' – he also treated works rules as modified by legislation. In his analysis, he conflated works rules with statute law to intervene in industrial relations. He offered as an example Japan's 1947 Labour Standards Act that contains detailed provisions governing the employer's responsibility for drawing up works rules and the procedures for doing so, their scope and the relationship between works rules and laws, collective agreements and contracts of employment:

> This Act has done much to transform works rules from a social norm established by the employer for ensuring the smooth running of the enterprise into a legal norm for protecting workers' conditions of work and employment – especially the large majority who are not covered by collective agreements (Ohta, 1988).

Adopting the system of unilateral employer determination of works rules, subject to certain legal limits, the Japanese Labour Standards Act shows its American influence in implicitly designating collective bargaining as the means whereby workers can press for improved pay and conditions. However, Japanese labour–management relations developed on the basis of the dialogue or consultation between enterprise unions and management. In recent years, the labour–management consultation system has developed considerably, particularly in large enterprises, as collective bargaining has declined. Conditions of work, according to Ohta, are frequently decided through some form of joint consultation machinery, such as the production committee. He noted that, of enterprises with 100 or more employees, 77 per cent had established a permanent system of consultation.

Similarly, in recent years direct participation along Japanese lines appears to have increased in Europe. In a paper for the European Foundation for Improvement of Living Standards, Fröhlich and Pekruhl (1996) considered whether it was primarily used as a management tool to decrease union influence. Their data suggested 'one general conclusion: In countries with a system of works councils or elected representatives at the establishment level, employee representatives are generally not by-passed by management' (Fröhlich and Pekruhl, 1996:138).

Legislative frameworks for works rules in other countries

Many countries have similar labour standards Acts or workers' charters to that of Japan, setting a framework for the determination of works rules by individual employers and companies. In France, the Code de Travail establishes a legislative framework that renders labour law somewhat autonomous and separate from general civil law (Wedderburn, 1987:2). In a recent judicial case in employment law in Spain, the High Court observed that the question of whether statute law (the Workers' Charter) prevailed over collective agreements or vice versa, for the purpose of determining remuneration for overtime, was controversial (Anon. 1992:314). In Italy, the *Statuto dei Lavoratori* (Workers' Statute) of 1970 deliberately refrained from imposing a duty to bargain in the same way as the US Wagner Act of 1933 but it did give rights to a 'unionized presence' constituted by workers' initiative at the workplace. Nielsen (1996:26, 35) has commented:

> The principles of equality of treatment and the prohibition of discrimination on any grounds such as race, colour, language, religion, political or other opinions, social origins, birth or other status are laid down in various international instruments (European Convention on Human Rights, UN Covenants, ILO Conventions etc.) and are enshrined explicitly or tacitly in the Constitutions of Spain, Portugal, Greece, France, Germany, Italy, Luxembourg, Belgium, Ireland and the Netherlands.

By contrast, seen from a continental European view, the Nordic source of labour law is remarkable because of the low constitutional protection of fundamental rights and high priority given to collective agreements. Similarly, it used to be thought the case that the law was largely absent from industrial relations in Britain. Nowadays, however, 'it is misleading to say that Britain, unlike most other developed countries, has no Labour Code. Statutory minimum standards already exist in respect of notice to terminate employment, maternity leave and pay, and guarantee payments, as well, of course, as in respect of health and safety' (Rideout, 1998:33).

Flexibility and procedures

Without statutory intervention or legislation, it has long been observed that one of the distinctive features of the employment contract is that its substantive content is never fully defined at the moment of engagement (and cannot be because of uncertainty about the employer's future requirements). It is then possible to argue that flexibility in the substantive content of jobs is regulated by the use of different 'procedures'. However, the operation of these procedures will also be affected by working practices. If the precise content of the job itself escapes definition and is 'defined by practice', it is clear that a precise account of the scope of procedures is impossible. They too will be defined by practice because practice has set the only standard of measurement that is available (Marsden, 1978:34).

Marsden raised the question 'how much flexibility is built into the content of a job and when does a manager's order take the worker beyond this margin and lead him (or her) into a new area? Clearly, management is likely to favour a more flexible interpretation than the employers or their representatives. From management's point of view, flexibility both increases managerial control over work organization and makes organization cheaper. From the employee's point of view, it is to his advantage that as inflexible an interpretation of his job content as possible should prevail so that he can make management pay for his co-operation. On the other hand, if management can enforce its flexible interpretation, no such opportunity exists' (Marsden: 40). It is obviously strategically vital for management to insist that global competition necessitates costless flexibility – without co-operation, in other words, there is a risk of no job.

Although Marsden was writing twenty odd years ago, the continuity of issues that were central to industrial relations then and to human resource management now is evident. To a degree, informality in employment relations and in the production process is inevitable (Terry, 1977). According to some studies, managers may depend on it to avoid chaos on the shop floor. In a study of a wire-processing mill in the USA, Juravich (1985:54) described how the machines were worked with wire beyond the tolerances specified for the wire-making machines. 'Everyone in the mill was aware of this. Thus everyone was in an ambiguous position that required a constant negotiation of the rules.' In Juravich's experience, this went on in other mills where official specifications serve only as general guidelines and where actual specifications were much looser. The issue of informal practices and health and safety procedures is well known, as it is in disciplinary procedures. These days, such informality is increasingly about deprofessionalization of the labour of occupations traditionally defined as professional. Expert systems, by codifying professional knowledge and skill, may facilitate the disempowering of workers at even the highest levels of organization, including those perceived to do professional work, such as doctors, lawyers, accountants and computer specialists, as well as strategic managers' (Rosen and Baroudi, 1992:228).

Question for discussion

'Industrial relations is about rules – but globalization knows no bounds.'

Where does this leave human resource management?

Flexibility now means much the same as Marsden outlined in 1978. In some contexts, the implication is to return full circle to the contract at will and contract prerogative. There tends to be an unfortunate duality in managers' minds between rules and procedures, and business needs, flexibility and commitment. Or, managers 'may believe in the importance of clear rules while insisting that they alone have the unilateral right to devise them' (Clark, 1993:80). According to Lord Wedderburn, the same pressure towards deregulation and flexibility has blossomed in France. Journals that once debated the autonomy of labour law now debate destroying the labour law code and discuss flexibility, scrapping the code's protections and loosening rules about dismissal (Wedderburn, 1987:15).

Selznick's argument (1980:137) that the contract of employment inevitably becomes a prerogative contract, a mode of submission, if provision is not made for employee participation in the continuing process of rule-making and administration, is compelling. This raises the question: if the collective bargaining model is seen as out-of-date, what is it being replaced by? Various writers have argued that unions ought to be moving away from collective bargaining, towards a more 'associational' model, perceiving a 'trend towards cooperative industrial relations based on a recognition of mutuality in the interest of industrial survival and individual fulfillment in the workplace' (Raskin, 1986:955).

It follows that human resource management models have to be participative, otherwise eliminating or reducing collective bargaining must entail a reversion or partial reversion to contract sovereignty or complete managerial prerogative. Human resource management is often in a no-man's-land between procedures and 'the complete flexibility/treat each case as it comes approach of the macho manager or other zealous believers in management's right to manage, irrespective of whether this is fair or reasonable' (Clark, 1993:80).

Wales joins tiger economies by undercutting the East

Fresh low-wage competition for skilled jobs is coming from the latest and least likely recruit to the ranks of the tiger economies: South Wales. The one-time heartland of heavy industry and labour militancy is undercutting the Far East, bringing back to Britain jobs long lost to the developing world.

The latest to come home is Ronson's highly successful petrol lighter, the Typhoon, heading for Cwmbran in Gwent after many years on the Pacific Rim.

With Korean wage rates pressing upwards as the country follows the trail blazed by the Japanese, Ronson's chief executive Howard Hodgeson has decided to bring the tools and the work back to Britain.

He disclosed that Korean pay averages £10,000–£12,000 a year, against £8,000–£10,000 in South Wales, while insisting the move back to Wales was not entirely based on relative wage costs. Manufacturing in Wales will eliminate shipping costs, he said, and allow Ronson to stick a Union Jack – whose kudos is 'con-siderable' – on the lighter.

Already Premier Pressings, the Typhoon's home-to-be, makes the far more complex upmarket Ronson gas lighters, and Mr Hodgeson is more than happy with the results. 'The British worker is not the worker that I grew up with in the 1960s, with his tea breaks and his strikes,' he said. 'Today's employee is a quality worker.' And, of the Cwmbran team, he added: 'We believe in them'.

But wage costs form a critical part of any calculation, and Mr Hodgeson is convinced that South Korea is mimicking Japan, transforming itself from a base for low wage manufacture of cheap and cheerful goods to a world-class economic player, home of international giants such as Samsung, Daewoo and Sinochem. In the process, incomes rise.

The Welsh can console themselves with the thought that in one country, at least, people will always be paid less than they are: China. Mr Hodgeson explained: 'The only labour cheaper than Chinese labour is no labour.'

Dan Atkinson, *Guardian*,
25 April 1996

Human resource management and participation

In 1987, Wolfgang Streeck considered the issue of participation in relation to human resource management. He suggested that alternative management styles to achieve organizational flexibility are consultation, participation and/or co-determination *or* unilateral use of managerial prerogative. Where flexibility is believed to be possible only under co-operative industrial relations, employers are faced with the strategic alternative between including independent trade unions in the constitutional structure of the workplace or excluding them.

Examples abound, particularly in the USA, of attempts to secure workplace co-operation without unions. Streeck reckoned that this provided the main impetus behind human resource management in that it aimed to create a substitute for unions. However, he concluded that 'even the most sophisticated human resource management may not be able, for political as well as technical reasons, to carry alone the immense burden of administering a complex internal labour market' (Streeck, 1987:281). Consequently, devolution of responsibilities to independent organizations of functional representation may be an effective way of increasing governability. In fact, he argued, this was apparently an important reason why German employers accepted works councils and co-determination.

Sub-contracting as alternative devolution

Unfortunately, in the light of hindsight, Streek can be seen to have been considerably over-optimistic. He should perhaps have been warned by his own reference to the 'complex internal labour market'. In the 1980s, some industrial relations professors, including William Brown, declared their dislike of the term 'internal labour market' as inappropriate for what was a set of internal administrative rules. Over the long term, however, it can be considered a very appropriate term. The laws of supply and demand and administrative rules may be considered synonymous if the firm is broken up – disintegrated – and there is no intervening agency. Since Coase's seminal article, many economists have tended to share his assumption 'that the distinguishing mark of the firm is the supersession of the price mechanism' (Coase, 1937:388). What can be internalized can relatively quickly be externalized:

> A hallmark of flexible production is vertical disintegration, meaning a central enterprise controls the final product and the key technology, while non-strategic functions are sub-contracted to other firms. The externalization of certain production functions gives firms the advantage of various cost savings plus external economies of scale (Ioannides and Debbage, 1997:229).

Sub-contracting is seen here as an external form of devolution of administration, avoiding the complexity that Streek observed when managers are compelled to recognize and bargain in good faith with a trade union. There is nothing new about this, although it may be justified and buttressed by new management jargon. The whole issue was researched by Margaret Chandler in her book *Management Rights and Union Interests*. Now a neglected classic, it contains important insights about sub-contracting, despite its origins in the full employment era of the 1960s.

> Chandler found that sub-contracting was double-edged: on the one hand, it was a means by which some managements shuffled off their responsibilities but, at the same time, it could be used to reassert managerial control and prerogatives by proxy. Sub-contracting offered an escape from some of the rebarbative and time-consuming obligations of the employment relationship itself (Aldridge, 1976:79).

More recently, it has been commented that 'before one extends rights or the protection of employees, one must consider the possibility that employers will resort to self-employment if pushed too far' (Rideout, 1998:34). This applies no less to legislation: 'If, as is suggested, zero hours contracts were forbidden for employees, it would be found very easy to avoid the protection by resorting to self-employment with little substantial change in working arrangements' (Rideout: 34).

The unions and their members are well aware of the threat of sub-contracting to their ability to defend living standards and tolerable working conditions. That is why the unions have attempted to reach a collective agreement limiting outside sourcing with each of the big car producing firms. Among the causes of the strike that rattled the apparent harmony at British Airways in July 1997 was the senior management's plan to increase sub-contracting of catering and baggage handling.

The participation that logically must take the place of collective bargaining if complete contract sovereignty is not entirely handed over to management may be a sham. It may be questioned whether direct participation is not primarily used as a management tool to decrease union influence. According to the EPOC (Employee Participation in Organizational Change) study of direct participation, the evidence is mixed. The EPOC data 'suggest one general conclusion which should be outlined: *in countries with a system of works councils or elected representatives at the establishment level, employee representatives are generally not by-passed by management'* (Fröhlich and Pekruhl, 1996:138).

In general, *direct participation* is a term that defies analysis, particularly when combined with *flexibility*. The EPOC team asserted that they were 'aware that they were dealing with a management-driven strategy that aims at the workplace level' but they nevertheless saw this as holding 'the idea of more consultative and/or delegative rights for individuals or for workgroups' (Fröhlich and Pekruhl: 20). Employee empowerment came into vogue in the 1990s as an example of initiatives to increase participation and involvement of employees. Empowerment initiatives were often part of a corporate culture change programme. The ostensible aim was to pass decision-making as far down the line as possible to give employees greater discretion and control over day-to-day tasks.

However, such initiatives are congruent with management perceptions of flexibility – not those of employees. According to a study of the training of low-skilled workers at Renault to work in semi-autonomous groups, the Confédération Générale de Travail (CGT) unionists kept out of this scheme in order not to support workforce integration 'in the Japanese way', in particular if job classifications were not revised to account for the workers' new skills. This was precisely the issue raised by Marsden in 1978 about flexibility but precisely the issue that management wants to avoid subjecting to rules and procedures. It was pointed out to researchers at British Steel that the company's Total Quality Production programme was not about workers' participation (Bacon, Blyton and Morris, 1996:46).

Making culture change of the 'control-by-commitment' type congruent with increased sub-contracting must be next to impossible. That sort of culture change usually emphasizes trust, loyalty and commitment. It is difficult to reconcile this with use of labour as a commodity under the direction of separate management and organization.

Conclusion – labour as a commodity versus industrial relations rules

A key question for those who believe that the study of industrial relations or comparative industrial relations is no longer relevant is 'will equilibrium wages prevail ?' The nub of the issue is encapsulated in Tony Blair's acceptance of the EU Social Charter, yet hedging it about with concerns about competitiveness. At the micro level, human resource management logically entails more participation if it does not mean a reversion to untrammelled contract sovereignty and management prerogative. There is tension between flexibility and rules and procedures. At the macro level, the EU Social Chapter, labour charters at national level and other societally approved methods of maintaining labour standards to prevent 'social dumping' run into strategies to increase corporate competitiveness. At an intermediate level, company mistakes in trying to increase competitiveness will incur investor disfavour, as in the case of the BA dispute of 1997 when top managers of financial institutions told BA senior management that a service industry depended on commitment and loyalty from its employees. Would they have demurred if the planned sub-contracting had not provoked a costly strike?

To the economist who believes in profit maximization, the question whether to use external contractors is one of economic efficiency in the neo-classical sense. If a social element is to be brought into wages and working conditions – not simply whether labour is a commodity in the moral sense of the Treaty of Versailles but how to make efficiency compatible with the firm as a dispersed social agency – this orthodoxy has to be somehow modified. Otherwise, as Chandler concluded (Chandler, 1964:163), it is 'easy to extrapolate to a situation in which the manager regained all his old rights in the employment relationship, while the worker moved back to the days before the Wagner Act', unprotected by trade unions and works rules governed by collective agreement.

8

Comparative Labour Law – Individual Employment Rights

Summary

In this chapter and the following chapter, the main factor underlying systemic differences in human resource management strategy – national employment law – is discussed. Labour law is conventionally divided into two parts: individual and collective. While this can be helpful in sub-dividing material, the inherent collective nature of the employment relationship means that what appear to be individual issues may soon shade into collective ones. Nevertheless, topics such as unfair dismissal and discipline are often treated as individual. In principle, at least, the contract of employment individualizes the employment relationship. As pointed out in the previous chapter, this can reassert complete contract sovereignty or managerial prerogative on the part of the employer. Some individual contracts are very precarious, particularly those of part-time workers. This is a key issue in the development of anti-discrimination legislation in Europe, as the huge majority of part-time employees are women. Part-time working and precarious employment is in itself a topic of vital importance, as for many employees the issue of interpretation of how secure their employment rights are is fraught with doubt and anxiety. However, most of this chapter is devoted to disciplinary law; first, because it relates very strongly to legislation on unfair dismissal and secondly, to demonstrate the thin and ambiguous line that separates individual discipline from collective labour law.

Industrial relations systems and labour law frameworks

One of the main ways in which countries can vary in their industrial relations and human resource management practices is by different employment law frameworks. Of course, such distinctions and contrasts do depend to a large extent on the notion of separate national industrial relations systems. For example, Kuruvilla (1996) has analysed links between national industrial strategies and industrial relations/human resource management policies, although in this study of Malaysia, India and the Philippines, the labour law framework was only a part of industrial strategy.

Labour law is that part of the law that deals with individuals and legal persons in their capacity as employees or employers, i.e. concerned with work and the relationships arising from it. Labour law is concerned with both the collective and individual aspects of the employment relationship. An important consideration in analysing national labour law is the extent to which it is *autonomous* in a particular country. That is to say, do the legal rules on labour and employment become a distinct discipline and the subject of special industrial legislation? If so, labour law may detach itself from the main body of civil law and become established as an independent judicial system with a specialist labour court. This is not unusual because the same might be said of maritime law, tax law or company law. Certainly, the need for autonomy in labour law has been a controversial issue in France. But not in the UK where employment law has been forced back on the (unsatisfactory?) foundation of contract and handled by the ordinary civil courts (except for the ill-fated brief reign of the Industrial Relations Act of 1971 and its National Industrial Relations Court).

Of course, 'autonomy' is a bit of an exaggeration; no branch of law can be completely autonomous from the body of judicial order as a whole. Labour law may, however, be to some extent distinguished from civil law by its collective character, its umbilical cord to the social facts. It must deal in categories of collective negotiation, rather than contract.

Consequently, it was suggested that, if the cornerstone of employment law in the UK was the employment contract, then perhaps it had a core of rubble (Rideout, 1966:127). The issue of the usefulness and validity of the employment contract has been raised in various ways (Leighton, 1984). One lawyer went as far as to claim that 'the nature of the exchange relationships in work cannot be gauged by reference to the so-called contract of employment' (Hepple, 1986). But, it follows that, once the concept of the contract of employment is rejected, the need to rebuild labour law more generally emerges (Wedderburn, 1987) which is why many countries have a Labour Standards Law, Workers' Charter or Code de Travail. However, it may be that 'it is misleading to say that Britain, unlike most developed countries, has no Labour Code' as 'statutory minimum standards exist in respect of notice to terminate employment, maternity leave and pay' (Rideout, 1998:33).

Individual and collective employment rights

The distinction between individual and collective employment rights is largely arbitrary and it may be difficult to draw a line between individual and collective. Disciplinary procedures are individual-based but the law surrounding administration of those procedures is by nature collective, needing to be laid down at the enterprise, occupational, industrial or state level. Nonetheless, the distinction is useful. When we talk about collective labour law, we generally mean employment law as applied to *collectivities* of employees (trade unions) and employers (could be in employers' associations). So, under collective labour law, we could be discussing trade union law – though not only that. This will be considered in the following chapter. Basically, individual employment law regulates the individual employment relationship as it arises from the contract of employment. However, in different countries, interpretation of the employment contract varies. As a concept, the employment contract is often vapid.

> As a concept, it has long been in crisis – one created by changes in relations of production that are not recent . . . But that crisis has been reinforced in recent decades by rapid fragmentation of the labour market, especially by the growth of so-called 'atypical' or 'marginal' relationships between workers and those for whom they produce value – the worker as part-time, casual, temporary or lump labour, homeworker, outworker or sub-contractor, let alone the trainee or the police cadet who are – unless special laws are passed – left unprotected because they are, in the eyes of judges, as reflected in the common law, *sui generis* – 'a class in themselves' (Lord Denning, quoted by Lord Wedderburn, 1987:6).

To illustrate this and expand on individual labour law, we will consider three main areas: teleworkers and part-time workers – to illustrate the ambiguities of contract – then disciplinary rules and, finally, unfair dismissal.

Homeworkers and teleworkers

Teleworking relies on three main ideas: organization, location and technology. More than 60 per cent of definitions are based on a combination of at least two of these ideas. It may be defined as 'work carried out in a location where, remote from central offices or production facilities, the worker has no personal contact with co-workers there but is able to communicate with them using new technology'.

'The relationship of teleworker to employer can be ambivalent. Certain conditions are similar to those of self-employed contractors because the workplace is located away from the company and work is performed more or less autonomously. On the other hand, teleworkers are dependent on the work given to them by the employer and they are also subject to the employer's authority in areas such as output. If the relationship between an employer and a teleworker is clearly recognized on both sides as one of subordination, then the teleworker is clearly entitled to the same working conditions and social security coverage as other workers in the same enterprise. He or she is entitled to the same dismissal procedure, sick pay, unemployment benefits, paid leave, minimum wage etc. However, if the relationship is formally one of self-employment but in fact involves substantial elements of subordination, the teleworker runs the risk of being deprived, without justification, of employment rights and social protection.' (Di Martino and Wirth, 1990:545).

Guidelines published by the CGT-Force Ouvrière (French trade union federations) point to the lack of information on the impact of telework and state that at this stage it is only possible to identify present advantages and disadvantages. These include saved commuting time, a more agreeable atmosphere achieved in small work groups and fewer apparent hierarchical constraints. However, these are outweighed by disadvantages such as isolation, fragmentation of work, erosion of work community and limited contact with trade union representatives.

Part-time workers

In an important case in Spain, the collective agreement between an airline and its ground staff stated that it applied to all the ground staff, with exceptions, including regularly employed intermittent workers and casual and part-time staff, who were to be covered by *rules* specifically drawn up for them. A trade union instituted proceedings demanding recognition of the right of intermittent and casual workers to the same wage levels as those established under the agreement for full-time permanent workers.

After the claim had been rejected by a lower court, the trade union appealed to the Central Labour Court which quashed the earlier decision. It considered that the Workers' Charter authorized the parties to determine the scope of collective agreements but specific groups of workers could not be excluded from that scope without *due cause*. The principle of equality laid down in article 14 of the Constitution and in a number of labour provisions – such as the Workers' Charter – required equal treatment in equal circumstances and did not allow different treatment unless there was sufficient justification. This principle was applicable also to collective agreements under article 14 of the Constitution and the ILO's Discrimination and Social Policy conventions which Spain had ratified. There is an answer here to the claim that it is misleading to say that Britain has no Labour Code. It is doubtful whether the minimum standards that exist would have protected similar workers in Britain. In fact, 'evidence of widespread alterations to the pre-existing terms and conditions and job security after business transfers, a situation which the law is supposed to prevent, clearly shows that the law is failing to regulate business transfers. These findings highlight a salient concern about how Compulsory Competitive Tendering (in the UK) generally results in a reduction in terms and conditions and, thus, undermines the purpose of the EU law relating to business transfers' (Hardy, Adnett and Painter, 1998:21).

The law of dismissal and employment practices in Japan and Britain

The Japanese law of employment dismissal has been established on the assumption of lifetime employment practice. This has been well developed in the larger companies. However, those who enjoy the benefits of lifetime employment and strict legal regulation of dismissal are regular and permanent employees only, *not* peripheral workers, part-timers, employment agency workers and temps, subcontract workers, fixed term contract workers, seasonal workers, day workers and 'side-job' workers. Lifetime employment applies to less than 30 per cent of employees and lifetime employment in practice does not mean that employees are guaranteed employment till retirement age, rather that this is expected to be the case. Nevertheless, the courts have denied the legal effectiveness of dismissals that don't have just causes as specified in collective agreements and also dismissals that do not satisfy substantive or procedural requirements stipulated in *shugyo kisoku* (works rules) are usually held to be void.

These assumptions have begun to collide with pressures for flexibility arising from technological change, the expansion of service industries and an ageing population and Japanese employers have been put under enormous pressure to bring down levels of permanent employees (especially white-collar employees). However, 'overall, Japanese employers' attempts to reduce the level of employment security for their core workers have not been extensive' (Morishima, 1995). The tendency for Japanese employers to stick to 'lifetime' employment practices was observed in previous recessions and again in the current recession. According to a study that examined more than 30 firms that took some sort of employment adjustment during 1992–4, only two of the firms surveyed laid off core workers. The main reason why employment security continues to be strongly protected in Japanese labour markets is that 'it is grounded in legal precedents set by the Japanese court that has made it almost impossible for employers to terminate or lay off regular status employees without employee or union consent' (Morishima, 1995). This will moderate even the changes set off by the economic downturn of 1998.

In a famous case, a worker at Hitachi's Musashi plant refused overtime at the end of a day, as ordered by his supervisor on the grounds that overtime should be entirely voluntary and he was busy that evening. He subsequently made up the backlog by working overtime the following day. His section chief tried to obtain a promise from him to comply with future requests to work overtime but he maintained his view that overtime should be voluntary. He was suspended for insubordination for fourteen days, after which supervisors tried several times to persuade him of his insubordination – to no avail. Relations between worker and supervisors deteriorated further until they ordered that he stay home to reflect – which he repeatedly refused to do. His employer then dismissed him, after consultation with the Musashi Plant labour union, invoking a written agreement between the company and the union on the extension of working time in certain circumstances. (The union had tried to save the worker's job by persuading him to admit insubordination but he refused to be represented by the union.)

The Tokyo High Court granted a temporary postponement, saying that disciplinary dismissal was too severe. Finally – after twenty-four years of legal wrangles – the Supreme Court in 1991 dismissed his appeal, saying that the agreement on overtime met the Labour Standards Law and, as provision was made in the works rules to order overtime work within the limits stated in the agreement, the worker had a duty to comply since the provisions of the works rules formed an integral part of the employment contract.

Ostensibly and theoretically, individual labour law may be to do with the individual contract and therefore is treated as encompassing dismissal and the law pertaining to dismissal, in particular, unfair dismissal. However, it has been argued by Brown and Rea (1995:365) that 'collective regulation – whether unilateral by management or jointly with unions – provides a means of lowering the costs of contracting by specifying rules common to all contracts'. They conclude that 'the nature of the employment contract is such that employers have to be sensitive to its inherently collective character' (Brown and Rea: 374) It is not necessarily clear how individual dissent may be distinguished from group indiscipline or refusal to accept changed working arrangements or rules. Crucial to this is the issue of works rules *versus* collective bargaining raised in the previous chapter.

According to one jurist, 'the decision of the UK Employment Appeals Tribunal in *Lewis and Britton v. E.Mason & Sons* is an indication of the depths to which British labour law has sunk in recent years' (Dolding, 1994:243). Britton was employed as a driver with the firm of E. Mason. A manager told him to drive one of the firm's lorries to Edinburgh. Discovering that the vehicle did not have a heater and not willing to spend the night in an unheated lorry cab in the middle of winter, he agreed to go provided he was given an extra £5 for bed and breakfast. The manager rejected this request and when Britton refused to go he was immediately dismissed. Another driver was asked to go but as he also stipulated conditions that were unacceptable to the manager, he too was dismissed. After a discussion among the workforce, including the two sacked drivers, it was agreed that Lewis, another driver employed by the firm, should negotiate on their behalf. He telephoned the manager and told him that if the dismissed drivers were not reinstated, the others would not come into work the next day. The manager replied that he would not be held to ransom and promptly dismissed Lewis and the others. Lewis and Britton took their complaint of unfair dismissal to an industrial tribunal. However, the tribunal found that they had been taking part in industrial action and therefore the dismissals were fair. 'That an employee who takes industrial action should thereby be in breach of contract and also lose protection against unfair dismissal is not immediately obvious to the student of labour law' (Dolding, 1994:246).

The bases of disciplinary law vary in ways that reflect the relative importance of works rules, collective bargaining and national legislation, as discussed in the previous chapter. In connection with the issue of discipline *per se*, Banderet (1986) carried out a survey that is quite useful in delineating the links between disciplinary procedures and law. It has been used as the basis for the discussion that follows.

Disciplinary procedures and the law

The main sources of disciplinary procedures are: (a) legislation; (b) collective agreements; (c) works rules; (d) individual contracts of employment and (e) case law built up on the basis of *just cause* clauses in collective agreements and added to the main body of disciplinary law. Case law might also be influenced by a code of practice on disciplinary procedures, such as that drawn up by ACAS in the UK.

(a)   Legislation on disciplinary law

According to Banderet (1986), France is the only country to have enacted legislation dealing with disciplinary law in its entirety. However, this development occurred in the Auroux laws on workers' rights that have had a limited effect in practice. In Japan, as exemplified above, the Labour Standards Law of 1947 legislates that discipline be covered by a clause in the works rules and puts limits on the amount of cash penalties that can be imposed. The USA has a considerable body of law governing prohibition of disciplinary measures, particularly those against employees engaged in union activities.

(b)   Collective agreements

In Austria, Belgium, France, Germany, India, UK, collective agreements constitute only a minor source of disciplinary law. They are more likely to be a significant source in the public sector. Connell (1991) reported on the deregulation of Telecom Australia and the effect on corporate discipline. In 1989, Telecom Australia had become a corporation, instead of a regulatory commission. If the disciplinary rules had not been revised, the new company might have been open to law suits for unfair dismissal. The union wanted the reintroduction of the former disciplinary code with minor amendments. The new disciplinary provisions, termed 'Agreed procedures' were accordingly incorporated in an appendix to an award under the newly legislated Industrial Relations Act, 1988, by consent between Telecom Australia and its employee organizations. Connell commented on the procedure that it requires a substantial industry base. It could not really be adapted for use in small enterprises where workers are necessarily dependent on either the courts or their unions. In a very large organization like Telecom Australia, the Appeal Board System ensures that disciplinary action is properly controlled internally, providing a much cheaper and speedier alternative to the courts.

(c)   Works rules

Works rules are usually the parties' and the judiciary's preferred basis for disciplinary law. They can take account of the specific culture of the workplace and can consequently be made more flexible. Some countries, such as France, have come to consider works rules as an obligatory source of disciplinary law. Others, such as Japan (see chapter 7) make them an obligatory source only where there are no relevant clauses in collective agreements. As Ohta (1988:999) pointed out, therefore, works rules and collective bargaining tend to be interchangeable. In all other countries, works rules tend to be an important source of law, especially in the UK and India. However, Banderet noted two countries where works rules did not usually enter into disciplinary law – Australia – where they were not a well-defined legal instrument – and Sri Lanka. In countries where co-determination is important – Germany and Austria, for instance – they may be negotiated with a works council where it is influential enough, generally in the larger enterprises.

(d)   Individual contracts of employment

Usually the contract of employment is of small importance in disciplinary law. Banderet pointed out that this is not really surprising because disciplinary law is by nature collective and so needs to be set out at the level of enterprise, occupation or state – an individual legal instrument cannot properly meet this purpose.

(e)   Case law

Of special significance is arbitration case law which has established a body of disciplinary law in the unionized sectors of the USA and Canada, on the basis of the *just cause* clause in collective agreements. However, since arbitrators do not have to follow precedents, the rules deriving from such case law are often controversial when used as guidelines. In the USA, Employment-at-will (EAW) is a common law doctrine stating that employers have the right to hire and fire whomsoever they choose, unless there is a law or contract to the contrary. In the 1960s a number of state courts began to create exceptions to EAW. 'Courts questioned the *fairness* of an employer's decision to fire an employee without just cause and due process. The courts in California and New York have taken two very different approaches to EAW. These positions represent the extreme ends of a continuum of approaches being taken nationwide. In New York, courts have refused to take EAW cases, saying that EAW is a legislative concern. On the other hand, in California, courts will take EAW cases almost without exception' (Mathis and Jackson, 1991:450).

Although, strictly speaking, it is not case law, the Code of Practice on discipline issued by ACAS in the UK has been used by judges in assessing the facts of a case and reaching a decision.

Substantive disciplinary law

According to Banderet, under all legal systems, if it is left to the employer to define offences, he will do so in most cases through the medium of works rules. However, does it follow that the employer must define precisely and exhaustively *all* offences rendering employees liable to disciplinary action?

Only Japan and Belgium appear to apply this principle strictly. Others – including Canada, France, New Zealand, Australia and the USA – do not on the grounds that breaches of discipline take such a wide variety of forms that it is impossible to draw up an exhaustive list of offences. However, Banderet reckoned that a comparison between Belgian and Japanese practices might well show that a fairly exhaustive listing of disciplinary offences is quite possible.

Limits on employers' powers to define scope of disciplinary offences are as follows:

1   offence must be work related (this limitation was breached by employers after the miners' strike of 1984–85 in the UK). In general, acts or behaviour in private life cannot be the subject of disciplinary action by the employer. An exception is substance abuse. Drug testing by employers is controversial but may be legal and appropriate if certain requirements are met. These are that the work consequences of abuse are so severe that they outweigh privacy concerns; that accurate test procedures are available; employees give consent in writing; results are treated confidentially and the employer has a complete drug programme, including counselling assistance to drug users;
2   employee's act or omission must be unjustified;
3   rules of which violation constitutes a disciplinary offence must be reasonable. The North American concept of *just cause* implies this sort of limitation – disciplinary rules must be reasonable, i.e. in keeping with the general framework and the activity of the organization.

Substantive disciplinary law – penalties

Only the French labour code contains a definition of penalties but it is poorly worded and open to varying interpretations. France generally prohibits cash penalties. Usually there are limits, as under the 1986 Wages Act in the UK. Other frequently used penalties are suspension (with or without pay) and deferment or suspension of pay rises.

Procedures in disciplinary law

The elements of the procedure include:

1   inquiry into the circumstances. In the UK, the code of disciplinary practice issued by ACAS recommends that employers promptly establish the facts so that they have reasonable grounds for believing that there has been a breach of discipline. The principle of *just cause* obtains in some states of the USA and all American and Canadian employers who are parties to a collective agreement must undertake an inquiry into the facts of the case;
2   employee's defence – a key element is the employee's right to reply to accusations;

3   representation and participation – there appear to be rules on this subject only in Germany and Austria where co-determination is necessary for the imposition of disciplinary penalties because the agreement of the works council is required;
4   imposing the penalty;
5   appeals.

Conciliation and arbitration

Obviously discipline is an issue that can often give rise to conflict and dispute. In some countries, disputes may be divided into disputes of *right* and disputes of *interest*. Disputes of right arise from the application or interpretation of an existing rule that is part of works rules, a collective agreement or individual contract of employment. Disputes of interests are about the making of new agreements or the revision of agreements that have expired. In many countries this distinction is crucial for the choice of mechanism to settle the dispute. Arbitration is often a cheaper and more convenient system for employers. 'In comparison with countries such as Canada and the United States, however, industrial arbitration is a rarity in Britain, though ACAS has always offered arbitration and a few employers regularly resort to it as a final stage in their internal disciplinary procedures' (Rideout, 1998:49). The 1998 Employment Rights (dispute Resolution) Act in the UK empowered ACAS to prepare a voluntary arbitration scheme as an alternative to employment tribunal hearings in unfair dismissal cases. This had been advocated (Dickens et al., 1985) as preferable to judicial determination of individual employment disputes on account of differences of personnel form, procedure, objectives and nature of the process.

In countries where the concept of disputes of rights exists, such disputes are handled by specialized labour courts or by the ordinary civil courts. In most European countries arbitration has little significance in the settlement of individual labour disputes. One reason might be the easy accessibility of the courts. Another reason might be that the validity of arbitration clauses in many countries is restricted by statute or case law. In the Nordic countries, however, collective agreements sometimes stipulate arbitration and permanent arbitration bodies for settlement of individual disputes.

'Labour Courts vary in their composition (single judge, bipartite or tripartite bench), procedures (adjudication or adjudication plus conciliation) and jurisdiction (individual employment conflicts or employment conflicts plus collective labour conflicts, for example works council claims)' (Rogowski, 1996). As previously discussed, 'Labour Courts also differ with respect to their autonomy from the ordinary judicial system and from the appeal structure. In Germany, for example, Labour Courts form a separate court system with the Federal Labour Court as the final instance of appeal in labour law matters. The independence of the Federal Labour Court has had a remarkable impact on the development of the field of labour law. The Court is in many instances the initiator of legal change which the legislator subsequently casts in statutory form' (Rogowski, 1996).

According to Rogowski, 'German labour courts handle three to four times as many dismissal claims as do the British industrial tribunals. They have a wide-ranging jurisdiction, including a number of claims beyond dismissal complaints that are related to the termination of employment (for example, references). Conciliation in court is a form of case management as a settlement does not require the judge to write a formal decision. Successful conciliation in Labour Courts depends on both the capability of the courts to engage in conciliation and the willingness of the parties to accept settlement proposals of the court. A counter-example is the French Labour Court system. The rate of conciliation has declined steadily in French Labour Courts and indicates a general loss of reputation of this lay court.' In general, the role of conciliation and mediation in individual labour disputes in Europe appears to be considerable, whilst that of arbitration is slight.

Although arbitration is widely used in the USA as a dispute resolution mechanism, comprehensive statistical data on its use are not collected by any organization, public or private. Every year, employees and management enter into thousands of collective agreements throughout the USA. Virtually all of these agreements provide for arbitration of unresolved disputes, including issues in such areas as discipline, dismissal, demotion, promotion, pensions and seniority. In fiscal year 1994, of nearly 5000 cases arbitrated by the Federal Mediation and Conciliation service, well over half were about working arrangements, rules and discipline, with dismissal and disciplinary cases totalling 2286.

Flexibility and dismissal protection

There are a wide variety of rules and procedures aimed at protecting workers from unfair dismissal. Demekas (1995) has analysed such regulation in relation to employment flexibility in Italy, noting that such restrictions would raise adjustment costs since 'atypical' or flexible contracts have lower fixed costs (at least in theory; in practice, he concedes that so-called flexible contracts may be saddled with restrictions that raise *their* fixed costs).

Rules on dismissals in most countries have been influenced by a legal tradition that the worker has a sort of property 'right' to the job and that being the weaker party he deserves protection by the state. 'In most of these areas of individual dismissal regulations, the Italian system has been more restrictive than that of other major EU countries' (Demekas, 1995:8).

Perhaps the most important restriction is the heavy penalty on the employer in case dismissal is judged unfair, particularly the rehiring requirement which is in addition to the mandatory compensation. This, together with the favourable rulings traditionally handed down by the courts to workers appealing against dismissals, has made the use of dismissal as an instrument of adjusting the size of the workforce very infrequent. According to European Commission surveys, dismissal protection regulations in the European Union have changed very little in recent years. In some countries, such as Italy, Spain and Ireland, they have been strengthened. In others – France and, especially, the UK – the protection has been reduced. In Germany, too, the statutory regulations on dismissal protection now cover only companies with more than ten employees (Winkler-Buttner, 1997:173).

The main legislative attempt to deregulate the German system of employment protection was the Employment Promotion Act of 1985. It tried to encourage ways around the unfair dismissal law by use of short-term contracts. However, according to Buechtemann (1993:291), the impact was limited. 'Despite intensive government propaganda extolling the benefits of the new regulations, the overwhelming majority (96 per cent) of firms in the private sector ignored the additional options offered.' German firms apparently preferred internal forms of workforce adjustment to external numerical flexibility – which perhaps could be categorized as a systemic or embedded human resource management strategy.

Another example showed the interconnection of collective and individual employment rights and how legal rights in some countries could protect workers from sub-contracting. Patrick, Australia's second biggest cargo handling company, sacked dock workers after announcing that the subsidiary companies that employed them were bankrupt. Patrick then replaced the sacked dockers with non-union workers trained in secret and hired on short-term contracts. The federal government strongly supported Patrick's coercive, rationalistic strategy.

Even so, the unfair dismissal law helped the dockers and their union. The union took legal action against Patrick in the Federal Court, which ruled that Patrick should reinstate the workers and not hire others in their place, finding that Patrick may also have broken the law forbidding the dismissal of people simply on the grounds of union membership. After Patrick appealed to the High Court – the ultimate appeal court – the ruling against the dockers' dismissal was upheld (Milliken, 1998). A human resource management strategy of flexibility and deregulation had run up against regulation in the form of individual employment protection law. Also, although the contract of employment may be individual, it cannot really be separated from the collective characteristics of the employment relationship, alongside other workers, as is explored in the next chapter.

Although many countries are trying to achieve more flexible labour markets, the role of labour law in the different countries remains quite distinct in regulating this common process. For example, one of the explanations for the rigorous policy of deregulation carried out by the Thatcher and Major governments in Britain originated in the typical British tradition of labour law. In pursuing a central policy of deregulation the (Conservative) governments of the United Kingdom did not have to remove many legal obstacles because few existed. Because it was voluntary collective bargaining, rather than regulatory legislation which was seen as the major obstacle to the growth of the flexible workforce, the main thrust of the United Kingdom's legislation was directed towards weakening collective bargaining.

By contrast, instead of *removing* collective and statutory regulations, countries such as France and Germany developed specific legislation to promote and protect the employment of atypical workers. In these 'juridifcation' models (Hepple, 1992), greater regulation by a law-driven state was seen as inevitable for a flexible restructuring of the labour market. In Germany, this has led to only minor changes in labour law. In France, the government acted as the prime mover in renovating the labour market by new legislation. Right-wing think-tanks such as the British Centre for Policy Studies continue to berate the Franco-German social model, yet British labour productivity continues to lag far behind that of both France and Germany.

Question for discussion

Discuss the meanings of the following, using different national examples:
(a)   contracts of employment;
(b)   employment at will;
(c)   employment rights;
(d)   due process;
(e)   just cause;
(f)   conciliation and arbitration in individual cases.

9

Collective Labour Law

An important aspect of collective labour law is the regulation of industrial conflict in the form of strikes or what is euphemistically called industrial action, and the opportunity is taken here to discuss comparative material on the right to strike. Undoubtedly, strikes are social phenomena of some complexity. Further, as the incidence of strikes has tended to decline in many countries – partly, if not wholly, due to more stringent legal regulation – any international comparison of strike activity is covered here, rather than in a separate chapter.

Collective labour law defined

Collective labour law deals with collective industrial relations behaviour and the institutions for the regulation of employment relations, such as trade unions and collective bargaining. Since collective bargaining does not always result in agreement without overt conflict, such as lock-outs, strikes or lesser forms of withdrawal of labour, collective labour law is mainly concerned with the regulation of such conflict.

According to Jacobs (1993:423), 'to classic legal minds the law of strikes is certainly one of the least palatable parts of the law. Those who go on strike seek to impose their stand on the adversary by simply inflicting harm but resolving a dispute by inflicting harm on the other party runs counter to all notions most dear to lawyers'.

Nevertheless, in the period from the end of the Second World War through to the 1980s, the practice of collective bargaining was generally accepted as the most suitable way to settle the terms and conditions of employment. This method carried the risk that, from time to time, the parties would not conclude their bargaining and negotiations successfully. There had to be a way of breaking the deadlock and that was that parties must be free to mount economic pressures to cause the adversary to make concessions.

The 'right' to strike

The right to strike or withdraw labour is a relatively new concept. Even in those countries that now have forms of constitutionally and legally protected democracy, collective bargaining, strikes and other collective action were historically outlawed, either by judge-made torts or legal precepts, or by specific legislation decreeing criminal liability, or by use of police and military coercion. At a later stage, they were restrained by the imposition of civil liability in the form of injunctions and damages.

One of the three main methods of trade unionism is legal enactment (along with mutual insurance – friendly society functions – and collective bargaining). As labour and working people began to secure more influence in the electoral process – sometimes through Labour or Social Democratic political parties – the laws suppressing strike action and expressions of collective solidarity were repealed and the laws on liability were reformed to be somewhat more favourable to labour than they had been. Trade union organization, collective bargaining and collective action, including strikes, were therefore granted legal approval. In fact, the first step in legally guaranteeing the right of union organization, collective bargaining and collective action was the state's establishment by legislation and administrative action of workers' freedom to participate in such activity. The state also exempted workers and/or workers' organizations from criminal and civil liability for those actions.

From works rules to collective bargaining

It may be useful at this stage to recall our discussion of works rules where Ohta's (1988) observation that collective bargaining tended to replace works rules, and Selznick's (1969) observation that collective bargaining modified the prerogative contract are relevant. It seems overwhelmingly likely that unions need legislative and/or institutional support to conduct collective bargaining properly. Sometimes the framework of what is permitted in collective bargaining and what is reserved for the unilateral decisions of employers is laid down by law. 'In the Nordic countries, the concept of employers' prerogatives has been used since the establishment of labour law as a legal discipline' (Nielsen, 1996:17). In the Basic Agreement in Denmark of 1899, the employers recognized the positive right of workers to unionize and, in return, the confederation of trade unions (LO) recognized the managerial prerogatives of the employers, 'in particular, the employer's discretionary power in matters of recruitment and dismissal, their right to direct and allocate work and their right to require foremen not to join the unions of the workers. In Sweden a similar development took place. In Norway the same development occurred in 1907. In other European countries no similar agreements exist and the employer's prerogative of hiring, firing, directing and distributing work is not viewed as an invisible, implicit clause in all collective agreements' (Nielsen, 1996:246).

In the first half of the twentieth century, there were varying approaches to regulating industrial disputes and industrial conflict. In Australia a distinctive system of compulsory arbitration was established at state and federal level. It gradually blended with collective bargaining to create a distinctive system of industrial relations, although by the 1980s it began to be perceived as inflexible and insufficiently responsive and was largely dismantled. In some countries, periods of totalitarian government and dictatorship resulted in complete bans on independent unions and industrial action. This was the case under fascism in Italy (1926–43) and Nazism in Germany (1933–45). Similar bans were imposed during the dictatorships in Portugal (1932–72) and Spain (1936–75) and Greece (1967–74). The Soviet Communist party rule of the eastern bloc countries suppressed strikes with bloodshed and used trade unions as an arm of the Communist party and the state. A different form of communism in former Yugoslavia permitted a controlled form of workers' self-management.

However, in most industrialized countries with some form of constitutional democratic government, the right to strike emerged after the Second World War as one of the hallmarks of a democratic regime. In fact, unions were seen by the Allied countries as countervailing power against corporate monopoly and totalitarian rule in Germany and Japan. The right to strike was explicitly mentioned in the constitutions of France (1946) and Italy (1948). 'In the 1970s, the southern European states – Portugal, Spain and Greece – followed the examples of France and Italy by inserting the right to strike as a fundamental right in their new democratic constitutions. Sweden also inserted this right in its new constitution' (Jacobs, 1993:424).

The USA as a model for collective bargaining and union rights

The model for this acceptance of collective bargaining was often the USA. It was the occupying power in Japan and influenced the position of unions and collective bargaining in the new constitution; as Ohta (1988) noted, the Japanese Labour Standards Act showed its American influence in implicitly designating collective bargaining as the means whereby workers could press for improved pay and conditions. The USA had legislated to regulate unions and collective bargaining before the Second World War with the Wagner Act or National Labour Relations Act (NLRA) of 1936. According to Selznick (1969), strictly speaking the Wagner Act was not concerned with the legal status and enforceability of collective agreements and yet with this Act, law entered decisively and affirmatively into employment relations. The National Labour Relations Board (NLRB) enforced the duty to bargain in good faith, made representation effective and enjoined discrimination against union members.

The honeymoon of American politicians with the Wagner Act and the National Labour Relations Board ended shortly after the Second World War. The advent of peace brought in swift resumption of overt conflict between labour and management. Strikes in the USA in 1946 set an all-time record for lost work time in the USA. Many Americans concluded that the frequency with which vital services were disrupted – often at great cost to the community – proved that the Wagner Act had swung the balance of power in industrial relations too far to the union side. The result was the passage of the Taft-Hartley Act (1947) that became the controlling law in industrial conflict. It greatly restored the salience of contract in US labour law. Its core is Section 301 which provides that 'suits for violation of contracts between an employer and a labour organization representing employees in an industry affecting commerce . . . may be brought in any district court of the United States'. By authorizing enforcement of collective agreements in the courts, this legislation implicitly recognized that a first stage of institution-building was past and that the legal status and outcome of bargaining would have to be clarified.

The earlier stage was mainly concerned with strikes launched to force non-union employers to enter into collective bargaining (Selznick, 1969:141).

The new law carried over almost intact the prohibitions on employer-committed unfair labour practices specified in the Wagner Act. However, it made illegal the closed shop (requiring workers to be union members at the time of hiring) and put limitations on the right of unions to negotiate contracts calling for the union shop. In addition, Taft-Hartley created for the first time a range of unfair labour practices by unions that were made subject to restraint by the NLRB. It also contained measures aimed at protecting individual employees against some labour organizations and gave employers the right to express their views on the merits of unionization, as long as there was no threat of reprisal or promise of benefit in their advice to employees. (This measure was later widely flouted when it came to certification elections for union recognition.) Yet another clause of the Taft-Hartley Act authorized the President to make a court motion for an eighty-day national emergency injunction to halt strikes that he deemed to be inimical to the national interest and secondary action was defined as an unfair labour practice. Known in popular parlance as the 'cooling off' period, this has been advocated in Britain in the past.

The remedial weight of the reformed NLRA greatly favoured employers. The main reason for this statutory imbalance is that the strongest unfair labour practice remedies were added to the NLRA in 1947 by an extremely pro-business Congress. Whenever a charge alleging an unfair labour practice was filed, the National Labour Relations Board is directed to seek an immediate injunction against the union to protect the employer's interests while the unfair labour practice proceedings are carried out.

But employers who commit unfair labour practices are not subject to mandatory injunctions. If a union files a charge alleging a violation by a business entity and the NLRB decides to issue a complaint, it may seek a preliminary injunction but it is not statutorily obliged to seek an injunction and if it decides against, there is nothing that the employees or union can do. In fact, the NLRB has rarely sought injunctions against employers although the number of employer unfair labour practices has increased over the last twenty years. Companies opposing union-organizing drives frequently fired the employees leading unionization.

Corporations defying the rights of their employees under the NLRA are generally motivated by the fact that the slight costs of unfair labour practice liability are outweighed by the perceived costs of unionization. These corporations are exploiting the inadequacy of Labour Board remedies and enforcement mechanisms that are too weak to do them much damage. There is a rare example of NLRB action against corporate unfair labour practice in chapter 4 (the 'Ruby Tuesday' case).

International conventions

Among international organizations, the International Labour Organization does not include explicitly the right to strike among the standards laid down in its constitution and numerous conventions. However, the right to strike was explicitly included in the International Covenant on Economic, Social and Cultural Rights (ICESCR) of 1966 and in the 1961 European Charter of the Council of Europe.

Although many countries' representative governments have established a positive right to strike as a constitutional right or with legal authority, other countries have only done this by limiting actions through the courts against unions and striking workers. Britain had a system of immunities against tort actions through the courts as long as the strike or other industrial action was 'in contemplation or furtherance of a trade dispute' from the Trade Disputes Act of 1906 through to the 1980s (with brief interregnums including the Industrial Relations Act 1971–4). In Denmark also, what is generally known as the right to strike is in fact a freedom to strike. 'The Danish system is quite distinct from all other member states (of the European Union). Its origins are to be found in the 1899 Basic Agreement under which the employers obtained a greater centralization of collective bargaining and union recognition of the management prerogative, while the unions were given joint responsibility for policing and enforcing collective agreements, even if individual employers and union members were unwilling or unable to fight for their implementation. The result is that several areas of working life – rules on overtime, shift work, notice of redundancy, maximum working hours, dismissals – which are determined by legislation in other countries are regulated in Denmark by collective agreements' (Barnard, Clark and Lewis, 1995:2).

In general, the view seems to have developed that the right to strike is implicit when constitutions and laws guarantee the right of association and the right to collective bargaining. When governments begin to reject collective bargaining as a model for conducting industrial relations, the policy-makers also restrict strike action and remove supports for union activity. Lammy Betten, who has researched the right to strike in EU law, specifically considered the criteria of the International Covenant on Economic, Social and Cultural Rights which refers to the right to strike in its Article 8. According to Betten (1985:1930), its wording seems to indicate that the right to strike under the Covenant:

1   should be seen as an *ultimum remedium* (last resort) in the case of conflicts;
2   can be denied to certain categories of workers in public or essential services;
3   can be regulated or restricted by national law.

Betten goes on to discuss how, in the international context, big problems have arisen about who may participate in a strike. In particular, the European Social Chapter experts have consistently criticized the total exclusion from the right to strike of civil servants in Germany.

On the other hand, closer European economic integration and EMU means that a disruptive strike in one country is a common concern for other EU countries. In the autumn of 1997 there was a French road haulage strike that obviously affected European cross-border trade. This was a straightforward trade dispute that incidentally had such side effects. However, the previous December there had been public sector strikes in France protesting against the massive public expenditure cuts required for EMU. *Le Monde* characterized the strikes as the 'First revolt against globalization'. The union representing the CRS, the French riot police, declared that 'officers will not serve as a buffer between those who demand work and the rich and privileged' (Simpson and Hines, 1996).

Distinctive comparative models of strike and collective bargaining regulation

Jacobs (1993:425) doubted whether it made sense to persist with the distinction between the 'right to strike' and the 'freedom to strike' and their legal consequences. However, this has turned out to be of vital significance in UK labour law and is the main reason why it is very difficult indeed to mount a fully lawful strike under UK law following the successive narrowing of the immunity of strikes against actions for damages by legislation through the 1980s and early 1990s. In general, the role of the individual employment contract – as Selznick correctly foresaw – is crucial. In countries that have only a 'freedom' to strike, the idea that a strike entails a breach of contract persists. In those countries with general legal recognition of a 'right to strike', the suspension of the employment contract is seen as the legal corollary to the right to strike.

What appears more important for comparative collective labour law are national differences in the extent of the right to strike or the degree of freedom to strike.

Limits on the right to strike

The sanctity of the right to strike is far from absolute and it is in divergences of national policy in this respect that we can find many differences in collective labour law. Canada in recent years has had a notably poor record of above average days lost in strikes, compared with other countries. As a result, federal and provincial legislators have moved to restrict the freedom to strike.

In Germany and the Netherlands, the law of strikes has been almost completely 'judge-made', rather than legislated, despite the fact that the German system has almost all areas of working life covered by statute law or executive orders based on statute law. This is because a system of labour courts regulates important areas of collective labour relations. During a lawful strike, employment is suspended and employees lose their claim for remuneration. If the employer's operations are not directly involved but, for example, a car manufacturer has to close down because he is cut off from suppliers (e.g. tyre manufacturers) who are engaged in a strike, the manufacturer's workforce has no claim for compensation even though they may be willing and able to offer their services. In a leading case, decided in 1980, the principle was laid down that the strike risk, i.e. the risk of losing compensation, has to be borne by the workforce, even if part of that workforce is not on strike but its lay-off is caused by the third party's dispute.

In 1984, the workforce of a supplier to the motor industry in Germany went on strike, leading to the lay-off of 400,000 staff employed by the car manufacturers. The metalworkers union claimed unemployment benefits of DM 200 million and prevailed in court on a technicality. In effect, though, the decision was seen to imply government-subsidized labour disputes, thereby undermining the balance of power between labour and management. In 1986, the federal legislature, at the behest of employers' associations, revised that section of the law on 'guidelines on neutrality in labour disputes', restating the principle of parity between labour and management and this was upheld on review by the Federal Constitutional Court.

'The hallmarks of the industrial relations system in the Netherlands include union pluralism; a strong degree of government influence; a comprehensive system of institutionalized consultation with organized interest groups on socio-economic policy issues; and a concentration of consultation and bargaining powers in the hands of leaders of centralized organizations. The result of these influences is a system in which legal regulation plays a major role, including the unusual provision which requires employers and employees dealing with dismissals and redundancies to apply to a semi-governmental agency for a permit if they wish to terminate the employment relationship unilaterally' (Barnard, Clark and Lewis, 1995:3).

In another group of countries, for example, the Scandinavian countries, the dominant idea is that the rules governing the right to strike should be decided among the social partners – unions and employers – themselves. However, again, changing economic conditions have led to legislative changes and intervention. In 1990 the Swedish government announced a strike ban with increased fines for wildcat strikes. 'The proposal, widely regarded as a violation of basic trade union rights, aroused a wave of protests from rank-and-file members and from many local union branches and workplace organizations. The collapse of the proposal forced the government to look for more consensual methods' (Kjellberg, 1998:89).

Unofficial strikes and 'wildcat' strikes

In various countries, including Germany, the Scandinavian countries, the USA and Canada, industrial conflict must be seen as almost completely complementary to collective bargaining. In other words, industrial action is permitted only if its purpose is the achievement of collective agreements. This approach makes an important limitation on the right to strike; it makes that right a collective (trade union) right, not an individual right. As a result, wildcat or unofficial strikes are unlawful because workers outside trade unions cannot conclude collective agreements. In Germany, 'wildcat' strikes for matters other than those agreed by collective bargaining are regarded as illegal and may allow immediate dismissal or a claim for damages.

In France, Spain and Italy, the right to strike is essentially thought of as an individual right for each worker. In France, the right to strike is regarded as a fundamental right under the Constitution of 1946. 'The law says relatively little about the regulation of strikes and the distinction between legal and illegal strikes is essentially left to jurisprudence' (Goetschy and Rozenblatt, 1992:437). However, as previously discussed (under the heading 'International Conventions'), the autonomy of a national system of labour law becomes an issue when one party to a collective labour dispute can coerce third parties, as in the French road haulage strikes of 1997.

The peace obligation – 'no strike' agreement

Often collective agreements contain a promise that there will be no strike or lockout for the duration of the agreement. In Germany, the Scandinavian countries and the USA, strikes in contravention of a collective agreement are unlawful. After the Taft-Hartley Act section 301 – which made collective agreements legally enforceable contracts in the federal court – employers' agreement to accept arbitration began to be treated by the courts as a quid pro quo for the union's promise not to strike during the term of a collective agreement. Grievance arbitration and the legal enforcement of collective agreements became inextricably linked.

In Britain during the 1980s there was controversy about so-called 'strike-free' collective agreements that typically contained explicit 'no-strike' provisions designed to restrict industrial action, usually accompanied by a clause for binding arbitration. However, there was really little new about this as virtually all collective agreements in the UK already contained express restrictions on the freedom of the parties to engage in industrial action. The much-vaunted 'no-strike' agreements were no more enforceable. The only real difference was that they typically stipulated pendulum arbitration requiring the arbitrator to choose between the union's last claim and the employer's last offer. This was again based on USA experience but is quite similar to 'straight choice' arbitration which has a long tradition in the UK.

Disputes of interest and disputes of right

As in individual labour disputes (discussed in the previous chapter), in the majority of European countries, a distinction is made in collective labour disputes between disputes of interest and disputes of right. Disputes of right are about the interpretation and application of existing contracts or collective agreements. Disputes of interest are more substantive, relating to changes in collective rules and may require that conflicting economic interests be reconciled. It follows that in cases of disputes of right, there should be no strikes or industrial action because these are now subject to the peace obligation until the expiry of the current contract or collective agreement. Disputes should therefore be settled by negotiation or by arbitration or the courts, often specialist labour courts.

> Why labour courts ? Traditional theory holds that the resolution of industrial disputes, in this case rights disputes, requires, in order to ensure social justice, that cases be heard and decided rapidly, at no or with minimum cost to the litigants, with a relative lack of formality and judicial trappings, and by bodies with a specialized capability in labour matters. Whether in the present situation labour courts in all of the industrialized market economies in which labour courts exist substantially meet these criteria is an open question. However, it is generally recognized that in respect of most of the elements mentioned, labour courts are more user-friendly than ordinary courts. This is so in spite of the fact that complaints are quite widely heard that labour courts in their operation, if not in theory, have become overly formal, particularly in terms of legal procedures (e.g. rules of evidence) and atmosphere of hearings (Gladstone, 1993:462).

The distinction between disputes of right and disputes of interest was made from the outset in Denmark and Sweden. 'The tenor of Nordic labour law has traditionally been collective labour law with collective agreements and case law from special Labour Courts as the main sources of law' (Nielsen, 1996:245). In these countries and also in Canada, New Zealand, Germany and Spain, industrial action relating to disputes about interpretation, administration or violation of labour laws or collective agreements is unlawful because the legislation provides procedures for adjudication. The *International Labour Review* (1992:314) reported on a specific instance by the Labour Court in Spain:

The Court noted that the collective agreement must invariably yield to the statutory provisions and regulations of the State which prescribe minimum contractual terms. But the settlement called for by the dispute under adjudication relied on section 3(3) of the Workers' Charter which gave precedence to whatever rule, taken as a whole, is more favourable to the worker.

Arbitration and collective labour disputes

As far as Europe is concerned, then, in the majority of the countries where the courts have an important role in resolving collective disputes on rights, conciliation, mediation and arbitration is of secondary importance. In a minority of European countries, however, there is no distinction between disputes of right and disputes of interest. In Britain and Ireland, collective agreements are not legally binding contracts. In Belgium the courts have no power to intervene in collective labour disputes whether they are about conflicts of interest or conflicts of rights. In these countries there is much more emphasis on procedures of conciliation, mediation and arbitration.

Only in a few European countries – Britain, France, Norway and Spain – has there been legislation providing for a specialist arbitration body for collective labour disputes. In most European countries there is no specific procedure for ultimate resolution of collective labour disputes and voluntary arbitration has little significance. By contrast, in the USA, third party intervention is widespread and decisions of arbitrators have historically been treated by the courts as final, binding and beyond appeal. It is remarkable that voluntary arbitration is so undeveloped in Europe compared to the USA.

Unlike US labour law, the compulsory arbitration system that formerly existed in Australia did not exclude collective bargaining. In effect, this system was intended to grant the unions' demand for collective bargaining but at the same time attempted to place a check on their power by restricting strikes. However, by 1992 this system was finished, replaced by a flexible system of workplace bargaining.

Types of industrial action and legal restrictions

In many countries solidarity or sympathy strikes are unlawful. But in Greece, 'there is even special statutory provision authorizing trade unions to call a strike in sympathy with another trade union of a multinational company which is on strike. At the other end of the spectrum are countries like Canada and Britain where almost every sympathy strike that has as its objective that of putting pressure on a secondary employer, is considered unlawful' (Jacobs, 1993:432).

Given the considerable legal restrictions on strikes in many countries, workers have occasionally resorted to alternative forms of industrial action, such as overtime bans, working to rule or going slow. Workers have also tried to put pressure on the primary employer by influencing consumers to boycott that firm's services or products. Local (union branch) 837 of the Allied Industrial Workers' Union, in dispute with A. E. Staley, a subsidiary of Tate & Lyle, made a conscious decision to avoid the strike weapon. Mail shots urged a public boycott of First America Bank Corporation which had cross-directorships with Staley. Other leaflets and publicity materials made much of the health and safety issue and a second line of attack was threatened, namely consumer pressure. 'Here, the likely target would appear to be Tate's Domino Sugar which is a household name and is stocked on the shelves of any US supermarket' (Tait, 1993). During a 1996 dispute, members of the Teamsters union demonstrated outside stores of the Giant Food supermarket chain, part-owned by Sainsbury's, handing out fliers showing a caricature of a thuggish, ermine-robed Lord Sainsbury striding across the north American continent, crushing innocent American workers underfoot. However, such boycotts are double-edged and if taken too far may result in permanent loss of market share and job losses.

Public service and essential services

'A last important limitation on the right to strike concerns strikes in the public service or in essential services. Strikes in these areas tend to victimize the public and sometimes threaten the whole economy. In various countries, the legislator has explicitly denied the right to strike to certain categories like the police, prison guards, the army, the firefighters, the intelligence services. The same has often happened to workers employed in the production and distribution of gas, electricity and water, the postal service, public health care, etc' (Jacobs, 1993:437).

It used to be thought that such restrictions are difficult to enforce. However, in the UK police strikes have been outlawed since the Police Act of 1919. In 1997 this was extended to prison officers when it was realized that 'the Prison Officers Association is not legally a trade union enjoying the legal immunities normally available to such a body in respect of properly called industrial action' but a professional association on a par with the Police Federation (Wasik and Taylor, 1995:128).

In 1981 President Reagan had no compunction in firing striking air traffic controller members of PATCO and authorizing the hiring of replacement controllers. This paved the way for more widespread use of the lockout. A controversial 1989 Supreme Court decision confirmed the employers' right to retain replacement workers after a strike is over. 'From the union's perspective, this is a powerful counter to a strike and it can result in the effective end of a union's influence in a company, as demonstrated by the UAW's return to work at Caterpillar when its CEO threatened to hire replacement workers. Union leaders have accused management of deliberately provoking strikes to allow management the opportunity to hire replacement workers who will decertify the union' (Anthony, Perrewe and Kacmar, 1996:622).

In India, the Industrial Disputes Act of 1947 is 'a crucial piece of legislation which aims at the speedy resolution of any conflict between labour and management through conciliation, arbitration and adjudication. This Act requires that fourteen days notice be given before a strike or lock-out can be declared in a public utility. The government has the power to declare any industry a public utility and most large industries have been so declared' (Ramaswamy and Ramaswamy, 1981:191). In Ireland the Industrial Relations Act 1990 repealed and replaced the Trade Disputes Act 1906. It was introduced to improve industrial relations and to facilitate a new economic ethos. However, the recent landmark decision in *'Nolan Transport v Halligan and others'*, although broadly in favour of the union, served as a reminder that issues such as trade union recognition lurk beneath the veneer of Ireland's recent economic boom (O'Keefe, 1998:347).

A secondary aspect of this case was the issue of whether the pre-strike ballot had been fairly conducted. An under-researched subject, the issue of variations in national practice about pre-strike ballots is nonetheless a key one for comparative industrial relations. The UK, Greece and Ireland are the only EU countries that require secret ballots before strikes can lawfully take place. More widely, ballots are also required in some Canadian provinces, Fiji and Brazil.

International comparisons of strike statistics

In the not-too-distant past, this topic would have demanded a chapter to itself. Although strikes are not homogeneous phenomena, they are among the more easily quantifiable and measurable statistics in comparative industrial relations. As such, international comparisons of strike activity used to be quite a popular research project – until strikes declined internationally. There were experts in the field, such as Michael Shalev (1980), who contended that industrial conflict was something more than an incident in the bargaining process. Predictably, the subject attracted attention from econometrics professors and 'the association between strike frequency and the business cycle is one of the clearest findings of econometric research' (Franzosi, 1989:353).

It cannot therefore be suggested that strike behaviour depends only on the national legislative framework for trade unions and collective action. Rather, 'findings suggest that the major direct influences are the structure of industrial relations and features of union organization. But, in addition to having some direct impact, political variables are important in shaping the structure of industrial relations. In other words, the analysis indicates that the most important output from the political system relates to union organization and bargaining structure, rather than the sorts of social policy variable emphasized by Korpi and Shalev' (Batstone, 1985:58).

Nevertheless, whilst the legislative framework may be a somewhat Procrustean bed for international variations in strike activity, it is justifiable to discuss strike statistics in the context of collective labour law, as those figures have declined in importance. Professors Brown and Wadhwani (1990:69) summed up the situation for the UK rather well:

> British strike activity has diminished substantially from the levels of the 1970s but since this is in line with a world-wide decline in strikes, it would be wrong to link it too closely to the legislation. The use of strikes has, however, been made more costly for unions. The increased opportunities for employers to use injunctions, and the increased risk for unions of having their assets sequestered, have encouraged them to observe greater procedural caution than in the past. This is reducing the scope for strike action, further reduced by the denial of secondary action. The balloting requirements have been important among the many ways in which the new laws are forcing unions to tighten up their internal organization and discipline.

Partly as a result of these restrictions, of countries that had available data, 'the UK had the fourth lowest strike rate in 1995, an improvement of two places since 1994. Of all the countries with relatively low strike rates (below 100 in the 1990s) only Portugal, Norway and Switzerland saw a fall in strike activity between 1994 and 1995. Over the OECD as a whole, 14 countries saw a rise in the rate over the whole year, seven showed a fall and one showed no change. The UK has now been below the OECD average since 1990' (Sweeney and Davies, 1997:130).

Strike statistics must be treated with extreme caution, a point emphasized by Shalev (1978:1–11). When making detailed international comparisons, even more care must be taken because of the different coverage of each country's statistics. In 1981, the United States revised its series of industrial stoppage statistics to include only those disputes involving more than 1000 workers, whereas previously the threshold had been six workers. It is estimated that this change reduced the recorded number of working days lost by between 30 and 40 per cent. In 1987 Canada revised the criteria for inclusion of an industrial dispute in its statistics – a response to unfavourable comparisons being made between the disputes records of the United States and Canada. Similarly, Danish statistics do not record disputes in which there are fewer than 100 working days lost. There are other important differences that may be significant when making international comparisons. For example, France and Portugal omit public administration strikes (Bird, 1990:610). Consequently, an exact comparison among countries is not possible on account of significant differences in methods used for compiling strike statistics in individual countries.

There was an overall decline in strike activity over the decade from 1986, with the UK rate considerably below both the EU and OECD average. The average rate in both the OECD and the EU more than halved, with only Austria, Denmark, Germany, the Netherlands, Switzerland and Iceland experiencing increases. 'Between 1991 and 1995, the average rate in the UK was 24 working days lost per thousand employees, a fall of 82 per cent over the previous five-year period' (Sweeney and Davies, 1997:130).

Evaluation and conclusions

Professor Jacobs (1993:451) remarked that 'it is tempting to compare the law on strikes in different nations with the varying pattern of industrial action in each'. However, he was forced to accept that 'it seems almost impossible to establish a relationship between the strike pattern and the legal system. This has led part of the doctrine to doubt whether industrial conflict can be controlled by legal regulation. It considers legal norms and sanctions as blunt instruments in shaping labour–management relations.'

Table 9.1 Labour disputes: working days not worked per 1,000 employees[a] in all industrials and services 1988–97

	1988	1989	1990	1991	1992	1993	1994	1995	1996	1997	Average[b] 1988–92	1993–7	1988–97
United Kingdom	166	182	83	34	24	30	13	19	57R	10	98	26	62
Austria	3	1	3	19	8	4	0	0	0	6	7	2	4
Belgium	66	44	34	22	65	18	24	33	49	..	46	..	..
Denmark	41	23	42	30	27	50	33	85	32	41	33	48	40
Finland	88	98	446	230	41	10	309	495	11	56	184	175	180
France	107	177	65	46	36	48	39	299R	57R	..	85	..	..
Germany[c]	2	4	15	5	47	18	7	8	3	..	16	..	..
Ireland	177	62	266	100	218	68	27	132R	110R	69	165	82	120
Italy	226	300	342	195	180	235	236	64R	135R	83	248	151	201
Luxembourg	0	0	0	0	0	0	0	60	2	..	0	..	..
Netherlands	2	4	37	17	15	8	8	115	1	2	15	27	21
Portugal	67	127	44	37	58	25	30	20	16R	25	66	23	44
Spain	1399	417	283	486	701	248	728	163	171	190	644	295	469
Sweden	199	101	191	5	7	54	15	177	17	7	102	54	80
Iceland	929	747	2	31	3	1	867	1889R	0	291	341	609	479
Norway	45	9	79	1	207	19	54	27	278	4	68	77	73
Switzerland	0	0	1	0	0	0	4	0	2	0	0	1	1
Turkey	264	415	480	536	151	74	31	601	31	20	366	147	249
Australia	266	184	210	250	148	100	76	79	131	75	211	92	150
Canada	423	312	427	216	183	130	136	131	276	290	313	194	253
Japan	4	5	3	2	5	2	2	1	1	2	4	2	3
New Zealand	313	163	279	85R	99	20	31	42	52R	18	189	33	108
United States	42	153	55	43	37	36	45	51	42	38	66	42	54

a Employees; some figures have been estimated.
b Annual averages for those years within each period for which data are available, weighted for employment.
c From 1993 data cover the entire Federal Republic of Germany; earlier data represented West Germany only.
R revised
.. not available
Source: Labour Market Trends, April 1999

Blunt instruments they might be but our inclusion here of international comparisons of strike statistics does seem to suggest that perhaps the relationship is rather closer to Professor Jacob's ideal than he dared imagine. In five countries that have experienced big decreases in average strike rates 1991–5 – the UK, the USA, Greece, New Zealand and Sweden – this had been preceded by more drastic legal restrictions on strike activity. In Greece, the new law 1915/1990 was comprehensively restrictive, 'abolishing most of the rights acquired by the unions in 1982, restricting the scope of lawful strikes, permitting the dismissal of unlawful strikers and imposing new limitations on strikes in the public services' (Kritsantonis, 1998:621). However, when PASOK returned to power in 1993, this legislation was repealed (Kritsantonis, 1998:521). By contrast, in the Netherlands, where the strike propensity rose, the legal framework has been somewhat loosened. After a series of short strikes against pay cuts for rail employees, the rail management brought legal proceedings against the unions under article 1410 of the Civil Code which provides that 'any unlawful act whereby damage is caused to someone else places the person through whose fault the damage has been caused under an obligation to make good such damage. In a remarkable decision for a country where there is no statutory protection for the right to strike, the lower courts referred to article 6(4) of the European (not EU) Social Charter of 1961 to reject claims that the action was unlawful, decisions which were upheld in robust terms by the highest court' (Ewing,1998:7). According to Betten (1995:205), 'the clearest example of the unofficial impact of the right to strike in the European Social Charter can be found in the development of the right to strike in the Netherlands'. But this was the only example that she could find of the 'influence of an international norm other than as an effect of supervisory procedures'.

Questions for discussion

1 'Law is a secondary force in human affairs and especially in labour relations.' Discuss the current reference of this statement in the light of international changes in human resource management.

2 Discuss the importance of the autonomy of national labour law systems.

10

Transnational Companies, Globalization and Industrial Relations

The guiding focus of this chapter is on what changes in industrial organization mean for labour and labour institutions internationally. The aim is 'to probe the unexplored link between the world of corporate strategy and the world of labour studies' (Campbell, 1992). There is a vast amount of published work on multinational companies which has been a popular area of academic research for many years. However, 'there is a relatively small body of research pointing to systematic differences in the ways in which MNCs of different nationalities manage their human resources' (Ferner, 1997:20). For example, according to Ferner, 'the foremost characteristic of Japanese companies referred to in both survey-based and qualitative studies is strong but informal centralized co-ordination of their foreign operations'.

This may well be so but it does not matter. Such studies may be valid but they are less and less significant. If there is any truth in the idea of globalization and in Ferner's suggestion that 'the activities of MNCs can be seen as a key transmission belt for the pressures of globalization, for example through the international dissemination of "best practice" in work organizations' (Ferner, 1996, review *ILLR*), then attaching MNCs to 'parent countries' may not mean very much – even if the data obtained through the comparison may still be informative. It may be that Japanese MNCs can be envisaged as 'transmission belts for the business and work organization practices of Japanese capitalism' (Ferner, 1997:20). Actually, if those work organization practices are seen as lean production, this idea is rather similar to the proposition about conver-

Biggest Global Organization

Country/Company by GDP/Sales

		$bn			
1	United States	7100	28	General Motors (US)	169
2	Japan	4964	29	Sumitomo (Japan)	168
3	Germany	2252	30	Marubeni (Japan)	161
4	France	1454	31	Thailand	160
5	United Kingdom	1095	32	Denmark	156
6	Italy	1088	33	Hong Kong	142
7	China	745	34	Ford Motor (US)	137
8	Brazil	580	35	Norway	136
9	Canada	574	36	Saudi Arabia	134
10	Spain	532	37	South Africa	131
11	South Korea	435	38	Toyota Motor (Japan)	111
12	Netherlands	371	39	Exxon (US)	110
13	Australia	338	40	Royal Dutch/Shell	110
14	Russia	332	41	Myanmar	108
15	India	320	41	Poland	108
16	Mexico	305	43	Finland	105
17	Switzerland	286	44	Nissho Iwai (Japan)	98
18	Argentina	278	45	Portugal	97
19	Taiwan	260	46	Wal-Mart Stores (US)	94
20	Belgium	251	47	Israel	88
21	Austria	217	48	Greece	86
22	Sweden	210	49	Hitachi (Japan)	84
23	Indonesia	190	50	Nippon Life Insurance	83
24	Mitsubishi (Japan)	184			
25	Mitsui (Japan)	181		*Source*: S. Canekin, 'It's Bigger	
26	Itochu (Japan)	169		than Turkey', *Observer*, 9 March	
27	Turkey	169		1998	

gence through human resource management advanced in the opening chapters of this book. More broadly, 'pressures for the diffusion of practices across countries will be shaped by the nature of dominant modes of production and their associated employment practices. These dominance effects arise out of cross-national differences in the nature of national business systems and, hence, are associated with those countries whose manufacturing sectors have performed strongly in recent decades, in particular America and Japan. Therefore the diffusion of practices within MNCs is likely to reflect these influences' (Edwards, 1998:7).

However, several factors appear to constrain the international diffusion of employment practices. Perhaps the most important is national employment law (see chapters 8 and 9). This can lend support to labour market institutions, such as unions (through legal support for union recognition) that can also constrain cross-border diffusion. Furthermore, as pointed out in chapter 6, the nature of a country's educational and training institutions may also restrict the range of decision-making choices of managers of a transnational company.

Strategy and human resource management in transnational companies

Despite the ambiguities of the whole concept of 'corporate strategy', it is probably right to suggest that studies of this would be more fruitful than nationally based studies of MNCs. Numerous companies, including British Airways, have espoused a global strategy. However, it is also important to make a distinction between the planned international strategy of firms and unintended strategic results. This reminds us of Karen Legge's four perspectives on strategy that were used to inform and clarify our ideas on human resource management in the opening chapter.

Karen Legge (1995) drew attention to reasons why the link between corporate strategy and human resource management that is so often assumed might be far from unproblematic and ought not to be taken for granted. It is a moot point anyway whether much that goes under the heading 'human resource management' is really strategic in any precise sense. But 'globalization' must entail some strategic orientation and impact on the management of the workplace – in terms of work organization, worker representation, working time arrangements, skills and training. Referring to the distinction between a 'differentiation' and a 'cost leadership' strategy, Jorg Sydow sketched how direct the consequences for labour can be:

> If you have a differentiation strategy, for instance, the organizations within the network would probably promote pooled research, promote high-quality production or have some target-oriented marketing of the manufacturing programme. If the network follows the other strategy of cost leadership, probably – and this is most important from a trade union point of view – they will focus on hiving off personnel-

intensive activities and building up some kind of transparent network-wide controlling system. This kind of network will have what has been called 'dependent, self-employed' people. It will have much more precarious employment conditions and be characterized by an externalization of labour. Strategic networks – and this is the potential of this new organizational form – are very good at combining these two competitive strategies, differentiation and cost leadership, especially if the firms organize themselves into some kind of pyramidical form, such as the Japanese *keiretsu*' (quoted in Campbell, 1992).

This little paragraph is quite pithy. It introduces the concept of strategic networks and the possibility of mixing the two strategies of differentiation and cost leadership. Networks will be discussed shortly but essentially – they are co-operative joint ventures that are not full mergers. Clearly it is more possible in networks for strategies to be mixed than in out-and-out mergers. When it seemed likely that BT would merge with MCI of the USA, despite the insistence of MCI's public policy director that there would be no change – 'We'll go on doing our thing and BT will do its thing' – the main British union was fearful. (Milne and Bannister, 1996). In the event, BT was outbid by an American consortium.

Transnational business strategy is hard to analyse even in a single MNC. Andrew Mair (1994) made a heroic attempt in his study of the character of the Honda Corporation as simultaneously a global and a local player. This study is useful in reminding us of another failed strategy, as it is made against the background of the failure of the so-called world car strategy that was tried by Ford, among others. Honda adopted a strategy of transforming its operations into a 'global local' company which Mair believes provided its springboard for success, the company having become an international manufacturer, operating with Toyota's production system but locating, first in the USA and later in the UK. Mair's distinctive approach is to contrast Western dualist management thought with the Japanese way of thinking. The idea is that the Western manager thinks dualistically of Taylorism v. flexibility; the Japanese think in a more holistic way that integrates these possibilities. Rover – before it was acquired by BMW – did seem to benefit from its partnership with Honda by way of a more participative and teamworking management style.

Ingenious as Mair's study may be, it is doubtful if it is a genuinely strategic approach, despite the use of the word. Strategy really needs to be broader in context, particularly amidst talk of global strategies.

Union-busting reputation a fear, say Seumas Milne and Nicholas Bannister

For all its company-loyalist cheer-leading of the BT–MCI merger this week, BT's main British union – the Communication Workers (CWU) – has reason to be nervous.

While up to 90 per cent of BT's 130,000 British employees are unionized and the company has already set up a cross-border European Works Council for employee consultation, MCI has a ferocious reputation as a US union-buster.

When the 600,000-strong Communication Workers of America (CWA) tried to organize a statutory ballot for union recognition in the late 1980s at MCI's Mid West regional calling centre, the company closed it overnight and sacked all 450 employees rather than face the prospect of legally-enforced union recognition.

The confrontation drew in Democratic congressmen such as Jesse Jackson and John Conyers and led to the establishment of a 'Jobs with Justice' campaign for non-violent action against US employers who refuse basic employment and civil rights to their workers. This is a long way from the set-up at BT which, despite some efforts to weaken union representation since privatization in 1984, still bears the mark of its previous incarnation as a nationalized industry.

'Our first priority is to prevent the MCI philosophy seeping into BT,' Roger Darlington, head of research at the CWU, says.

'Our second challenge is to work to bring about a more tolerant view of trade unions on the MCI side.'

The hope is that union support for the MCI–BT merger case to regulators in the US and Britain can be traded for representation rights on the US side of the tie-up. But Robert Stewart, MCI's public policy director, insists there will be no change: 'We'll go on doing our thing and BT will do its thing.'

Larry Cohen, CWA organization director, backs the British union approach to what he calls MCI's 'horrendous labour relations policy'. The key question for employees, he believes, should be: 'Does this company respect collective bargaining rights on a global basis or not?'

The contrast in the two firms' cultures partly reflects their origins at opposite ends of the commercial spectrum. BT grew up under the wing of a government monopoly, but MCI, only founded in 1968, has been an upstart company seeking to join the big league. Small, flexible and strong on marketing, it has won over 20 per cent share of the US long-distance market, previously dominated by AT & T and expects to take on more staff as it expands with BT.

In recent years the gap between them has narrowed. BT has shed 110,000 jobs since 1991 to keep profits buoyant, while MCI has tripled the number of its employees to 52,000 over the past decade.

Further MCI growth is unlikely to compensate for the extra BT redundancies its chief executive Sir Peter Bonfield says will result from merger, though these are expected to be relatively modest compared to the jobs lost over the past five years.

The BT takeover of MCI has been structured to reduce cultural conflict and great care has been taken to give the impression that it is a merger of near equals, though BT's market value is twice that of MCI. At BT boardroom level, there will be the sweetener of boosted salaries to match MCI levels.

BT is hoping that it will be able to speed its penetration of new markets in Europe with the help of MCI's well-established marketing skills. Yet MCI is used to doing things at a faster pace than its partner. Whether BT's management and workforce will be able to adapt to that without stooping to MCI's more extreme management style remains to be seen.

Guardian, 6 November 1996

International human resource management approaches – ethnocentric to global

The HRM literature has used four terms to describe MNC approaches to managing and staffing their subsidiaries. The idea is that these approaches are determined to a large extent by the attitudes of top management at headquarters and the strategy-structure mix. This rather begs the question but the four approaches are:

1   *Ethnocentric* – little autonomy for subsidiaries with strategic decisions made at head office and key jobs held by headquarters managers;
2   *Polycentric* – the MNC treats each subsidiary as a distinct national entity with some autonomy;
3   *Regiocentric* – uses a wider pool of managers but in more limited way than the following, geocentric approach;
4   *Geocentric* – a worldwide business strategy affords the possibility of successful promotion within management ranks entirely on merit without reference to nationality (Dowling and Schuler, 1990:35).

This would be of limited use as a guide to the approach that should be taken in implementing a strategy for the HRM of a transnational company. The trouble is that such thinking is wedged in the mindset of *strategy as planning*.

'Most *Fortune* 500 companies engage in some type of strategic planning. There are, of course, instances in which strategic analysis played an important role in shaping a corporation's actions, but more often than not, strategic planning and formal strategic analysis plays a secondary role. Many business breakthroughs result from an opportunistic response; someone has a new idea, it matches a market niche and soon a new business is budding. Only after the fact are premeditated designs attributed to these outcomes' (Pascale, 1990:53).

Strategic thinking identifies the underlying context. 'The choice of a global geocentric or polycentric approach to human resource management is not dictated by product-market or industry-market logic; each approach represents a different way of coping with the different socio-cultural environments of a multinational company. Thus firms in worldwide industries where divisions and subsidiaries are interdependent would be advised to adopt global human resource strategies: the costs of such strategies would be outweighed by the potentially enormous returns of a successful global strategy. Firms where divisions and business elements can be discreetly and independently defined would be advised to adopt cheaper polycentric human resource strategies. Some of the disadvantages of either extreme position can be counteracted by the use of subtle management processes' (Evans, 1980).

Accepting the four approaches as clearly defined is evidently too close to the rationalistic, deliberate, purposive perspective on strategy. The emergent and systemic perspectives have also to be considered, especially in the international context. It may be better to view the four approaches – ethnocentric, regiocentric, polycentric and geocentric – as possible stages of development of multinational companies. The ethnocentric firm is at the initial stage of internationalization. The regiocentric firm is the next stage when control is devolved but only to specific regions. More decentralization takes place at the polycentric level where human resource management coincides with business operations in each foreign location: 'How management adapts its operations to foreign environments and alters policies in different ways depending on the particular country or issue' (Hutchings, 1996:58–71). Finally, it used to be thought that the 'global firm manages its global workforce in a centralized or at least a coordinated way. Corporate policy on human resource management is relatively specific and influential' (Dowling and Schuler, 1990:37). This necessitates numerous guidelines, policies, principles and corporate values.

The global stage – are we there yet?

Of course, the 'stages' idea may be overly schematic and too chrono-
logically clear-cut. Although a recent survey of chief executives of
377 of the world's leading corporations found that only 6 per cent
claimed to have a fully integrated corporate culture that crosses national boundaries and values, they regarded the creation of such a
unifying force among employees as a key objective (Warner, 1998).
This suggests a tendency to corporate globalization but in a much
more diffuse form than had been previously thought. 'Many things
can be globalized – goods, services, money, people, information, effects of the environment, as well as less tangible things such as ideas,
behavioural norms and cultural practices. Globalization can come
about in at least four ways: two-way interactions, emulation, telecommunications and institutional isomorphism (the tendency to become
alike). The quintessential example of all four processes at work is to
be found in the expansion of market globalization, the principal motor
of which is the discourse of free trade' (Higgott, 1997).

Some would go further and say that the triumph of the American
model has been an integral part of globalization through the transfer
of capital. Indeed, the word 'globalization' may be something of a
misnomer because what is happening is not so much a homogenization of different forms of economic organization and management
as a worldwide emulation of the American economy. In 1998, the
Asian economic model and the finance-capital policy of Japan were
discredited. Yet the American multinational companies had already
begun to adopt the lean production practices that had originated in
Japanese human resource management.

The majority view seems to be that the tendency towards the lean
production model is the present logic of the situation. The main regions of the world 'are the settings for some largely irreversible macro-
forces in the political, socio-cultural, technological and ecological
arenas' (Perlmutter, 1992:7). These macro forces have three aspects:

1 a globalizing process;
2 an increasing level of interdependencies, regionally and globally, shown in patterns of competitive/co-operative alliances;
3 a greater degree of value-sharing as a result of these alliances.

At the business sector/industry level, these forces have caused a global shake-out. 'From accounting to zippers, there is a globalizing of

markets and co-operative agreements to stay competitive in webs of alliances. Some industries can now be conceptualized as sets of global enterprise networks' (Perlmutter, 1992:11). There is a concern with similar values – such as standards of cost, quality and service, concern with environmental impacts and productivity and efficiency – across all industries. Examples range from aerospace, with its web of international co-operative projects, to motor vehicles and semi-conductors.

Opposition to globalization – globalization as a myth?

It has been said that 'claims about globalization are themselves not particularly new', and furthermore, 'the dramatically overused notion of globalization is largely based on misinterpretation of evidence and it is most frequently used by those with a vested interest of one sort or another. What better way for corporate spokesmen and women to justify an attempt at changing work practices or gaining acceptance for a small pay settlement than to say that in a global market failure to compete will result in death ?' (Miles, 1997). The three-month strike of 1998 at General Motors in Flint, Michigan, was explicitly about globalization. Workers were resisting GM's attempts to work them harder with the company pleading that it was under pressure from cheaper plants and competitors throughout the world. One of the voices in support of the strike was Pat Buchanan, erstwhile Presidential candidate and right-wing demagogue who turned populist defender of the American worker against the scourge of the global economy.

The opposition to the idea of globalization may be supported by the fact that, typically, only about 5 per cent of the overall financial assets of the private sector are international. The UK and the Netherlands have a relatively high degree of international diversification but even there only about 15 per cent of assets are claims on foreign governments or companies.

Hirst and Thompson (1995), in assessing 'whether there is such a thing as a globalized economy', concluded that 'globalization has not taken place and is unlikely to do so', though acknowledging that some of the conditions of globalization are present. In their own terms, their argument is bound to prevail as the main feature of their model globalized economy is that 'distinct national economies are subsumed and rearticulated into the system by essentially international processes and transactions'. Whilst accepting that there is a wide and increasing range of international transactions in the present world-wide economy, they believe that 'these tend to function as opportunities or constraints for nationally-located actors and their public regulators'.

Their argument is therefore about a truly global international system and is quite compatible with Perlmutter's view of global corporate strategy. What they do provide is a useful corrective to exaggerated versions of global strategy. For instance, in the airline industry there is much talk of global strategy and even planned action to achieve it but it continues to run up against the bilateral regulatory framework that constrains any genuine 'open skies' approach to global competition. In 1997 BA and American Airlines reached agreement about a joint venture but the move was held up by the US Department of Transportation and the EU who wanted safeguards for competition; recessionary concerns led to postponement in 1998. It remains possible to argue then that 'the notion of the global corporation transcending national boundaries is, very largely, myth. For very few of the world's largest companies is production highly internationalized; thus less than a score of the *Fortune* top 100 companies have more than half their production facilities or their workforce outside their country of origin' (Ferner, 1997:19).

However, parent company production facilities, are hardly a very useful criterion. According to Ioannides and Debbage (1997:237), 'One of the hallmarks of post-Fordist production systems in the manufacturing sector is vertical disintegration or externalization of peripheral services through sub-contracting'. They go on to remark that 'contracting out of services has become so common in the airline industry that many carriers have been turned into "virtual airlines" whose business focus is to carry passengers and freight'. At any rate, it is generally accepted that 'multi-centred corporations are increasingly emerging as the world economy becomes integrated and production more globalized. Large multinationals are now characteristically made up of a number of strategic business units which are, in turn, often subdivided into profit centres with further devolution of management responsibility. Divisions are increasingly organized internationally or even worldwide, rather than country-by-country. One example is Nestlé which has moved from a tradition of strong functional departments to a structure based on seven new strategic business units with worldwide responsibility for different product groups (such as coffee and beverages)' (Ferner, 1994:81).

The forces that drive businesses to compete on a global stage

The advent of the global company has been widely predicted in recent times – and in many ways 1997 was the year in which the soothsayers were at last proved right. *Roger Trapp* examines a trend that could change the way companies do business.

Globalization was on everyone's lips as business in a range of sectors sought to explain away their need to merge, acquire or restructure – usually with the loss of several thousand jobs, even though the era of 'downsizing' was supposedly over.

Price Waterhouse – which, incidentally, is one of the four accountancy and management consultancy firms planning megamergers, has put globalization at the top of its list of 'eight trends driving companies into 1998 and into the new millennium'.

Scott Hartz, global leader of the firm's management consulting practice, said: 'Globalization is the single biggest force driving corporate change. It affects organizational structure, technology, communications, product development, service delivery, people and training. Global 500 companies need to transform their organizations into global enterprises to compete successfully in the future.'

As such language suggests, this is not a trend to be welcomed by the fainthearted. Though much is made of the benefits for the customer or client of being able to obtain goods or services from anywhere in the world at the touch of a phone button and the flash of a credit card, the ramifications for the businesses seeking to meet these ever-more-demanding consumers are huge.

Not surprisingly, more than one senior partner of an accountancy firm has harked back to a golden age of less frenzied days, when clients could be told without fear of reprisals that their problem would be dealt with as soon as the appropriate people became free.

The pressure to compete on an international stage is also apparent in the increasing use of the term 'world class'. No longer is it enough – except perhaps for the moment in such comparatively regulated countries as France and Spain – for a company, for example, to be the best widget maker in Britain. If its customers can buy better widgets from overseas that is a completely worthless claim.

As Douglas Lamont, a Chicago-based consultant and academic on international business points out in his recent book *Salmon Day*, globalization is – in the current parlance – a 'zero-sum game'. Some organizations will win and some will lose and there is no option of simply muddling through.

It is partly because of the likely extreme outcomes – for example, Barclays' decision to sell off much of BZW immediately led to the assumption that the rest of Britain's investment banking business was doomed – that globalization is widely seen as anything but a benign force.

Certainly, those involved in running government and in watching it have long been fearful of what they see as a threat to the nation state. Much of this has to do with the sheer size of companies such as Ford, General Motors, Sony, Unilever and Shell. As Rosabeth Moss Kanter, another US management thinker, points out in her book *World Class*, such organizations tend to be seen as 'imperial corporations' that control the flow of money, goods and information across the world.

This is the thinking that goes along with the idea of large companies having larger annual revenues than the gross domestic products of many developing countries. And while Ms Moss Kanter regards it as probably 'far fetched' to say that international corporations replace governments, she accepts that 'their ability to operate effectively in more than one place gives them immense bargaining power in negotiations with governments'. She then quotes Percy Barnevik, the creator of Asea Brown Boveri, the Zurich-based engineer that has garnered shelves full of excellence awards without ever making much impact on the collective mind, as saying that his power to influence government was limited when he was merely head of Asea. But 'today I can tell the Swedish authorities that they must create a more competitive environment for R & D or our research there will decline'.

But it need not be all negative. The old slogan of 'What's good for General Motors is good for America' signals the sort of approach that the Blair government seems to be buying into by seeking to forge as many partnerships as possible with the business community. Since business has such great power it might as well be harnessed for the greater good, it is implied.

Not that it is size alone that is driving the globalization of business. For a start, many of the companies that are at the head of the globalization bandwagon are smaller in terms of numbers of people employed than they were 10 or 20 years ago. Second, the development that is pushing the globalization of business is new technology, in particular, the Internet.

While it might have been possible for some time for large organizations to use their economic power to buy what they want from wherever they want, such desires have been purely wishful thinking for the man or women in the street until comparatively recently. Now, though, an ordinary consumer equipped with a personal computer and a modem can buy a book that until recently would only have been available in the United States or can bypass travel agents and book a room in a beachhouse on a Far Eastern island.

In short, the Internet is a great leveller. Just as it enables consumers to start enjoying the same sort of access to goods and services that has long been available to corporations, so it enables a just-founded company to have the same sort of global marketing reach as a well-established organization employing thousands of people all over the globe.

The downside to this, of course, is that right from the start the little guy finds himself competing with the big boys. And the result is that – for all but a few exceptions – business success is set to be even more fleeting than in the past. Companies will be able to enjoy huge expansion in sales on the strength of dominating a technology or a niche of the market while constantly at risk from newcomers like themselves.

Roger Trapp, *Independent*,
30 December 1997

The individual transnational company level

From the company level perspective, globalization looks much more feasible. Indeed, it seems much more sensible to argue – as Perlmutter does – that the transnational corporations are driving globalization with their competitive and co-operative activities increasing the interdependence between countries. This is more or less the same as the idea that the activities of multinational companies can be seen as a transmission belt for the pressures of globalization, for example, through the international dissemination of 'best practice' in work organizations (Ferner, 1997:20). This, in turn, leads to the sharing of similar production values, i.e. for worldwide standards and behaviour.

There remains a wide range of global strategies for individual firms because although they have in common the tendency to inter-firm co-operative alliance strategies, there are variations in the forms and stability of alliances. BA has espoused a strategy of globalization since 1992. The company has pursued this through equity stakes in US Air, Qantas, TAT , Deutsch Air and Lot (Poland). However, a direct merger with KLM collapsed – not least on account of human resource factors. Consequently, for the alliance proposed in 1997, both BA and American Airlines proposed to avoid the equity or full merger route, wisely as it turned out.

In electronics and information technology, Philips has a 32 per cent stake in Grundig and the pair joined forces for video and cordless operations. Olivetti made an alliance with Canon. Fujitsu took over ICL with immediate consequences for human resource management.

In automobiles, Ford and Volkswagen have a joint enterprise in

Brazil. General Motors and Toyota have NUMMI in the USA. General Motors and Suzuki have CAMI in Canada. As motor vehicle manufacturers began to suffer from over-capacity in the industry during the 1990s, there began a process of rationalization through mergers. Renault's planned merger with Volvo fell through but Jaguar was sold to Ford and Rover to BMW. Mergers often disguise bankruptcies; heavy debt loads and collapsing sales often cause motor manufacturers to join forces. Ostensibly, this was not the case with the mega-merger of Chrysler and Daimler-Benz in 1998 that was supposedly 'untypical of the industry because the two companies did not compete in geographical or product markets' (Simonian, 1998). Even though the US auto union thought that the deal could be a win–win situation, Daimler boss Jürgen Schrempp was known as an enthusiast for the US brand of capitalism, complete with shareholder value and flexible labour markets.

Siemens has many co-operative agreements in telecommunications (with Ericson and Toshiba), semiconductors (General Electric, Philips), robotics (Fujitsu) and computers (Fujitsu and Microsoft). Cadbury's who had purchased Dr. Pepper – a direct competitor with Coca-Cola – made an agreement with Coca-Cola to carry out bottling and distribution in the USA.

Books and articles have begun to appear about making alliances work and co-operating is an organizational expertise that companies such as Siemens seem to have achieved. Evidently, global alliancing has become a vital component of strategy and, as the transnational company becomes a more global enterprise network, it is being transformed into a different sort of institution. 'Some travel-related sectors realize that the formation of strategic network alliances allows an effective pooling of resources, improved marketing coverage and technology sharing. Already a number of regionally-based integrated computer information reservation management systems have been developed in Europe and North America. These systems provide information (and sometimes reservations) for the components making up a region's entire travel and tourism product. Importantly, they enable small and medium-sized tourism enterprises to amass collective bargaining leverage when dealing with CRS operators and other powerful industry players' (Ioannides and Debbage, 1997:238).

The trouble with all this information is that it tends only to 'clarify that our knowledge about the impact of characteristics on personnel management in international joint ventures lacks specificity', according to Zeira and Shenkar (1990:17). Their recommended approach is

Union warms to win–win for Chrysler

Reaction to the Chrysler/Daimler-Benz merger from the influential Union of Automotive Workers, which represents more than 70,000 employees at the US car-maker, has been as favourable as the companies could have hoped.

Steve Yokich, UAW president, said on Thursday the deal could be a win–win situation, although he also acknowledged there were many questions still unanswered. 'We're taking a good, hard look at it – not just today, but three years, six years and 10 years down the road' he said.

But, he added: 'At the moment, I think it's good for the Chrysler workers and good for the union. I don't believe it weakens us at all.'

As US labour experts have already pointed out, the deal could offer the UAW advantages. Although the union still has the muscle to cause serious disruption to the Big Three car-makers if it wishes, its influence has declined over the past two decades as membership has dropped.

Today, it represents about 770,000 workers, about half the peak level of 1.5m in 1978.

Importantly, the UAW has had a mixed record when trying to organize at the foreign-owned car plants which have set up on US soil.

It failed to secure a foot-hold at the independent Japanese plants – those not in joint venture with US car-makers – owned by the likes of Nissan, Honda and Toyota. But, following the Daimler deal, it may now sense an easier entrée into some European-owned facilities. Daimler-Benz itself has an assembly plant in Alabama, employing about 1,500 people which the union is eager to add to its membership, and BMW has a separate facility in South Carolina. Neither are organized at present.

In addition, the German approach to labour representation is conciliatory, with union members given supervisory board representation. Union attitudes in the US have varied on this issue of whether it is better to achieve goals through collective bargaining in the broader political arena or through having a stake in management.

However, the UAW said yesterday it would like to participate fully in any worker board arrangement.

Two former presidents of the UAW – Douglas Fraser and Owen Bieber – have served on Chrysler's board in the past.

Finally, in productivity terms, US plants compare well with those in Germany. That – coupled with the assurances from Mr Eaton and Mr Schrempp that the merger is about opportunity rather than rationalization may have helped to assuage fears of job losses. As M. Yokich pointed out: 'Our job is to protect American jobs.'

Out in the plants the dominant attitude seemed to be one of 'wait and see'.

'There are mergers going on everywhere – it's hard to know what will happen,' said one employee at Chrysler's Belvidere assembly plant in

Illinois. Others have pointed out that employees stuck by the US car-maker during its problems in the 1970s and 1980s, and have expressed hopes that this would not be forgotten.

Meanwhile, dealers' reaction seemed to be generally enthusiastic – although there was initial confusion over whether upmarket Mercedes would be sold next-door to minivans. (The companies will retain exclusive dealerships, and do not expect to co-mingle brands.)

Nikki Tait, *Financial Times*,
9 May 1998

to investigate for each parent company's characteristic or combination of characteristics, how each employee group is affected and the nature of problems faced by that group. For instance, how does the size of the parent company influence the promotion of foreign expatriates in the international joint venture? How does the number of parent companies influence communication between foreign parents' expatriates and host parent transferees? How does a reputation gap between the parent firms affect the loyalty of third country expatriates of the international joint venture? How do differences in parent company objectives influence the evaluation of host country nationals? How does the flow of resources affect the communications between foreign parent expatriates and foreign head office executives? While these may be the right questions, however, this sounds a very complex approach.

Effect on labour and labour institutions

The effect so far of competitive and co-operative alliances on labour has been mixed but full takeovers appear to mean rationalization and job cuts. There are daily reports on the need for cost control and employment reduction or new work practices as part of global competitive strategies of firms.

In the USA, Caterpillar's management held firm against a lengthy strike, saying that its survival was at stake against foreign competition. In Europe, Caterpillar integrated its forklift truck joint venture with Mitsubishi. One of the main achievements of the joint venture was to introduce *kaizen* or continuous improvement techniques. The Japanese were also instrumental in developing local suppliers' quality standards. Rover, before being taken over by BMW, had a co-operation agreement with Honda that influenced a radical change in work practices. At the beginning of this chapter, union concern at BT's proposed merger with the fiercely anti-union MCI of the US was noted. A Canadian firm announced in 1996 that it wanted to change its corporate culture from being a family environment to one that is 'lean and mean'.

Tate & Lyle extended its global network of subsidiaries by buying A.E. Staley after a successful hostile bid in 1988. On the expiry of the collective contract in 1993, Tate & Lyle tried to impose flexible working practices at Staley, halving the workforce and altering shift patterns. Faced with opposition from the United Paperworkers International Union, the management locked out the workers and tried to use unlimited sub-contracting, apparently to undermine the union. The dispute became a damaging war of attrition, ending finally after two and a half years when the workers voted to accept a contract in which Tate & Lyle made limited concessions. However, the union did not recommend acceptance and continued legal action against the company (Eaton, 1997).

In general, the fear for workers and their unions is of relocation for cost-cutting reasons and the use of this threat to stifle collective bargaining and extract concessions of flexibility and productivity. In a case well publicized in a BBC TV documentary, BPI, Britain's leading supermarket plastic bag manufacturer, shut its factory in Telford, sacked all 150 employees and shipped all the machines to Guangdong province, South China, where wages were one eighth of the British level. Inside Europe there are moves to lower cost sites: Hoover, for example, moved production from Dijon to Cambuslang in Scotland and in November 1998 the chairman of Rolls Royce aero engines referred to the additional costs in social benefits of manufacturing in Europe and warned that the company could move production to America 'if Britain introduces costly European labour laws' (Harrison, 1998).

Social dumping, trade unions and works councils

It may be no exaggeration to say that some 'multinationals have ruthlessly played one country or region against another, accepting the highest subsidies and lowest controls over pollution and workers' welfare. Environmental and employee legislation in their home countries has been cynically avoided by transferring production overseas. Trade unions have been slow and largely ineffective in providing employee protection to match the activities of global managers' (Price, 1997:39).

French jobs lost in EU lottery

Villers-la-Montagne

French factory workers who are losing their jobs on a hi-fi assembly line, because their Japanese employer is concentrating production in Scotland, will tell a government minister today that they have been the victims of a European Union subsidies lottery.

A delegation of nine women, representing 243 workers who assemble mid-priced hi-fi systems for JVC in the industrial zone around the village of Villers-la-Montagne, in eastern France, claim the company is leaving because it has exhausted EU subsidies for their blighted former steel area and now intends to profit from hand-outs in Scotland.

The company – which manufactures televisions at East Kilbride, near Glasgow – last year expanded its Scottish operation to include the production of mid-systems previously made at the factory near the border with Luxembourg.

The French plant is now due to close at the end of January.

'When they have finished in Scotland they will return to the Far East, having spent 10 years benefiting from subsidies and securing a foothold in the European market,' said Catherine Leblan, a 30-year-old production line worker.

Meurthe-et-Moselle, where the JVC factory opened in 1988, is one of dozens of European industrial regions – including parts of Wales, northern England and Scotland – which competed for the attention of hi-tech businesses during the 1980s.

In return for investing in former mining, steel and ship-building areas, the companies received billions of pounds in government and EU grants, and secured European markets.

For the likes of Aline Radosevic, whose father was a steel worker and was laid off at the age of 38, the departure of JVC is proof that eastern France is heading for its latest depression.

'JVC got a grant of Fr2 million (£225,000) to expand its television assembly plant outside Glasgow,' she said. 'Last year, they transferred part of our audio production there. JVC had already received EU money here; it's like robbing Peter to pay Paul.'

Pointing to her inflamed left elbow, she said: 'They recently took some of our machines to Scotland. On the assembly line we have to push the hi-fis manually along the band.'

But Mrs Radosevic, who will be laid off at the end of January unless a buyer to take over the factory is found, does not resent her Scottish colleagues, even though she believes they are paid considerably less than the Fr6,554 (£710) gross monthly minimum at Villers-la-Montagne.

Sitting behind a pile of documents which would humble an average financial director, Isabelle Banny explained Miss Leblan's prediction. 'The market in hi-tech equipment – such as televisions, video recorders and hi-fis - has slumped by 30 per cent in the past three years.'

'Glasgow's industrial history is similar to ours, but they must be warned that Far Eastern investment provides no future. Employers' costs may be low in Britain but still they cannot compete with Malaysia.'

Miss Banny and her colleagues – some of them supporting their husbands and many of them single mothers – are far from resigned to their fate. Last week, they held hostage five of the company's directors for a day. On Thursday they plan a one-day strike.

The women – who are mostly aged under 35 because French employers receive grants to employ young people – are not drawing up plans for a buy out. 'There is no market for hi-fis,' said Miss Leblan.

'The best we can hope for is that the factory will be sold and some of us re-employed.'

Even if that happens, the women know they will be just the latest example of the transformation of an area where people once had father-to-son jobs for life into one of 'le-relay factories'.

This growing phenomenon sees companies move into a blighted area and receive grants, and then leave when the incentives or profits run out.

Before JVC's eight-year-tenure of the factory, it was owned for two years by Thomson electronics, which employed 100 people. Yesterday, a compact disc manufacturer was looking around the site.

Miss Banny said: 'We want our experience to serve as an example of how things should not be done. We shall tell the minister that when companies apply for grants in development zones they must promise not only to create jobs but to stay for 10 years.'

While France has not, as yet, descended into an autumn of discontent to match that which paralysed Paris last winter, small private sector companies are increasingly the scene of strife. In Normandy, workers for Moulinex are currently protesting against 2,000 job cuts. South of Villers-la-Montagne, riot policy recently ended a three-month sit-in by workers who had been laid off at a clock factory.

The localized private sector uproar has come at a time of rising indignation over foreign investments and takeovers – seen as being agreed with few job guarantees. Last week, the French government sold part of the state-owned Thomson group to Daewoo, of South Korea.

Trade union activism is very limited in France's private sector – only 40 of JVC's 243 staff at Villers-la-Montagne are union members. National unemployment is 12.5 per cent, and higher in areas such as the east.

Maria Lamagra, aged 32, said: 'We have our determination, though. There are jobs in Luxembourg, just a few miles away, but they are falling in number.'

'This area used to be known as Black Texas, because of the coal and iron ore. Now all that industry has gone and we are seeing that the painful, partial recovery we made was for nothing.'

The company's personnel manager, Régis Spor, denied that JVC had let down its workers. 'We brought eight years of employment to this area and in 1992 we employed 300 people. We have paid Fr26 million in taxes and Fr75 million in social charges.'

He said the company had received Fr22.3 million in grants from the French state and from the EU, but had invested Fr80 million.

He conceded that the European audio market had been in decline since 1993, while denying that JVC was in the process of abandoning Europe.

But a JVC official added: 'It would be suicide for anyone to open an audio plant anywhere in Europe now. All production is going back to the Far East.'

Alex Duval Smith, *Guardian*, 31 October 1996

Reasons for relocating Scotland's strong cards

- Manufacturing productivity annual growth rate of 5.2 per cent;
- Less onerous restrictions on labour. UK workers put in an average 41 hours a week against EU average of 39;
- Days lost to industrial disputes in the UK were 24 per 1,000 workers, according to latest Eurostat figures in 1992;
- Success of other inward investors attracts more companies. Inward investment in Scotland announced this year is more than £2.7 billion.

Guardian, 31 October 1996

France's drawbacks

- Manufacturing productivity; annual growth rate of 2.7 per cent;
- Higher cost of labour: up to 25 per cent more than the UK;
- Days lost to industrial disputes: 37 per 1,000 workers;
- Total remuneration costs 37 per cent higher than the UK as benefits in France are more extensive;
- Wages councils under Social Chapter can set pay;
- Output per hour in manufacturing about 80 per cent of UK level.

Guardian, 31October 1996

However, some multinational companies are far from being antagonistic to trade unions. ABB, formed from a merger of Sweden's Asea and Switzerland's Brown Boveri in 1988, is an example. The attitude of the British union, RMT (National Union of Rail, Maritime and Transport Workers), who had extensive negotiations with ABB over the closure of the BREL engineering works at York, is conciliatory: 'ABB is certainly not a soft employer but the management is comfortable with trade unions. They come from an environment where trade unions are accepted and recognized. Unlike some companies, they don't regard trade unionists as people who have arrived from Mars' (Milner, 1997).

To reconcile company competitiveness with co-operation may appear possible in principle, as the UAW attitude of 'win–win' towards the Chrysler/Daimler-Benz merger showed. However, while they sought to fit in with the conciliatory German approach to labour representation, there were signs that breaking away from the German system was part of the rationale for the deal. Co-operation may be a Trojan horse that will defeat the unions. It seems both a necessity and a risk for, as a manager noted, a company's recognition of the importance of human resources may mean that employees come to believe 'that they don't need a trade union because they have a correct situation in the company. This may explain why the trade union movement – which is too largely based on confrontation and not on co-operation – has had some difficulty in the last ten years. To a certain extent, I would say that management is playing the role of the union' (Campbell, 1992:74).

In chapter 7, it was suggested that part of the impetus behind human resource management was the aim to provide a substitute for unions. A few years on, this seems less realistic. In the European Union, the Commission appears to recognize the role of trade unions in social dialogue at the same time as trying to develop a culture of partnership. In relation to multinationals, the European Works Council directive was adopted by the Council of Ministers in 1994. This may help trade unions and union representation in multinational companies, as will be discussed in chapter 12. However, such policy pertains mainly to core or permanent workers and does little or nothing for the periphery or excluded workers (roughly defined as part-time, sub-contract and temporary workers). In this connection, social dimension legislation for higher labour standards and employee rights has supposedly been a part of the EU's policy. Its effectiveness in counteracting social dumping and the feasibility of introducing minimum labour standards into international trade is discussed in the following chapter.

Questions for discussion

1 Discuss the compatibility of human resource management policies and trade union recognition and consider key factors that
could induce a transnational company to recognize trade
unions in one or more of its national locations.

2 'The transnational company has the flexibility for globalization,
the management of global interdependencies and the sharing
of values within national states.'

Discuss and consider the implications for labour.

3 'Where foreign direct investment occurs in a context of high
levels of demand and there are effective rules of the game that
limit the destructive aspects of competition, then foreign direct
investment may have a positive effect on nations and communities.'

Discuss.

11

Minimum Standards in International Trade

The basic issue here may be seen as the old one of free trade versus protection. However, to say that is also to be somewhat misleading, although it is true that the main issues can be set out very simply: 'The idea that international trade agreements should include a social clause laying down minimum or fair labour standards, though far from new, has lost none of its immediacy. The argument is that if a country allows its workers to be employed under deplorable/exploited conditions of work (and the precise meaning of this would have to be defined), it can then export its products at lower prices and thus acquire an unfair advantage over its competitors. Hence the proposal that such a country should be obliged to guarantee minimum rights to its workers under international trade arrangements' (Servais, 1989:423). Opponents may see this as protectionism – an indirect but effective way of raising tariff barriers against imports from developing countries. This is denied by advocates of social clauses who say that they are intended to correct exploitative practices and improve the conditions of workers in the exporting countries too.

Nevertheless, a kind of protection of social standards and prevention of 'social dumping' is the rationale behind the EU Social Charter, Social Dimension and Social Action programme. The principles and main outcomes of the EU Social Dimension will be examined later. However, the chapter starts with a consideration of the problems entailed in trying to establish and enforce minimum standards in international trade generally.

History

The aim to establish links between international trade and labour standards dates back to the formation of the International Labour Organization (ILO) after the 1919 Versailles Treaty, which also drew up the first international Labour Charter (see chapter 7). Labour standards have always been a prime concern of the ILO because the preamble in its constitution declared that 'the failure of any nation to adopt humane conditions of labour is an obstacle in the way of other nations which desire to improve the conditions in their own countries'. In 1998, the European Parliament Committee on External Economic Relations adopted a report prepared by André Sainjon on labour standards in international trade. The report called for debate within the World Trade Organization to establish measures guaranteeing observance of fundamental social rights by all states that were signatories to multinational trade agreements and for the European Commission to adopt a code of minimum conduct, based on ILO principles, that could be ratified by multinational companies.

Theory and practice

This area of economics is one in which economic theory in itself is of limited use. The idea of 'positive' economics does not help very much. In terms of 'positive' economics, the idea would be that the analyst does not consider the ethics or morality of policies, but rather looks at the policies that can make people better off. However, this may be a nonsense since frequently the work practices themselves are mixed with cruelty in developing countries. The degrees of exploitation and labour intensification can often not be separated from practices that are unacceptable by any standard: children are employed in dangerous factory jobs; labour laws are not enforced; every year trade union organizers are harassed, jailed, disappear or are murdered.

Against these cruel practices, a social clause would aim at improving labour conditions in exporting countries by allowing sanctions against exporters who fail to observe minimum standards. Typically, a social clause in an international trade agreement makes it possible to restrict or halt the importation of products from countries where labour conditions fall below certain minimum standards.

However, the main comparative advantage of the Third World is its poverty. The inward investment attracted by lower wages is welcomed by the governments concerned because otherwise such investment would go elsewhere. Further justification is sometimes made that the workers – although on desperately low wages – are at least better off than if they were unemployed. Even some aid agencies have been reluctant to condemn instances of child labour for similar reasons. Mainly, though, like Oxfam, they argue that the rights laid down by the International Labour Organization, covering areas such as forced labour and employment discrimination, should be linked with trade obligations imposed by the World Trade Organization.

International trade union organizations may not have much bargaining power but they have been active in monitoring and uncovering exploitative and cruel treatment of workers in many countries. Bill Jordan, General Secretary of the International Confederation of Free Trade Unions, reported in 1997 that 'trade union research has uncovered terrible practices carried out in factories in Central America and Asia which include punishing women by forcing them to stand with chairs above their heads for hours on end or making them do 24-hour shifts without pay' (letter to *Independent*, 18 April 1997).

Jordan also reported that 'the reality of globalization means Pakistani children stitching footballs for Euro 96 (halted after union pressure), the death threat hanging over a trade union activist in Indonesia and troops rounding up whole villages in Burma to force them to build a new road for the tourist trade'. Furthermore, he argues, every defeat for workers in the developing world has a knock-on effect for workers in the West as well because it gives employers an excuse to strip their employees of hard-earned rights by pointing to the completely deregulated labour markets in the developing world. Therefore, those who say that codes of conduct based on international standards are an unwarranted and unrealistic interference in international trade are wrong – in the sense that unacceptable conditions and cruelty are often not far removed from what might be seen as low pay necessarily due to low national income and low economic development.

A report by the World Development Movement about workers in three factories in Haiti – all sub-contractors for the Disney Corporation – concluded that the factories were keeping wages down to the lowest level legally allowed; forcing workers to work overtime with little additional pay; sacking workers who joined unions; and refusing sickness and maternity leave. Of course, the issue is far from clear-cut. In terms of low pay – e.g. a daily wage in 1997 of £1.35 for workers in the Haiti sweatshops sewing T-shirts – there is another

Nike trips up over poverty pay for Asian labour force

American women's groups are attacking Nike, the sports goods multinational, for what they call its abusive treatment of the female labour force in its Asian factories. The women's coalition has targeted as hypocritical a television ad campaign aimed at female consumers.

The Nike commercials depict well-toned female athletes in images designed to persuade American women that if they buy into the popular brand name they too will be powerful. The problem, according to a coalition of 15 women's groups, is that the ads obscure the truth – that the Indonesian, Vietnamese and Chinese women who manufacture Nike's shoes are weak and powerless.

'Nike's slogan is catchy, "There is no finish line," ' said the letter to Nike chairman Philip Knight. Unfortunately, this motto also applies to some of the factories overseas where women, according to pay-slips from Nike factories in Indonesia, work from 100 to 200 overtime hours a month (to make ends meet).

'While the women who wear Nike shoes in the United states are encouraged to perform their best, the Indonesian, Vietnamese and Chinese women making the shoes often suffer from inadequate wages, corporal punishment, forced overtime and/or sexual harassment.'

The letter, whose signatories include the vanguard feminist National Organization for Women and the celebrated author Alice Walker, seeks to expand the propaganda offensive against a colossally successful multinational, which so far appears to remain immune to a sustained onslaught by international labour organization.

A biting report on Nike's labour practices, issued recently by the Hong Kong Christian Industrial Committee, has barely made a dent on the consciousness of the sports-shoe buying public, but it is in large measure from that report that the US women's coalition derived the impetus to lodge their protest.

The report noted that, over thirty years, Western sports shoe companies have been relocating factories or seeking sub-contractors in Asia where wages are lower and 'where systematic repression of labour movements promises a "docile" workforce'.

Initially they looked to Taiwan and South Korea, where political authoritarianism and repression of workers' rights were at their peak. In time, however, workers in those countries fought successfully for higher wages, whereupon companies like Nike shifted production to countries where labour was still cheaper, such as Indonesia, Vietnam and China. Investigation of conditions in factories that manufacture Western brand-name sports shoes demonstrated a pattern of abuse by management, the report said.

"But poor conditions in the factory are not simply the result of having a particularly harsh factory owner. It is actually the multi-nationals, not the subcontractors, that ultimately set the pace of production as well as the wages of the workers.

'. . . When the multinationals squeeze the subcontractors, the subcontractors squeeze the workers.'

In the case of the female workers, they squeeze them literally. The US women's coalition letter to Nike pointed out that in Vietnam, where Nike has been in operation for two years, factory officials have been charged with sexual abuse.

The women's coalition says Nike has been blinded to these violations, as well as the systematic exploitation of its Asian workers, by the spectacular profits it has made from the huge gap between the Third World wages of the workers who make the shoes and the spending power of those in the First World who buy them.

Nike's response is that it is playing a beneficial role in Asia, by providing jobs that pay better wages than those of Asian-owned factories.

John Carlin, *Independent*,
28 October 1997

side to the story in a country where 80 per of the population are unemployed. The workers do not want companies moving out but they do want their rights to union membership respected.

Code of conduct for labour standards

Bill Jordan of the ICFTU reckons that a code of conduct based on internationally agreed labour standards is a step in the right direction but in order to operate properly, it must be independently monitored and the trade unions that represent the workers at the factories must be involved. Current schemes where supposedly independent monitoring teams visit factories in the presence of company managements to ask workers about their rights and report back 'no complaints' are clearly not adequate.

What standards should be included in a social clause? There are various suggestions, all related to ILO standards from the 168 ILO conventions. A review of eight different labour/social clause proposals found that the following standards were mentioned by all of them:

1 freedom of association;
2 the right to organize and bargain collectively;
3 freedom from discrimination in employment on grounds of race, sex, religion, political opinion etc.

4   freedom from forced labour;
5   minimum age for employment of children;
6   occupational safety and health regulation.

Problems and complications

Problems arise in the first place because of failures to agree any international policy on minimum standards as a result of policy differences among national governments. There have been disagreements among the European Union member states about the amount of labour market regulation that measures against social dumping should entail. Between industrialized and Third World countries, the scope for disagreement is obviously greater. The ultimate sanction of blocking trade could make it less rather than more likely that the use of child workers could be phased out and better health care and educational provision – absent from the core standards usually mentioned – introduced.

According to Richard Thomas (1996), 'this is why poorer countries, such as India, oppose the idea, pointing out that Britain's transformation from agricultural to industrial economy was built on the sweat of 10-year-old miners and factory workers'. Many developing countries therefore detect more than a whiff of moral imperialism in the air. Developing countries are suspicious that industrialized nations are using a professed concern over human rights to cloak straightforwardly protectionist aims. Their doubts were shared by Peter Sutherland, director general of GATT, when he argued in March 1994 that drastic remedies against so-called social dumping were the wrong approach: Such politicization of trade policy-making turns it into the equivalent of breaking off diplomatic relations or suspending aircraft landing rights' and introducing it into the co-operative WTO framework 'would place the system at immediate risk of collapse' (Williams, 1994).

It was the USA that set the stage for disagreement in 1994 by insisting that worker rights be put on the agenda of the World Trade Organization – the Clinton administration had been under some pressure from US labour unions to take a tough position against social dumping. In fact, no country has taken such far-reaching action in the area of international trade and minimum labour standards as the USA. Since 1983 US trade and investment policies have been linked to labour rights in at least four laws. For example, under the Generalized System of Preferences (GSP), the US government is obliged to remove from the list of countries receiving duty-free benefits any country that denies workers' rights. In 1987, Romania and Nicaragua lost GSP beneficiary status, leading the AFL/CIO to accuse the then Reagan administration of using the GSP politically. However, Chile also subsequently lost GSP status.

Enforceability

Gary Fields (1996:571) makes a sound point when he says that rules and regulations need to be modest in scope. If not, it will be hard to point the finger at alleged violators and get them to change what they do. 'What country could say with a straight face that it is honouring the ILO's convention regarding equal remuneration for work of equal value but another country is not? When codes are generally honoured, violations are more clear-cut and the rate of compliance on core matters is likely to be higher as a result. Though there are many labour *standards* (defined as those workplace processes and conditions that we would rather have than not have), there are manageably few labour *rights* (defined as workplace processes and conditions so fundamental that it would be better to have no production at all than to have production in their absence – which would amount to production using illegitimate means). Adoption of the 'illegitimate means' criterion would mandate the setting of labour rights at a level appropriate to all working people in rich and poor countries alike, and the promulgation of international agreements to guarantee those rights.'

Fields's own list of rights that would fit this definition are as follows:

1   No person has the right to enslave another or to cause another to enter into indentured servitude and every person has the right to freedom from such actions;
2   No person has the right to expose another to unsafe and unhealthy working conditions without providing the fullest possible information;
3   Children have the right not to work long hours whenever their families' financial circumstances allow;
4   Every person has the right to freedom of association in the workplace and the right to organize and bargain collectively with employers.

There are ways in which governments, trade unions and non-governmental organizations can make a difference. 'One example, quoted in a recent World Development Report, has been the action in the deep-sea fishing industry of Cebu in the Philippines where large numbers of small boys were employed in dangerous sea-diving. A task force was established, including non-government organizations, to persuade villagers to stop sending their children to work. The boys were given incentives to go back to school, grants were given to establish soap-making, weaving and pig-rearing projects and the boys' mothers were given financial help with retraining. Pressure was then applied on employers who agreed not to recruit any boys aged under eighteen' (Balls, 1995). According to this author, 'regulation in developing countries is generally more effective when it is agreed and enforced at a local level between employers and trade unions, and regulation to eradicate child labour is more likely to be effective if it is in the interests of children and parents and goes with the grain of development'.

Business ethics and international trade

According to an editorial in the *Financial Times* in March 1994, 're-pugnant as child labour or wilfully dangerous working conditions are, efforts to ban them simply by imposing standards from outside could easily increase deprivation in really poor countries where no alternative legal source of family income exists. Such efforts would in any case be credible only if backed by threat of sanctions which would risk further impoverishing third-world economies'.

Interest in business ethics has revived and this is undoubtedly an issue for business ethics. Geoffrey Chandler, former senior executive for Shell, has suggested that 'there are arguments of self-interest as well as principle which should cause rethinking in boardrooms, even if recent reports of Shell in Nigeria and BP in Colombia fail to shake corporate complacency more broadly. Abuse of human rights threatens the stability essential to long-term investment' (Chandler, 1996). In October 1996, Sainsbury's and Asda supermarkets reportedly welcomed a campaign that aimed to highlight the human rights abuses of some of their suppliers. *Change the Rules*, launched by Christian Aid, urged shoppers to lobby supermarkets to stop them stocking produce from developing countries where workers suffer unacceptably low wages or work in dangerous conditions (Bellos, 1996).

In the USA a similar campaign was begun against Nike, the sports shoe producer, sharply criticized for exploiting its mainly female workforce. The company was accused of turning a blind eye to abuses by its local managers and sub-contractors – despite its attempt in

Basic labour standards – the dilemma of global trade.

1994 to impose a code of good conduct on its suppliers. Women making shoes that are later sold under the Nike brand name are said to be beaten and to suffer sexual harassment.

The basic question is, do relativist arguments carry all before them (for example, is forced overtime really an oppression in a society where paid work of any kind is scarce?) or are there moral absolutes and are they enforceable? In the USA, Nike came under pressure from a coalition of women's and religious groups. However, will consumers sympathize sufficiently to want to pay extra?

The EU Social Charter, Social Dimension and Social Action Programme as minimum standards in international trade

Ruth Nielsen (1996) observed that 'in external relations between the EU and the rest of the world, there is a growing interest at EU level in including collective labour law in world trade regulation in order to protect the European Union against social dumping'. At a meeting in March 1995, the Council of the EU discussed a memorandum on the social dimension of world trade that proposed guarantees of basic social standards. Although most members were in favour, there was some concern about protectionism. Consequently, 'in the course of the debate flowing from the adoption of the EU Social Charter and Social Action Programme in 1989, a vigorous argument has been made against any further extension of the European social policy on the grounds of its harmful economic consequences' (Deakin and Wilkinson, 1994:289).

The terms of this debate are essentially similar to what has been discussed but in an EU context. There is not space to consider the debate in detail but a central issue is the additional costs for employers entailed by the social dimension. To begin to consider that, it is necessary to see just how much of the EU Social Charter has been put into effect.

The Social Charter

The Social Charter of 1989 contains twelve fundamental social rights:

1   Freedom of movement – enables every worker to engage in any occupation in the EU in accordance with the principles of equal treatment as regards access to employment, working

conditions and social protection in the host country;

2   Employment and Remuneration – 'equitable' wages. That is to say, the freedom to choose an occupation and the right to a fair wage;

3   Improvement of living and working conditions (originally, it was declared that the completion of the internal market must lead to an improvement in the living and working conditions of EU workers, including employment regulation, such as procedures for collective redundancies. However, since the adoption of the Single European Act, the emphasis has shifted significantly from harmonization to adoption of minimum standards.);

4   Social protection – adequate levels of social security benefits, whatever the status of the worker and whatever the size of undertaking where employed;

5   Freedom of association and collective bargaining – every worker and every employer to have the freedom to join or not to join professional organizations or trade unions of their choice. These organizations to have the right to negotiate and conclude collective agreements. The dialogue between the two sides of industry at European level which must be developed, may, *if the parties deem it desirable,* result in contractual relations in particular at inter-occupational and sectoral level;

6   Vocational training – every EU worker must be able to have access to vocational training throughout their working life;

7   Equal treatment of men and women;

8   Information, consultation and participation for workers – collective labour law still differs fundamentally from country to country (see chapter 9) and is therefore the most difficult part of labour law to integrate into EU law. Many proposals have failed but finally in 1996 the European Works Council directive was adopted. This to apply especially in companies in two or more EU member states;

9   Health, protection and safety at the workplace – every worker must enjoy satisfactory health and safety conditions in the working environment;

10   Protection of children and adolescents – minimum working age; limitations on working hours and access to training and education;

11   Elderly persons – living standards during retirement;

12   Disabled persons – entitlement to additional measures aimed at improving their social and professional integration.

Hence the 1989 Social Charter was prima facie a framework declaration of normative rights. It has no legal force but is supposed to demonstrate the identity of Europe in the social field and contains, in the originating Social Charter, an action programme designed to implement the principles laid down in the Social Charter by means of directives of the European Council.

Emperor's New Clothes or practical measures?

European trade union officials initially believed that they could use the Social Charter to lobby the Commission to create a uniform set of rules for co-ordinated EU-wide collective bargaining. Otherwise, they argued, the Single European Act would trigger an irreversible shift in the balance of social power against labour. However, 'labour's weak position economically and politically in the early 1990s, particularly at the national level, prevented the ETUC and their member confederations from winning support for their version of the Social Charter, since they could neither credibly threaten recalcitrant governments with social unrest nor convincingly offer them electoral aid' (Silvia, 1991:626). Indeed, it seemed as though all the Social Charter proposals were simply idealistic aspirations, bogged down in the decision-making processes of the European Council. Discussing this issue with some Danish economists in 1992, the Social Charter was evidently regarded by European trade unionists as equivalent to Hans Christian Andersen's 'Emperor's new clothes'.

Nevertheless, since then 'virtually all of the substantive proposals stemming from the Action Programme (designed to implement the principles laid down in the Social Charter) have either been enacted into law or are close to becoming law' (Addison and Siebert, 1994:5). This was despite the fact that the UK governments (until 1997) regarded the rights contained in the Social Charter as 'old-fashioned' and at odds with their deregulatory labour market policies.

The UK 'Opt-out' from the Social Charter

During the Maastricht negotiations about the single market, the UK opposed the widening of the social dimension of the EU Treaty. Hence a protocol on social policy – then referred to as the 'Social Chapter' – had to be appended to the Maastricht Treaty.

This agreement led to seemingly endless – and exasperating – press reports and statements by Conservative MPs and government ministers that referred to the UK as having an 'opt-out' of the Social Chapter. However, although the UK was able to negotiate temporary exemptions from particular individual European Council directives under the Action Programme on Social Policy, it was always fundamentally bound by the Treaty of Rome and Articles 117–122 and therefore to eventual progress to adoption of the measures under the Social Dimension, Social Chapter, or whatever it was called. This point was well elaborated and argued by Derrick Wyatt, a lawyer specializing in EU law, in 1989: 'In the UK, the principles of direct effect and the supremacy of Community (now EU) law are secured by sections 2 and 3 of the European Communities Act 1972. Whatever EU law says must be given legal effect without the benefit of further implementation shall be given the force of law in the UK. Parliament defers to the founding treaties and EU law is given full force and effect.'

An example in December 1994 was the rejection by Michael Portillo, then Secretary of State for Employment, of the measure that extended proportionate or similar rights to part-time workers as those enjoyed by full-time workers. This was at first phrased in the press as 'a government decision, expressed by Portillo, to reject the principle contained in a decision by the House of Lords in August 1994 that – under Equal Opportunities legislation – part-time workers (being mainly female) had to have similar or proportionate rights (dismissal, sickness, pregnancy) to those of full-time workers'. A week later, Portillo and the government were compelled to admit that the UK was bound to accept that part-time workers had similar rights to full-time workers.

A further example preceded the announcement by the European Commission in December 1994 that there was no intention of weakening the Transfer of Undertakings Protection of Employment (TUPE) directive that aimed to protect wages and conditions when a new employer took over a business from another. A month previously, former Leyland DAF workers won their industrial tribunal case that receivers Arthur Andersen had repeatedly failed to observe statutory regulations and proceeded to recover compensation from the government under the EU directive on insolvent companies.

It was conceded in November 1997 that the previous Conservative governments had evaded their obligations to ensure that working conditions were protected when private businesses took over public services under the Compulsory Competitive Tendering policy. In the British interpretation of the EU Transfer of Undertakings law, only private sector workers in commercial undertakings were protected. However, the EU directives on which UK law was based protected all workers.

In its Trade Union Reform and Employment Relations Act of 1993, the government was obliged to include sections that were out of character with the rest of the Act. Changes to the law on consultation where redundancy may take place originated in EU legislation. Redundancy consultation now had to include ways of avoiding the dismissals, reducing the numbers to be dismissed and mitigating the consequences of the dismissals with – significantly – a view to reaching agreement with trade union representatives. In March 1994, the European Court of Justice ruled that workers must be given a statutory right to representation where jobs are threatened – which appeared to entail legislation to restore collective bargaining in firms where employers had derecognized unions and put staff on individual contracts. British governments up to 1997 were unable to resist important changes to maternity pay and leave as a result of the Social Dimension, requiring amendments to national and local agreements. These stemmed from the European Commission pregnant workers directive that was also introduced by the 1993 Trade Union Reform and Employment Relations Act.

In fact, opting out made passage of the directives easier. The Social Chapter made two fundamental changes to facilitate EU social legislation. It provided for qualified majority voting in five important areas of social policy: improvements to the working environment to protect workers' health and safety; working conditions; information and consultation rights of workers; gender equality and integration of persons excluded from the labour market. Majority voting ensured that the limit on working hours of forty-eight per week could be passed. However, the vast array of exemptions (air, rail, road and sea transport) and the voluntary character of the directive further exemplified the limited effect of some parts of the Social Dimension.

Nevertheless, the Working Time Directive contains very real benefits for employees and unions. When the Directive came into effect in October 1998, employment lawyers believed that there would need to be case law to establish the scope of the regulations. In March 1999 this occurred with the case of *Barber and others v. R. J. B. Mining*. The case concerned Regulation 4 about the maximum working time of forty-eight hours a week. It was brought by five members of the UK colliery supervisors union, NACODS. They had refused to sign opt-out agreements issued by the employer, R. J. B. Mining, and applied to the court for a declaration clarifying their legal position. The judge held that employees are entitled to such a declaration to clarify their position under their contracts of employment.

> The implications of this judgment for employers are enormous. The common perception was that the (Working Time) Regulations would only be enforced in the UK through criminal proceedings brought against the employer by the Health and Safety Executive. This case disproved that: Employers can ask their employees to work in excess of 48 hours a week in emergencies but employees can refuse. Where they agree, they should be asked to sign individual opt out agreements. This case shows that the Regulations give employees a powerful negotiating lever. It may be the first case under the new legislation but it will not be the last (Dawson, 1999).

Majority voting also allowed for belated passage – after many attempts – of a directive on the establishment of European Works Councils for information and consultation in EU-scale enterprises and companies. This is discussed in the next chapter on workers' participation.

The second main innovation introduced under the Social Chapter was to accord the 'social dialogue' an enhanced role in the formulation of social policy. Article 118B of the Single European Act requires the Commission to further the dialogue between organized labour and capital with a view to 'establishing relations based on agreement'. This may be construed to mean that 'at the second stage of consultation, the social partners can press for a collectively bargained solution in lieu of the Commission's proposed legislation' (Addison and Siebert, 1994:21). However, although Article 3(4) of the Agreement on Social Policy stipulates that the social partners can inform the Commission of their desire to embark on a process of negotiation, the main emphasis in the Social Action Programme 1998–2000 is on 'social dialogue' and developing a European industrial relations partnership culture.

Conclusion – costs and mandated social benefits

The social benefits resulting from the Social Charter are mandated, i.e. they are legislated and then employers and/or employees meet the costs. The Social Charter Action Programme is not insulated from the EU's anxieties about unemployment and competitiveness. It is debatable, however, just how costly are the mandated benefits that so far have flowed from the Social Charter. Addison and Siebert (1994:16) believed that 'the adjustments required could be extensive, particularly for the United Kingdom, with its relatively unregulated labour market and distinctive industrial relations system. The directives may be expected to affect the poorer member states as well because of their (de facto) lower labour standards. One puzzle to be explained is why the latter have not raised more objections to the mandates.'

It is argued that the poorer member states – Greece, Ireland, Portugal and Spain – may have most to do to comply with EU mandates. However, to some extent these countries have high standards. For example, dismissal is difficult if legally contested and there are extensive health and safety regulations. Enforcement is less certain partly because of family workers and unofficial employment in Greece and Portugal but the EU influence will increase enforcement.

An important rationale and justification for the Social Dimension is to protect attained levels of real wages and benefits from competition in 'free trade' from countries where labour costs and social standards are much lower. The term 'social dumping' has been used to apply to outcomes disadvantageous to labour that might result from the operation of the single market under conditions of wide differences in labour standards and costs. There could be an incentive for capital to move from high labour cost countries to those with lower labour costs, resulting in unemployment and lower wages in the higher labour cost countries. The findings of Erickson and Kuruvilla (1994) confirmed that there is a labour cost incentive for capital mobility but their analysis of foreign direct investment during the period 1980–8 showed that capital flows to lower labour cost countries were actually not much larger than capital flows to higher labour cost countries.

Addison and Siebert (1994) theorize that two conditions are necessary for mandated social charter benefits to increase the welfare of workers. It is necessary for the previous, pre-mandate, freely contracted situation to be inefficient, but even then, there needs to be wage flexibility and the money wages must fall to reflect the cost of the benefit. Otherwise, the cost to firms of the benefit will be greater than the value placed on it by the workers. The mandate becomes a tax on employment. 'Unless mandates are working to correct a pre-existing market failure and wages are flexible, the full wage will increase for some workers but at the expense of unemployment for others' (1994:25).

For Deakin and Wilkinson (1994:293), 'the essence of the response is that labour markets are characterized by structural imperfections – various kinds of uncertainty, limited information and sunk costs – to the extent that they can never be fully competitive in the sense specified by neoclassical models of equilibrium and that in no sense can a return to the common law (contract) be said to represent a restoration of the competitive ideal'.

Transnational standards are perhaps best seen as setting a minimum floor below which state regulation may not fall, thereby seeking to prevent destructive competition among countries and companies. The nature of EU social legislation as a 'floor of rights' is emphasized in the directives. Article 118A refers to the adoption of directives laying down minimum requirements in the field of the working environment. The framework directive on health and safety is without prejudice to national provisions that are more favourable. The maternity leave directive sets minimum provisions, rather than requiring every state to adopt Denmark's generous standards. Similarly, the working time directive does not require every state to adopt Germany's tough restrictions on night and weekend working for a working week lower than the forty-eight hours required by the directive which, in any case, has numerous exceptions.

Globally, the task is much more difficult. The international institutions that regulate trade, economic development and wealth creation can be undermined by excessive deregulation. Consequently, 'analysis and debate which have so far been mired in the question of pros and cons of deregulation, need to re-focus on such questions as the form to be taken by transnational standards, the degree to which procedural norms are used to buttress substantive regulation and how far guidance through recommendations and opinions is to be preferred to binding norms in directives and regulations' (Deakin and Wilkinson, 1994:310)

Questions for discussion

1   Discuss what is meant by 'social dumping'.

2   Discuss the feasibility of minimum labour standards as part of international trade agreements.

3   The EU Social Dimension entails mandated social benefits.

Discuss the contention that such mandates are a tax on employment, with the result that firms and all worker groups become worse off.

12

Participation: Partnership or Teamworking for Productivity?

Participation has become a portmanteau word, meaning all things to all people. In industrial relations, it generally refers to workers' participation in management. Formerly, in countries with high trade union membership and density, workers' participation was regarded as an addition to collective bargaining by unions, rather than an alternative. The idea of replacing unions and collective bargaining by non-adversarial participation that envelops worker representatives in the responsibilities of management is not new and was often a facet of paternalistic companies in the form of profit-sharing or joint consultation. It has been suggested that 'theorists of worker participation make a distinction between pseudo-participation in which management define the issues to be considered and substantive participation in which the employee voice is less narrowly circumscribed, more independent and influential'. The former can be called *employer-led participation* and the latter *negotiated participation* (Lowell Turner, 1997:309).

Human resource management and the idea of direct participation

The fundamental question about participation is whether, as collective bargaining has declined, it is necessary to look for replacements (see chapter 7). 'Where restoration of productivity is only possible under co-operative labour relations, employers are confronted with the strategic alternative between including independent unions in

the constitutional structure of the workplace or excluding them ...
Examples abound, particularly in the United States, of attempts at
establishing co-operation without unions – attempts that are often
accompanied inside the managerial structure by a conspicuous shift
of responsibility for labour relations from traditional IR staff to a
newly created Human Resource Management function' (Streeck,
1987:299). The implication was that a fair and accountable human
resource management may need to include provision for alternative
types of representation and participation. In chapter 10 a manager
from a multinational company was quoted as suggesting that, to some
extent, human resource management substituted for trade union representation. Logically, this implies some form of participation.

True enough, in the current period of global transition of economies and societies, an array of different forms and approaches to
participation have been tried. They include quality circles and Total
Quality Management and empowerment; teamworking and team
briefings; economic and financial participation, such as employee
share ownership and profit-sharing schemes.

To the extent that it can be argued that there is any global convergence of human resource management, these approaches do seem to
have in common that they do not usually contain explicit roles for
unions. 'Nowadays, participation schemes have become more and
more key elements of management demands, motivated by purely
economic objectives, with employees and their representatives pursuing partially different interests. This fits well into the generally
accepted hypothesis that management has become the key actor in
the ongoing process of decentralization and human resource management' (Keller, 1995:323).

However, this observation is sometimes true by definition. As the
authors of a 1996 survey of participation in Europe put it, 'whenever
we use the term *direct participation,* we are aware that we are dealing
with a management-driven strategy that aims at the workplace level,
that holds the idea of more consultative and/or delegative rights for
individuals or for workgroups' (Fröhlich and Pekruhl, 1996:20). The
same authors did not find that direct participation was always used
as a management tool to decrease or supplant union influence. According to a survey by Eaton and Voos (1992), union firms make
more use of all the types of direct participation than non-union firms,
with quality circles and job enrichment most likely to be found in
moderately unionized companies, whereas Quality of Working Life
committees were more likely to be found in highly unionized environments. However, the type of distinction suggested by Lowell

Turner between pseudo-participation and substantive participation is possibly obscured by this idea of direct participation in the Frohlich and Pekruhl study.

Knudsen (1995:5–8) did not think so, as he set out a typology of participation, according to whether it is direct or indirect:

(a) direct participation based on law, such as the 1982 Auroux laws in France;
(b) direct participation based on collective agreements;
(c) direct participation based on unilateral employer decisions, as in the Frohlich and Pekruhl research;
(d) indirect participation based on law, such as works councils and employee representation on company boards;
(e) indirect participation based on collective agreement as in collective bargaining itself;
(f) indirect participation through unilateral employer decision.

There is still an enormous diversity of worker participation schemes and institutions. In many countries, they are part of the framework of collective labour law and may be adaptable or hard for new management practices to assimilate. The data from the EPOC survey itself suggested one general conclusion that the authors felt it was necessary to emphasize at the outset: 'In countries with a system of works councils or elected representatives at the establishment level, employee representatives are generally not by-passed by management' (Fröhlich and Pekruhl, 1996:117).

The diversity of participation schemes

So direct participation is not necessarily incompatible with indirect, representative, collective and institutionalized participation. In the European Union, such participation is specifically provided for companies of at least 1,000 employees within the member states and at least 150 employees in each of at least two member states. These mandated representative forums are a far cry from the incremental, eclectic approaches instigated by management at the establishment level. Managers are often opposed to legislated participation but they may have to adapt to it. For instance, when Deutsch Bank was taking over Morgan Grenfell, Morgan's chairman was quoted as saying that the German tradition of two-tier boards and group decision-making was 'not the best way of doing investment banking' (Willcock and Eisenhammer, 1994). However, subsequent events and lack of financial control at the London office may have convinced the parent company that their way was still the best way.

Moreover, 'although the formal and actual rights of German worker representatives are among the most favourable in Europe, formal and actual management control is also among the most highly developed' (Lane, 1989:232). The real location is not the supervisory board but the works council which has not fundamentally changed the balance of power in the workplace but has secured worker participation decisions that are elsewhere reserved for management prerogative.

In the following discussion, first of all a recent cross-national comparison of teamworking (as an example of 'direct' participation) is summarized. Then there is some comparison of formal legislated worker participation mechanisms in various countries, such as that of Germany. Finally, the possible impact of the European Union-legislated works councils is discussed.

Murakami's cross-national comparison of teamworking

Murakami (1997:748) set out to ascertain how much autonomy is ceded to work teams by the managements of car companies that are seeking to move from Fordism to MIT's 'lean production' model. Hence his research was very relevant to one of the themes of this book: to what extent is there convergence of human resource management practices, originating in the Japanese human resource management model that includes *kaizen*, Total Quality Management and lean production? If there was substantial genuine convergence across countries, we would surely expect to see it in a single industry such as automobiles.

Murakami constructed a questionnaire to elicit information from auto work team members. The questionnaire allowed construction of indices of autonomy based on nine task areas identified by Jon Gulowsen, the Norwegian researcher, in 1979:

1   the selection of the team leader;
2   new member on the team;
3   distribution of work;
4   time flexibility;
5   acceptance of additional work;
6   representation outside of team;
7   methods of production;

8   production goals (output);
9   production goals (quality).

Murakami then made a survey of nineteen plants:

Toyota	Kyushu, Japan
Nissan	Kyushu, Japan
Nissan	Sunderland, UK
GM Opel	Russelsheim, Germany
GM	Bochum, Germany
GM	Eisenach, Germany
GM	Vienna, Austria
GM Saab	Usikapungi, Finland
Mercedes-Benz	Sindelfingen, Germany
Mercedes-Benz	Bremen, Germany
Volkswagen	Wolfsburg, Germany
BMW	Bavaria, Germany
Ford	Cologne, Germany
Ford (Engines)	Bridgend, UK
Jaguar	Birmingham, UK
Rover	Cowley, Oxford, UK
Vauxhall	Luton, UK
Rolls-Royce	Crewe, UK
Peugeot	Coventry, UK

'In summary, team autonomy in the task area of team leader selection could not be detected in the majority of plants in this study because the average level of participation only scores 2.5 on a 1–4 scale' (Murakami: 753). The average score of autonomy in the case of new members reached 1.4 which is just above pure management prerogative. There was some autonomy (2.8) on 'work distribution within the team' but this was halved on 'time flexibility' where the average is 1.4.

Overall, aggregating the nine task areas, 'teams in Toyota and Nissan rank on or slightly below 2 (participation). German teams do not rank much higher, only reaching 2.2 on average. Teams at GM-Eisenach (2.7) and GM's Finnish Saab plant (2.6) rank highest. In none of the task areas was the average team awarded full autonomy' (Murakami, 1997:755). Teams are given considerable autonomy for one of the core elements of lean production, quality. However, this would not resolve the contentious issue of whether 'empowerment' is really responsibility without power. According to a study of the training of relatively low-skilled workers at Renault to work in semi-autonomous groups, the CGT trade unionists kept out of this scheme in order not to support workforce integration 'in the Japanese way', in particular if job classifications were not revised to account for the workers' new skills (Fröhlich and Pekruhl: 144). A study of 'Japanese style' teamworking in an autocomponents plant in south Wales found that it 'resulted in an intensification of work effort on the factory floor' (Danford, 1998:428).

Murakami concluded that full autonomy was not found in any of the teams studied and in fact, the level of autonomy given to teams was far below full autonomy and even below the level of co-decision-making. 'Therefore management's power in prime task areas of production within the car industry remains unchallenged by the introduction of teamwork' (Murakami: 755). Continuing the logic, it would appear that collective bargaining – that was quite prominent in the car industry – has not been replaced by any substantial participation, despite the introduction of human resource management.

It could be argued, however, that trying to judge whether union bargaining has been replaced by other forms of participation by use of the yardstick of teamworking is too stern a test at this early stage of HRM. It could be that other forms of involvement in other industries will provide the basis for growing participation. Unfortunately, the available evidence does not suggest this. A study of British and German steel industries (Bacon et al., 1996:46) noted that 'the adoption of strategies to promote individual rights and participation (were) increasingly important'. However, a craft union representative informed the researchers that British Steel management had called in union representatives and said 'Let's get one thing straight – Total Quality Production is not about workers' participation' (Bacon: 46).

A more recent example of employee involvement has been employee empowerment, 'virtually unheard of until the early 1990s within industrial relations circles', according to Cunningham and his fellow researchers (1996:143). To learn more about this apparently new approach, they conducted a survey of thirty-eight British organizations and then concentrated on the fifteen that claimed to have introduced empowerment programmes. They concluded that 'empowerment in the UK context is adopted to suit the practical needs of organizations in the flexible labour market and in this respect is much closer to the traditional hire 'em and fire 'em philosophy than the Japanese job-for-life and also mirrors the hard-edged HRM concept of tough love, whereby the needs of the organization are paramount and employees are seen as disposable resources' (Cunningham, 1996:153).

Direct Participation in Organizational Change

(European Trade Union Information Bulletin 2/98)

The European Foundation for the Improvement of Living and Working Conditions released an analysis of the results of a survey undertaken in the autumn of 1996 into the extent of direct participation in European enterprises. The survey was undertaken as part of the EPOC project (Employee Direct Participation in Organizational Change). Direct participation is defined in terms of the EPOC projects as individual consultation and delegation and group consultation and delegation. Some of the key results of the 1996 survey were:

- Direct participation is more likely in workplaces with white-collar occupations, task complexity, team activity, high qualifications and internal training;
- Four out of five workplaces practised at least one form of direct participation but only 4 per cent had the complete array of all six forms;
- There was little evidence of the adoption of the Scandinavian model of group work;
- Productivity and quality of working life concerns far outranked other motives in all countries in the decision to introduce direct participation;
- All forms of direct participation were considered to have a strong impact on economic performance. In the case of quality, nine out of ten respondents reported a strong impact;
- Around one third of respondents reported a reduction in absenteeism and sickness;
- The introduction of direct participation was accompanied by a reduction in the number of employees or managers in around one third of all workplaces; however there was more likely to be reductions in employment in workplaces without direct participation than those with it;
- The more employees that were informed, the greater the economic effect.

Direct versus indirect participation – the role of works councils

It has to be said that use of the adjective 'direct' to describe teamworking and other forms of employee involvement has rather muddied the waters and has not aided clarity. Forms of participation through works councils that are common in some European

Union countries, notably Germany, are hardly indirect. The distinction is more that employer-promoted 'direct' participative forms are independent of collective institutions. In the Lowell Turner distinction, noted in the opening paragraph, direct participation would be *employer-led*, while works councils generally (though not always) pursue *negotiated participation*.

It is the controversial role of works councils and similar institutions that is more likely to influence whether participation is strong or weak. In turn, the strength of works councils often depends on the legislative framework of individual countries. 'In many countries they are consulted over the introduction of new technology or a revised hours pattern. In Germany, stronger co-determination councils may also be involved in investment decisions or product development. Spanish works councils can call a strike' (Fernie and Metcalfe, 1995).

However, despite British employers' hostility to collective participation, it seems that they have little to fear – at least, not from its weaker form. A moderate form of participation and accountability that presupposes taking account of the importance of industrial relations, seems to be successful (Edwards, 1987). Fernie and Metcalfe investigated the links between the existence of joint consultation (JCC) (a weak form of works council) and workplace performance. There was not a single unfavourable link between the existence of a JCC and the various economic and industrial relations outcomes. Other things being equal, a workplace with a JCC had faster productivity growth and a better climate of industrial relations.

Comparative analysis of industrial relations is obviously interested in where and why participation is strong and whether its strength relates to national legislation or continuing trade union power. studies on this are quickly dated. In one, published in 1990, the data was collected much earlier. It considered the introduction of new technologies and the level of participation in product and labour market strategies and investment on the one hand, and participation in work organization on the other. Both management and employees (45 per cent of each) believed that employees were not involved in decision-making on product market strategies or investment. However, the great majority (80 per cent for both groups) believed that they were involved in issues such as work organization or health and safety. The researchers coined the term 'participation paradox' to describe their findings. Participation is limited at the planning stage where the possibility of having an impact is greatest and increases at the implementation stage when this possibility is much less. Denmark and Germany showed a high level of participation in the planning *and* implementation stages. Italy and Spain showed a low level at each. Belgium and the UK were somewhere in between (Van Ruysseveldt et al., 1995).

Country-by-country assessment

A brief country-by-country survey may go some way to illustrate the range of participative forms.

Germany

The Works Constitution Act specifies that works councils can be elected at all establishments with at least five employees. Obviously, in practice, they are stronger in big workplaces. It is estimated that more than 70 per cent of German employees are represented by works councils that have co-determination rights about daily working hours, bonuses or similar performance-based pay. In a study (Muller, 1997:618) of the German banking and chemical industries, most interviewees – managers and works councillors alike – described the industrial relations climate in their company as one of high trust. 'Concerning the future of workplace representation in Germany, the transfer of bargaining functions from the industry level to the works councils has already strengthened and will further strengthen works councils. Nevertheless, there is an expectation that new forms of work organization could lead to new forms of direct participation which could supplement or even replace representation by the works council' (Muller, 1997:619).

Denmark

Shop stewards are seen as the backbone of the relatively strong Danish trade unions that represent 85 per cent of all wage earners. They are the prime movers in the various participation schemes: the co-operation committees; the safety committees (that consist of equal numbers of management and employee representatives) and representation on company boards. The committees are not permitted to deal with issues that are settled by collective bargaining or local wage settlements. Therefore shop stewards' activities are divided into grievance handling and collective bargaining on the one hand, and co-operation and participation rights on the other.

France

It is possible to 'disagree with the English translation of the French comité d'entreprise as works council, rather than enterprise committee' (Rogowski, 1996:150). 'The French body is not an exclusive body of employee representation but is chaired by the head of the enterprise. Its bipartite character and its lack of real veto powers prevent unequivocal representation of employee interests' (Rogowski, 1996:149). Be that as it may, Delamotte (1988:221) reported that these committees had become more union-influenced. Managements seemed to have three basic strategies to deal with them (admittedly according to a union survey by the CFDT): first, it might try to neutralize and marginalize the committee; second, it might be accepted but with preferential treatment accorded to less truculent unions, such as Force Ouvrière. However, most managements did take a participative approach. The role of these committees is mainly consultative, though they do have managerial powers over social activities. They are not set up in every workplace where their establishment is required by law, the reason being lack of candidates for committee membership.

Supermarket comités d'entreprise are not very active and exert little influence. In electronics, they have a small influence on staff training. In Air France, the committee had a sizable grant from the employer and was able to employ its own permanent staff. Its main expenditure was on welfare and solidarity activities (28 per cent); canteens (27 per cent) and leisure, sporting and cultural activities (12 per cent). Under a 1983 Act that aimed to democratize the public sector, the staff training plan had to be submitted to the comité d'entreprise for approval (Delamotte, 1988:225).

Legislation of 1982 was designed to encourage 'groupes d'expression' to comment on the content and organization of their work and extended shop steward (delegue du personnel) power. 'The idea backfired somewhat, though, with the union representatives tending to alienate themselves from the workforce and the 'groupes d'expression' serving as a useful forum for apolitical discussion. Indeed, although the 'groupes d'expression' are no longer obligatory, many companies kept them running. Therefore, measures intended to reinforce union power have to an extent ended by undermining it' (Lawrence and Barsoux, 1990:203).

Sweden

By contrast with the model of works councils as formally separate from union organization in Germany and the Netherlands, in Sweden and the other Nordic countries, union workplace 'clubs' are the main form of representation at the workplace level. The unions press for greater co-determination rights but in some ways the co-determination law may be seen as a step too far by Sweden's unions as it 'represented the replacement of the spirit of co-operation by confrontation' (Kjellberg, 1998:82). Employers were faced with an obligation to provide appropriate information for collective bargaining and trade unions were to enjoy a status quo provision in relation to the interpretation of collective agreements. They also secured wage-earner funds for capital growth sharing. However, 'the labour movement was forced to retreat on wage-earner funds, not least as a result of the employers' successful campaign on the issue' (Kjellberg, 1992:100). 'The employers, encouraged by the social democrats' loss of office after 44 years (1932–76), launched a strong ideological and political counter-offensive. SAF refused to conclude an agreement under the Co-determination Act until 1982; the agreement reinforced negotiating rights in the event of major changes within enterprises [but] beyond that it contained no substantive rules of co-determination' (Kjellberg, 1998:82). Although the union clubs have jurisdiction in the settlement of conflicts over the interpretation and application of laws and agreements under the Law on Co-determination, production issues have become more prominent.

Israel

Israel is characterized by highly centralized collective bargaining. Formal involvement of workers in management exists only in enterprises collectively owned by the Histadrut or General Federation of Labour, where there are joint management committees (four a side), with board level participation (Bar-Haim, 1988:127).

Kibbutzim – the traditional participative management organization of Israel – did spread from agriculture to manufacturing during the 1960s. This created problems for the kibbutz principle in that it was necessary to hire wage-earning workers alongside the founding kibbutz members. 'The response of kibbutzim to this challenge to their way of life was to attempt to keep the numbers of hired workers within bounds' (Barkai, 1977:223) but this policy tended to undermine the other kibbutzim principles in their manufacturing enterprises. In the agricultural kibbutzim there was great informality and little specialization of job functions. This informality had to give way in manufacturing establishments where production entailed repetitive work, more specialization and stricter co-ordination. Nevertheless, more recent human resource management emphasis on empowerment and decentralization may permit some resuscitation of latent kibbutzim principles in teamworking.

Canada

Gunderson and his research team at the University of Toronto perceived 'employee buyouts as part of the growing trend towards employee involvement in various facets of the workplace that includes workplace democracy, empowerment, employee participation schemes, team production and quality circles, joint committees, profit-sharing, representation on the board of directors, worker capital or solidarity funds and employee ownership in general' (1995:457). They examined the employee buyout of Algoma Steel, Ontario. The parties agreed that the union and employees would be full partners in the redesign of the workplace and in implementing the change programme. The contract established an Algoma Joint Steering Committee to develop jointly a workplace participation process. There was some criticism of the steelworkers' approach to the agreement as just another form of co-option but early evidence was of successful operation with profits up in 1993 and 1994.

USA

Workers' participation in the USA is very much in the minority and of the employer-initiated gain-sharing variety. However, extensive restructuring as a result of deregulation in the 1980s led unions into previously unheard of levels of co-responsibility and co-ownership in an effort to keep some companies in the airline industry in business. Unions made concessions on pay in return for profit-sharing. However, a feature of some of the company policies for participation is that they are not new. 'Lincoln Electric's incentive management programme has its roots in a system of elected employee representative to an advisory board first established in 1914' (Donkin, 1995).

The Chrysler/Daimler-Benz merger announced in 1998 seemed to offer advantages to the United Automotive Workers Union. This would follow from the view that 'the German approach to labour representation is conciliatory with union members given supervisory board representation. Union attitudes in the USA have ranged on this issue from whether it is better to achieve goals through collective bargaining or through having a stake in management. However, the UAW said it would like to participate fully in any worker board arrangement (Tait, 1998).

Japan

In Japanese industrial relations, managers of large firms often utilize the joint consultative committee system in order to avoid disputes with labour. A study by Morishima (1992:405) describes two such uses of the system, information-sharing and pre-*shunto* pay discussions.

Joint consultative committees, comprising senior managers and high level trade union officials, are one of the most common labour–management institutions in Japan. They are participation mechanisms but they also must be seen as strategic tools used by Japanese employers to obtain labour's consent and co-operation in potentially conflictual situations.

Transnational works councils

The preceding brief sketches are intended only to suggest the continuing importance of legal, institutional and systemic factors that affect participation and hence human resource management strategies. Muller (1997:619) emphasized the continuing vitality of the legislated German worker councils but pointed out that new forms of work organization could lead to new forms of participation that could supplement or replace them. However, the Chrysler–Daimler and Deutsch–Morgan Grenfell mergers show that a key issue is the compatibility of participation arrangements with multinational corporate management structures. So, by way of conclusion, we need to return to the transnational level.

In his research on the British and French gas industries, Parsons (1997) has provided one of the few company level studies of how participation works with very different models of union organization. He tried to find reasons for the continuing diversity of industrial relations systems with a strategic analysis of how management and unions have used the machinery of participation. The former public utilities that were previously nationalized and national have begun to be very much internationalized after privatization, often attracting foreign takeover bids, as in the case of the British electricity companies. BA has been pursuing an avowedly global strategy since the early 1990s.

Global strategies have provoked calls from international trade unionists for 'world works councils for each major international company' (Hutton, 1995). However, as unions search for common policies on industrial relations, the divergences are more glaring than the common bonds. A solution could be to take the best of all worlds: European industrial democracy or co-determination, plus short work hours, combined with American protection of workers and Japanese employment security and flat pay differentials, linked to teamworking. Of course, this sounds very utopian but the concentration of several industries into fewer hands makes possible the conclusion of a truly world agreement on labour relations and social organization in the workplace.

This is not quite as utopian as it sounds. Company councils are not new, though they have never been very strong. Moreover, 'there is a long history of European Union measures to improve the position of workers in EU-scale undertakings; particularly in respect of measures for the information, consultation and participation of employees in decisions' (McGlynn, 1995:78). After many years of deadlock, the European Commission finally agreed a directive on the establishment of European Works Councils implemented in 1996.

'The principle of autonomy of the parties is evident in the Directive: flexibility is the overriding basis for many of the provisions' (McGlynn: 80). The Directive will not apply if at the date of its implementation (22 September 1996) there was already an agreement providing for transnational consultation and co-operation with employees (Article 13). Such an agreement had to cover the whole workforce which was not stipulated as being confined to the workforce of EU member states. Consequently, not only was there an incentive to reach a voluntary agreement but this could – in principle – be extended to include in the works council representation of workers in non-EU countries.

In the event, according to Cressey (1998:67), 'the period before the deadline was one of frantic activity in many of the largest companies in Britain as they sought to negotiate Article 13 agreements that allow for voluntary agreement inside enterprises. These negotiations have determined the form and substance of works councils and allowed those companies exemption from the statutory provisions encased in the directive. The list includes household names like ICI, BT, NatWest, GKN, Scottish & Newcastle Breweries, Pilkington Glass, British Steel, United Biscuits and Courtaulds.' In fact, of the many voluntary agreements concluded throughout the EU, the UK has the highest proportion.

Cressey traced the path taken by NatWest when the senior managers decided to take action and become the first financial services company to implement a works council as a result of the Directive. He also explored the strategy that inaugurated a worldwide, rather than a European works council. In conclusion, he reckoned that 'management values the ability works councils give them to communicate corporate strategy, to allow discussion of change, to foster international contact and to encourage an identity among staff of belonging to an international company' (Cressey, 1998:78). Trade unions appear glad of any activity that can give them some formal authority. For example, it was reported that unions in the UK might take legal action 'against the works councils that have been organized at BP, Marks & Spencer and the Japanese companies Honda and Sony, on the grounds that they were established without complying with the EU directive' (Taylor, 1996).

The unions may have hoped that European works councils would be a means of recovering their bargaining status. 'Following the report of the Davignon committee, activity is being directed towards an instrument for rights to consulation at domestic level in companies with over 50 employees' (Cressey: 78). However, despite the belief that the new Labour government in the UK might favour such development, it was reported in March 1998 that 'Downing Street has been trying to head off a European directive to give employees enhanced rights to consultation and information' (Clement, 1998). The lobbying helped to determine UNICE, the European employers' confederation, to decline to meet their union counterparts to agree a voluntary code. Consequently, the European Commission would have to draft a detailed directive for works councils for companies of 50 employees – clearly a huge task. President Jacques Santer and Padraig Flynn, the employment commissioner, expressed their disappointment with the UNICE decision, saying that it undermined the whole concept of partnership that was at the heart of European decision-making and that they would call a mini-summit on the future of 'social dialogue' (Clement, 1998).

It is true that there are concerns about competitiveness arising from the European works council (EWC). The Engineering Employers' Federation, one of the UK's biggest employer organizations, reckoned that they would cost UK multinational companies at least £1 million each annually. UNICE, the European employers' organization regarded disruption to business decision-making caused by the EWCs would be more important. 'It can be argued that the EWC will not add additional power to the side of the workers but will merely make up for the power lost by national representatives due to increased internationalization. In the long run, employee involvement on a European scale through EWCs might even be seen as a factor increasing long-term competitiveness, just as *Betriebsrate* in Germany have played a positive role in German economic development' (Dorrenbacher and Wortmann, 1994:206).

In the chapter on multinational companies, it was noted that the American autoworkers' union believed that the Daimler-Benz/Chrysler takeover would benefit the union because German works council arrangements would be incorporated under German law. The United Autoworkers Union takes one of three trade union places among ten worker representatives on the Daimler–Chrysler supervisory board. This sort of outcome to mergers involving German companies and the EWC suggest that the German co-determination (*Mitbestimmung*) will survive. However, continuing integration of the European economy and monetary union will highlight the relative efficacy of models of corporate government in the various EU countries and it must be rather doubtful whether the full panoply of the German model, including works councils at workplace level, will be transplanted elsewhere.

Questions for discussion

1   Discuss the different meanings of participation in management in relation to Total Quality Management, empowerment and collective bargaining.

2   Discuss the role of employment law in relation to participation in management and the idea of convergence.

3   Why do foreign corporations have problems coping with the idea of works councils?

13

Conclusion: Prospects for Comparative Industrial Relations

What has been attempted in this book has been a guide to the literature and theory of comparative industrial relations. It would be impossible to attempt to survey all the relevant publications of the last
decade. However, one important aim has been to include a good
proportion of the introductory articles that provide a basis for further study and link with international human resource management.

Limitations

In one or two of the individual chapters, a limited recourse to country-
by-country studies has been unavoidable. Chapter 2 concentrated
on employment relations inside Japan in order to show how the 'sacred treasures', including lifetime employment, had faced pressure
from corporate restructuring. Ironically, the more flexible features
of Japanese human resource management had already been
influential in reshaping the management of employment in the USA
and Western Europe, as discussed in chapter 3. In chapter 5, it was
considered necessary to utilize a survey of several countries, including Britain, to explore whether global economic competition had
enforced convergence and a weakening of distinct national collective bargaining systems. For the most part, however, the discussion
has been confined within a thematic framework with a view to providing food for thought of an analytical kind, especially for the student new to the subject of comparative industrial relations. For this
reason, the author does not apologize for extensive use of the con-

cept of convergence/divergence and for reference to perspectives on human resource management strategy, such as the systemic perspective embedded in a particular national system. Neither is national culture a concept to be derided, so long as it is regarded as merely a starting point for further exploration of the main constituents of national culture.

Another obvious drawback of this sort of study is its susceptibility to becoming rapidly out of date. No matter how the writing attempts to convey the impression of a moving train of continuous industrial relations change, of unfinished business and of government or management policy responding to a dynamic yet largely uncoordinated global system, the salient themes of the text may seem old-fashioned on publication.

Industrial relations writers often rely on the idea that we learn from history. In the economic and social sciences we do so because we can refer to theories and comparative analyses that have gone before and point out that it's not like that now.

If not a post-mortem then – because we hope that the subject of comparative industrial relations is alive and kicking – it is necessary for a concluding chapter to try to delineate the main themes and developments that seem to be important at the beginning of the next thousand years.

The prevailing winds of change

In any attempt to forecast, or at any rate, estimate the longevity of current trends, the economic bases and the factors of production are fundamental. If one economic motif was dominant during the late 1990s it was 'sayonara' to Japan as a model economy. It was also becoming somewhat difficult to insulate the prescriptions of the ideal model of Japanese-style human resource management from the realities of bankrupt Japanese businesses.

There was a 'back-to-the-drawing-board' feel about publications and journals that, earlier in the 1990s, had been praising the Asian tiger economies, such as Malaysia and Korea, for their economic policy and organization. As they used to chant at British soccer games: 'they've all gone quiet over there'.

Nevertheless, the Japanese HRM model of lean production and continuous improvement through harnessing teamworking and peer group surveillance has been gradually – if far from smoothly – incorporated into American capitalism and production management.

The moral panics and fears of the 1980s that American companies could not keep pace with Japanese now seem almost ludicrous.

It was once believed that learning from Japan involved study of the 'sacred treasures', such as seniority wages, long-term skill upgrading (or 'white collarization') and enterprise unions. It has turned out that lean production methods learned from the Japanese involve less reliance on skills and more emphasis on numerical flexibility through sub-contracting.

This disparity between productivity and real wages has macro-economic causes and consequences. The giant corporation managements can continuously cut costs by contracting out as much production as possible to smaller firms who pay less. Simplification of production through use of cheapening technology means that contract suppliers can perform most jobs as cheaply as the parent company. 'When the parent company awards contracts to various satellite manufacturers, it does so as part of a strategy to keep costs down. Moreover, US companies who do this save more than do companies in Japan where a good many workers in the satellite companies receive the traditional benefits of Japanese industry' (Head, 1996).

The rhythms of the trade cycle can upset trends. Since 1950 Japan had taken pride in unemployment rates lower than almost any industrial country. Then in 1999 the Japanese rate hit a post Second World War record of 4.8 per cent. These higher rates damaged the implicit employment contract that was markedly different from many other countries. Unlike the US, the corporate sector had adapted to economic restructuring, not by laying off workers but by moving them around subsidiaries of the same parent company.

Similarly, when companies needed to cut costs, they did not cut jobs but instead reduced workers' salaries. By 1999, the system looked too rigid to cope with the scale of change required. There was change but some critics claimed that the shift towards flexibility was still too slow to significantly affect corporate productivity levels. Corporate restructuring and the reduction in lifetime employment had created a market for 'outplacement services'. In practice, many companies were still protecting their core job-for-life staff – at the expense of the more vulnerable, a point made in chapter 2.

As lean production has economized on numbers employed and held down wages in manufacturing, a whole vista of service industry employment has opened up. In the UK in 1981 there were nearly six million people employed in manufacturing and two and a half million in financial and business services. By 1998 the two sectors were equal at four million each. Many of the service industries have their own approximations to lean production. This is generally by use of information technology to re-engineer and streamline many of the routine activities.

In the UK and other countries, despite continuous and severe fiscal squeeze on their employers' pay and conditions of work, public services continue to be the largest sector of employment. Here, the two-tier employment structure created by sub-contracting in manufacturing and private sector services is replicated, not only by sub-contracting but also by persistent management attempts to create a meritocracy of higher paid employees.

Creation of such elites is a pragmatic, even desperate, device to hang onto highly skilled professionals despite the public sector pay squeeze that is widening the gap between average public sector pay and average private sector pay for comparable work. The idea seems to be that, using performance-related pay, perhaps a conjuring trick can be brought off and a type of money illusion of expectancy prevail. Against all rational expectations, the hope seems to be that capable lower-paid workers will stay in the public services in the hope of one day also achieving merit pay or promotion.

Dual or segmented economies

A policy of performance-related pay may be fine in principle – and may even be made to work – at the micro level of the company or organization. However, the implied two-tier dual labour market has macro-economic implications.

In the USA, the real average weekly earnings of production and non-supervisory workers fell by 18 per cent between 1973 and 1995, from $315 per week to $258 per week. The real pay of corporate chief executives increased by 20 per cent. The move to flexibility in Europe will attempt to emulate American levels of pay inequalities but without American levels of employment.

The mopping up of labour by US service industries that has contributed to job creation can be viewed more critically:

> If the US economy were entering an era of sustained productivity gains, there would have to have emerged a new and more efficient relationship between labour input and national output. Fewer people would be needed to do more – or they would be able to perform their tasks in less time. Yet the hiring of an additional 12 million workers since 1993 is just what we would predict on the basis of the persistently slow

productivity growth and the 15 per cent growth in national output over that period. The unemployment rate would not have plunged to a 28-year low had there been a new relationship between jobs and the production of goods and services. Like it or not, in many respects the 'new economy' is conforming quite closely to many of the old economy's fundamental relationships. In a true and lasting productivity revival that would not be the case (Roach, 1998:159).

In Europe, accentuating the two-tier labour market, flexibility adds to growing inequality without improving the responsiveness of pay to unemployment and therefore not attaining US-style job creation. In Spain by 1990, temporary jobs accounted for 30 per cent of all employment. However, the new casualized peripheral labour force makes it easier for a firm to lay off these workers in a downturn, rather than imperilling the jobs of core workers.

In addition, hours worked in the USA are longer than in any other industrialized country and Europeans are catching up in productivity (Coyle, 1999). Meanwhile – rather against convergence – France was being hailed as Europe's tiger economy. Employment minister Martine Aubry claimed that the rapid fall in unemployment should be partly attributed to regulatory policies, including a reduction of standard working hours from thirty-nine hours a week to thirty-five (Lichfield, 1999).

In the secondary labour markets of Europe, wages are actually flexible as a result of low security and increasing competition for jobs. For people in this second tier, job prospects are poor, there is a high jobs turnover and, despite all the rhetoric about social inclusion, there are few training opportunities. 'This is not the stuff of open-ended prosperity' (Roach, 1998:159). As the flexible sector grew in the 1990s, Britain's economic apartheid became reinforced, with those in peripheral employment suffering from job uncertainty and falling relative earnings.

Poverty at the periphery

A growing number of marginalized, jobless households have only tenuous contact with the world of work. In 1998 it was reported that the UK had one of the worst poverty levels of all industrialized nations. The report - from the UN – stated that 13.5 per cent of the UK population are below the poverty line and 22 per cent 'functionally illiterate', meaning that they are unable to perform simple tasks, such as reading a story to a child or the label on a medicine bottle. Of the industrialized nations, only the USA has a greater proportion of the population below the poverty line and only Ireland has worse literacy rates. At the other end of the scale, of course, Ireland has been growing rapidly. This growth is built on commitment to education and a skilled workforce, implying a clear-cut two-tier economy of human resource development alongside social exclusion.

The impermanence of 'permanent' jobs

It could once be argued that the degree of labour market insecurities was exaggerated and that core workers actually benefited from the insecurity of the casual workers. However, the proximity of manufacture and an integrating labour market act to make more previously permanent workers join the ranks of the insecure. In car assembly in Mexico, high levels of productivity can be achieved at very low wages through a combination of seemingly contradictory forms of work organization. This must exert severe downward pressure on the pay and working conditions of car workers in the USA. There must be a similar effect from Skoda, now owned by VW, on German car workers. Again, there must be consequent effects on purchasing power and effective demand.

Against convergence and universalist tendencies

In the preceding chapters all these pressures were treated as the main storyline in the latest version of the convergence hypothesis. Remember that this is not new. Its previous manifestation was in 'Industrialism and Industrial Man' (Kerr et al., 1960). The contemporary version has also relied heavily on the impact of technology, though this time on information technology and the business process re-engineering that it facilitates. Yet this hypothesis is far from being completely accepted. The main opposing argument originates in what we have called (following Legge, 1995 and before her, Whittington, 1993) the systemic perspective on human resource strategy. Human resource management may be strategic in intention but that does not change the fact that it is embedded in particular economic and political contexts, dominated though these may be by global competition. The market is not, according to this view, the dominant co-ordination form. 'Price mechanisms are only said to be the most efficient coordination form regarding financial services on the continental and world level' (Sjogren, 1998:161) – and after the débâcle of long term capital management and so-called hedging funds in 1998, even that must be debatable. 'Regarding all other types of private products and services, networks and associations are seen as more efficient' (Sjogren, 1998:161). Trust has been rediscovered as an important element in the co-ordination of markets. Moreover, there are several elements of national business systems that constrain the diffusion of employment practices.

Not much convergence even in Europe?

There is little evidence as yet of anything approaching a European labour market, except perhaps at the highest level or the most casual type of employment (where law breaking is connived at by employers). 'In comparison with Japan, the Pacific rim or the United States, there is little evidence of significant convergence of labour markets or institutions. Work and employment are, and are likely to remain, substantially national issues' (Brewster, 1997). The convergence hypothesis has also been rejected on the grounds that it often fails 'to distinguish adequately between centripetal tendencies at the level of policy and any underlying confidence of national structures through which policies are implemented' (Scott, 1997:572).

Reconstructing the theory of comparative industrial relations

All the arguments opposing convergence have perhaps been encapsulated by Boxall (1996:5): 'Undergraduate textbooks on Human Resource Management in the Anglo-American world often propagate the view that what is presented as "best practice" has universal implications. Such an assumption, implicit or otherwise, is untenable. We must confront the reality of diversity in Human Resource practices around the globe and the unpalatable possibilities, if not truth, that models of labour management outside the Anglo-American world may well be more economically efficient.'

Boxall then attempted to lay the foundations for a comparative theory of the management of labour in its broadest sense. First, he genuflected towards the definition that 'comparative industrial relations is a systematic method of investigation relating two or more countries which has analytical rather than descriptive implications' (Bean, 1994:4). Secondly, he focused on two critical variables: workforce capability and labour productivity. The former is obviously vital 'for comparative analysis because national institutions continue to exercise a decisive influence over education and skill formation' (Boxall, 1996:7) as discussed in chapter 6. Thirdly, he tried to steer comparative Human Resource Management away from 'international Human Resource Management where the focus on management and the firm is so strong that other actors tend to become invisible. Comparative Human Resource Management should try to avoid this trap and thus qualify some of the more unrealistic and inappropriate claims of writers in the school of international Human Resource Management. Educationally, this must be one of the primary functions of any course in comparative Human Resource Management' (Boxall, 1996:11).

Divergence rules, OK?

Boxall reminds us significantly about the dangers of determinism. The superstructure of international human resource management discourse and rhetoric is all pervasive but predictable behaviour of the economic base of employment and the transaction with labour to secure productivity cannot be assumed. I hope that – alongside the underlying premise of convergence – this book has also conveyed the continuing uncertainty and diversity and continuing conflict in the distribution of economic rewards.

A crucial role is played in the institutionalization of such conflict by trade unions. There has been plenty of evidence in the preceding chapters that trade union collective bargaining power has declined drastically in the 1990s. Unions are faced with transnational companies becoming more global enterprise networks. 'There are daily reports on the need for cost control and employment reduction or new work practices as part of global competitive strategies of firms' (Perlmutter, 1992:27). The development of multinational enterprise networks has dramatic effects for labour and also collective bargaining. This organizational form entails the erosion of organizational boundaries and a more intricate situation for regulating labour. Traditionally based on clearly defined enterprises and business units, it is now faced with erosion of these boundaries. Attempts by governments or trade unions to regulate labour conditions are problematic. Moving employment across international boundaries is an important development and throws into question the role of the nation state as overseer of industrial relations. It is nonetheless a continuation of earlier human resource management strategies that shifted work regionally.

The impotence of national governments

Comparative industrial relations differences are revealed in the systemic perspective on human resource strategy. Management policies and practices are embedded in national laws, culture and institutions. These issues were explored in chapters 8 and 9 on employment law. Yet, national governments have been pusillanimous in upholding national laws and regulations that protect working conditions. Governments and finance ministers, far from trying to control globalization, have accepted it as a fact of life. UK Chancellor Gordon Brown, at the Ottawa summit of Commonwealth Finance Ministers in October 1998, stressed that, in his view, the answer to the global crisis was 'not less globalization but more' (Paterson, 1998). He went on to argue that the existing international financial architecture was not sufficient to regulate world markets effectively.

Little has been done to develop global institutions to police and control multinational companies. On the contrary, nation states, weakened by global forces, tend to become obsessed with law and order. Excelling in the job of 'precinct policeman', according to Bauman (1998) is the best (perhaps the only) thing that national government can do to cajole footloose multinational capital into investing in citizens' welfare. They are no longer citizens with rights but consumers with choices – often therefore no choices.

Minimum standards in international trade

One possibility is for combined intergovernmental action to control social dumping and erosion of living standards and working conditions by enforcing minimum standards in international trade. It may be a theoretical possibility that a more federal European Union will gradually discover the means to temper multinational corporate development. The recent developments do not support this outlook, as exemplified by the failure of trade unions to utilize the Social Chapter as a vehicle for multinational collective bargaining (Silvia, 1991:626) and connivance of national governments in attempts to evade the forty-eight-hour limit on working hours discussed in chapter 11. There may also be a possibility of countervailing power through workers' participation as in the EU works Councils. However, this prospect seems muffled by the overpowering rigmarole about 'direct participation' that was discussed in chapter 12.

Deconstructing comparative industrial relations?

There will be opposition to globalization, as in the USA, where the 1998 strike at General Motors in Michigan was explicitly *against* it. There will be opposition, as in developing countries such as St Lucia, where two unarmed banana farmers were shot dead by police in 1993 during a strike when farmers blocked the road in protest at the low prices paid for their bananas. The roadblock inconvenienced tourists who had to be airlifted to their hotels. The local politicians reprimanded the demonstrators and accused them of sabotaging the tourist industry, fearing that the visitors might go elsewhere (Pattullo, 1998).

However, opposition is increasingly emasculated by international structures. As mentioned in chapter 9, in the European Union in 1998 a transport strike in France that blocked the highways was stigmatized by the British press and politicians as a strike against the goal of full European union. So we have to take seriously Bauman's contention that globalization makes it 'increasingly difficult, perhaps impossible, to reforge social issues into effective collective action' (Kane, 1998).

Bauman's emphasis on *collective* action is important. It seems that individual rights, broadly interpreted to mean the 'rights of consumers', may be used by multinational companies *against* collectivities of employees or communities:

> A most revealing document published by a leading firm of solicitors is entitled 'Incorporation of the European convention on Human Rights: Implications for Business'. It seems rather curious that a treaty designed to protect human rights could have any implications for business, other than as a source of restraint. Yet, as the document points out, companies, as well as their members and directors, are afforded significant rights and freedoms under the convention. Indeed, cases have been taken by companies, their members and directors, to the Commission and the European Court of Justice alleging breaches of the right to a fair hearing, the right to freedom of expression and the right to peaceful enjoyment of property. The cases on these questions

have dealt with a wide range of issues, including arbitration, restraints on advertising, the expropriation of land and shares, planning decisions, the withdrawal of trading licences, illegal share dealing, takeover bids and competition law, taxation and patent applications.

This seems a perversion of principle. We might or might not agree that companies should be treated fairly. But it is surely extraordinary to say that multinational companies have human rights and that as such they are entitled to enlist the support of the courts to protect their affairs from regulation by the State in the interests of the community as a whole. Yet the European Convention on Human Rights is not the only jurisdiction to have empowered creatures of the State in this way. The same is true of the Canadian Charter of Rights and Freedoms where a drug store invoked the principles of religious freedom successfully to challenge Sunday trading laws. Even more remarkable is the more recent decision of the Supreme Court of Canada in which it was held that legislation restraining tobacco advertising violated the cigarette manufacturer's right of free speech. Freedom of expression is not confined to political speech but applies also to commercial speech and this is as much true of the European Convention on Human Rights as it is of the Canadian Charter (Ewing, 1998:2).

Such is the power of advertising and the religion of individual consumer choice, then, that a world has been created whose values are essentially those of the atomistic, maximizing consumer in the marketplace. But the consumer is not sovereign because important protective legislation can be subverted by corporate appeal to those very rights. The so-called theory of post-modernism, with its rejection of productionist values and reason, has not helped. An even more threatening Trojan horse of policy that will allow multinational companies to override the rights of elected governments to protect people against exploitative labour conditions and the destruction of the environment is the Multilateral Agreement on Investment. This seems likely to overwhelm the feeble attempts to establish minimum standards in international trade. Moreover, public health will be imperilled 'as national and local authorities risk being sued if they try to promote safety at work, a clean transport policy or food standards' (Pilger, 1998).

Robert Reich, who was Secretary of Labour in the Clinton administration, forecast that 'there will be no national products or technologies, no national corporations, no national industries. All that will remain rooted within national borders are the people that comprise a nation' (Hatfield, 1998:12). If that is the case, there will be virtually no comparative industrial relations. The main feature of national differences in laws and institutions will be eradicated and all that will remain is sporadic opposition to the totalitarian managerial discourse and culture, opposition that will be pilloried as interference with consumer rights. To recoin a phrase, comparative industrial relations will be largely informal, largely fragmented and only slightly autonomous.

Question for discussion

'Globalization is creating a global class system with a divide between a rich and cosmopolitan class and a widening class of socially excluded.'

Discuss.

References

References to Chapter 1

C. Berggren (1993), 'Lean Production – The End of History?' *Work, Employment and Society*, 7(2).

L. Black (1993), 'Downsizing towards a Disparate Workforce,' *Independent*, 25 March.

P. Cappelli (1995), 'Rethinking Employment,' *British Journal of Industrial Relations*, 33(4).

J. Clark (1995), 'Is There a Future for Industrial Relations?' *Work, Employment and Society*, 9(3).

C. Crouch (1994), *Industrial Relations and European State Traditions*, Clarendon Press, Oxford.

J. T. Dunlop (1958), *Industrial Relations Systems*, Holt, New York.

C. L. Erickson and S. Kuruvilla (1998), 'Industrial System Transformation', *Industrial and Labour Relations Review*, 52(1).

J. Eyal (1996), 'Conspiracy of Silence', *Guardian*, 12 January.

R. Florida and M. Kenney, (1991), 'Organization v. Culture: Japanese Automotive transplants in the USA', *Industrial Relations Journal*, 22(3).

J. Goddard (1997), 'Managerial Strategies, Labour and Employment Relations and the State: the Canadian Case and Beyond', *British Journal of Industrial Relations*, 35(3).

H. Henderson (1993), *Paradigms in Progress*, Adamantine Press, London.

C. Kerr, J. T. Dunlop, F. H. Harbison and C. A. Myers (1962), *Industrialism and Industrial Man*, Heinemann, London.

S. Kuruvilla (1996), 'National Industrialization Strategies and their Influences on Patterns of Human Resource Practices', *Human Resource Management Journal*, 6(3).

K. Legge (1995), *Human Resource Management: Rhetorics and Realities*, Macmillan Business, Basingstoke.

P. Marginson (1994), in R. Hyman and A. Ferner (eds), *New Frontiers in European Industrial Relations*, Blackwell, Oxford.

M. Morishima (1982), *Why has Japan Succeeded? Western Technology and the Japanese ethos*, Cambridge University Press, Cambridge.

M. Morishima (1995), 'Embedding Human Resource Management in a Social Context', *British Journal of Industrial Relations*, 33(4), December.

G. Muller (1997), 'Institutional Resilience in a Changing World Economy? The Case of the German Banking and Chemical Industries', *British Journal of Industrial Relations*, 35(4).

P. Ormerod (1994), *The Death of Economics*, Faber, London.

C. Piganiol (1989), 'Industrial Relations and Enterprise Restructuring in France', *International Labour Review*, 128(5).

A. Pollert (1988), 'The Flexible Firm: Fixation or Fact?', *Work, Employment and Society*, 2(3).

P. Pringle (1995), 'The Cold War is Over, the Bosses Won', *Independent*, 3 January.

M. Prowse (1995), 'Australians Top World Bank's Wealth League', *Financial Times*, 18 September.

R. Rogowski (1997), 'The Regulation of Employment Relations', *Work, Employment and Society*, 11(1).

C. Sabel (1982), *Work and Politics: The Division of Labour in Industry*, Cambridge University Press, Cambridge.

A. Sorge and W. Streeck (1988), 'Industrial Relations and Technical Change: The Case for an Extended Perspective', in R. Hyman and W. Streeck (eds), *New Technology and Industrial Relations*, Blackwell, Oxford.

A. Sorge and M. Warner (1980), 'Industrial Relations, Organization Structure and Social Context, in A. W. Thomson and M. Warner (eds), *The Behavioural Sciences and Industrial Relations*, Gower, Farnborough.

K. Taira (1996), 'Compatibility of Human Resource Management, Industrial Relations and Engineering Under Mass Production and Lean Production: An Exploration', *Applied Psychology: An International Review*, 45(2).

H. Thomas (1995), *Globalization and Third World Trade Unions: The Challenge of Rapid Economic Change*, Zed Books, London.

K. Thelen (1991), *Union of Parts: Labour Politics in Post War Germany*, Cornell University Press, Ithaca, New York.

K. Urabe (1988), 'Innovation and the Japanese Management System' in K. Urabe, J. Child and T. Kagono (eds), *Innovation and Management*, Walter de Gruyter, Berlin.

G. Van Liemt (1992), 'Economic Globalisation', *International Labour Review*, 131(2).

R. Whittington (1993), *What is Strategy and Does it Matter?*, Routledge, London.

P. Wickens (1993), 'Lean Production and Beyond: The System and its Future', *Human Resource Management Journal*, 3(4).

K. Williams et al. (1987), 'The End of Mass Production?' *Economy and Society*, 16(3).

K. Williams, J. Williams and C. Haslam (1989), 'Do Labour Costs Really Matter?' *Work, Employment and Society*, 3(3).
K. Williams et al. (1992), 'Against Lean Production', *Economy and Society*, 21(3).
J. P. Womack, D. T. Jones and D. Roos (1990), *The Machine that Changed the World*, Rawson Associates, New York.
A. Wood (1995), *North-South Trade, Employment and Inequalities: Changing Fortunes in a Skill-driven World*, Clarendon Press, Oxford.
World Bank (1995), *World Development Report 1995: Workers in an Integrating World*, Oxford University Press, Oxford.

References to Chapter 2

J. Abegglen (1958), *The Japanese Factory: Aspects of its Social Organization*, Free Press, Glencoe, Ill.
J. Atkinson (1984), 'Manpower Strategies for Flexible Organizations', *Personnel Management*, August.
D. L. Asher (1996), 'What Became of the Japanese "Miracle"?' *Orbis*, Spring.
C. Berggren (1993), 'Lean Production – The End of History?' *Work, Employment and Society*, 7(2).
S. H. Best (1984), 'Now for Something Completely Different', British Steel Corporation.
M. Bronfenbrenner (1988), 'An Essay on Negative Screening' in T. Shishido and R. Sabo (eds), *Economic Policy and Development: New Perspectives*, Croom Helm, London.
N. Chalmers (1989), *Industrial Relations in Japan: The Peripheral Workforce*, Routledge, London.
M. Cusumano (1985), *The Japanese Automobile Industry: technology and management at Nissan and Toyota*, Harvard University Press, Cambridge, Mass.
D. Dirks (1998), 'Restructuring and Human Resource Management in Japan', *Management International Review*, 38(2).
R. Dore (1973), *British Factory – Japanese Factory: the Origins of National Diversity in Industrial Relations*, Allen & Unwin, London.
Economist (1995), 'Mitsubishi's Company Man', 9 December.
S. Jacoby (1995), 'Recent Organizational Developments in Japan', *British Journal of Industrial Relations*, 33(4).
S. Kamata (1984), *Japan in the Passing Lane*, Unwin Paperbacks, London.
C. Kerr, J. T. Dunlop, F. H. Harbison and C. A. Myers (1962), *Industrialism and Industrial Man*, Heinemann, London.
K. Koike (1988), *Understanding Industrial Relations in Modern Japan*, St. Martins Press, New York.
M. Morishima (1982), *Why has Japan Succeeded? Western Technology and the Japanese Ethos*, Cambridge University Press, London.
M. Morishima (1991), 'Information Sharing and Collective Bargaining in Japan: Effects on Wage Negotiation', *Industrial and Labor Relations Review*, 44(33), 469.

M. Morishima (1995), 'Embedding Human Resource Management in a Social Context,' *British Journal of Industrial Relations*, 33(4).

H. Odagiri (1991), *Growth through Competition, Competition through Growth: Strategic Management and the Economy in Japan*, Clarendon Press, Oxford.

M. Paci (1981), 'Class Structure in Italian Society', in D. Pinto (ed.), *Contemporary Italian Sociology*, Cambridge University Press, Cambridge.

G. Palmer (1983), *British Industrial Relations*, Allen & Unwin, London.

K. Rafferty (1995), 'Mr International Signals the Demise of Jobs for Life', *Guardian*, 22 April.

W. Craig Riddell (1986), *Labour–Management Co-operation in Canada*, University of Toronto Press, Toronto.

D. Rollinson (1993), *Understanding Employee Relations*, Addison-Wesley, Wokingham, England.

S. Prakash Sethi, N. Naniki and C. L. Swanson, (1984), *The False Promise of the Japanese Miracle: Illusions and Realities in the Japanese Management System*, Pitman, Marshfield, Mass.

K. Taira (1996), 'Compatibility of Human Resource Management, Industrial Relations and Engineering under Mass Production and Lean Production: An Exploration', *Applied Psychology: An International Review*, 45(2).

K. Urabe (1988), 'Innovation and the Japanese Management System' in K. Urabe, J. Child and T. Kagono, (eds), *Innovation and Management*, Walter de Gruyter, Berlin.

D. Whittaker (1990), 'The End of Japanese-Style Employment?' *Work, Employment and Society*, 4(3).

W. F. Whyte (1987), 'Human Relations and Human Resource Management', *Industrial and Labour Relations Review*.

J. P. Womack, D. T. Jones and D. Roos (1990), *The Machine that Changed the World*, Rawson Associates, New York.

References to Chapter 3

P. Adler (1993), 'The Learning Bureaucracy: New United Motors Manufacturing, Inc.', *Research in Organization Behaviour*, 111–94.

C. Berggren (1993), 'Lean Production – The End of History?' *Work, Employment and Society*, 7(2).

S. Caulkin (1993), 'British Firms Resurrected Courtesy of Japan', *Guardian*, 8 May.

J. Clark (1995), 'Is there a future for Industrial Relations?' *Work, Employment and Society*, 9(3).

R. Delbridge, P. Turnbull and B. Wilkinson (1992), 'Pushing back the Frontiers: Management Control and Work Intensification under JIT/TQM Factory Regimes', *New Technology, Work and Employment*, 7(2).

R. Dore (1973), *British Factory – Japanese Factory: the Origins of National Diversity in Industrial Relations*, Allen & Unwin, London.

C. Evans (1993), 'Human Resource Management in Japanese Financial Institutions Abroad: The Case of the London Office', *British Journal of In-*

dustrial Relations, 31(3).

J. Fisher (1994), 'New Management Techniques', *Federation News*, 44(3).

R. Florida and M. Kenney (1991), 'Organization v. Culture: Japanese Automotive Transplants in the USA', *Industrial Relations Journal*, 22(3).

P. Garrahan and P. Stewart (1992), *The Nissan Enigma: Flexibility at Work in a Local Economy*, Mansell, London.

L. Graham (1995), *On the Line at Subaru-Isuzu: the Japanese Model and the American Worker*, ILR Press, London.

S. Head (1996), 'The New, Ruthless Economy', *New York Review of Books*, 29 February.

H. C. Jain (1990), 'Human Resource Management in Selected Japanese Firms, their Foreign Subsidiaries and Locally Owned Counterparts', *International Labour Review*, 129(3).

K. Koike (1988), *Understanding Industrial Relations in Modern Japan*, St. Martin's Press, New York.

J. Lie (1990), 'Is Korean Management Just Like Japanese Management?' *Management International Review*, 30(2).

G. Palmer (1996), 'Reviving Resistance: the Japanese Factory Floor in Britain', *Industrial Relations Journal*, 27(2).

M. Parker and J. Slaughter (1988), *Choosing Sides: Unions and the Team Concept*, South End Press, Boston, Mass.

J. Rinehart, C. Huxley and D. Robertson (1997), *Just Another Car Factory: Lean Production and its Discontents*, ILR Press, London.

G. M. Saltzman (1995), 'Job Applicant Screening by a Japanese Transplant: A Union Avoidance Tactic', *Industrial and Labour Relations Review*, 49(1).

G. Sewell and B. Wilkinson (1992), 'Someone to watch over me: Surveillance, Discipline and the Just-in-Time Labour Process', *Sociology*, 26(2).

C. Smith and T. Elger (1994), 'Researching the Toyota Effect', *Human Resource Management Journal*, 4(4).

C. Smith (1996), book review of Graham, 'On the Line', *Work, Employment and Society*, 10(2).

G. Strauss (1996), book review of Graham, 'On the Line', *British Journal of Industrial Relations*, 34(1).

K. Taira (1996), 'Compatibility of Human Resource Management, Industrial Relations and Engineering under Mass Production and Lean Production: An Exploration', *Applied Psychology: An International Review*, 45(2).

S. Watanabe (1991), 'The Japanese Quality Control Circle: Why it Works', *International Labour Review*, 130(1).

R. Wickens (1993), 'Lean Production and Beyond: The System and its Future', *Human Resource Management Journal*, 3(4).

S. Wood (1991), 'Japanization or Toyotaism?' *Work, Employment and Society*, 5(4).

References to Chapter 4

J. T. Addison and J. Wagner (1994), 'UK Unionism and innovative activity: Some cautionary remarks on the basis of a simple cross-country test', *British Journal of Industrial Relations*, 32(1).

C. Barrie (1997), 'Lift union ban says Hyundai', *Guardian*, 4 February.

J. Benson (1994), 'The Economic Effects of Unionism on Japanese Manufacturing Enterprises,' *British Journal of Industrial Relations*, 32(1).

D. G. Blanchflower and R. B. Freeman (1992), 'Unionism in the United States and other advanced OECD countries', *Industrial Relations*, 31(1).

R. Boyer (1995), 'The Future of unions: Is the Anglo-Saxon model a fatality or will contrasting national trajectories persist?' *British Journal of Industrial Relations*, 33(4).

J. Bridgford (1994), *The Politics of French Trade Unionism*, St. Martins Press, New York.

G. Brunello (1992), 'The Effect of Unions on firm performance in Japanese manufacturing', *Industrial and Labor Relations Review*, 46.

G. Chaison (1996), *Union Mergers in hard times: The view from five countries*, Cornell University Press, Ithaca, New York.

S. Deery (1995), 'The Demise of the Trade Union as a representative body', *British Journal of Industrial Relations*, 33(4).

J. Eaton (1996), *Globalization and Human Resource Management in the Airline Industry*, Avebury Press, Aldershot.

F. Fitzroy and K. Kraft (1985), 'Unionization, wages and efficiency', *Kyklos*, 38(4).

A. Flanders (1970), *Management and Unions*, Faber, London.

R. B. Freeman and J. L. Medoff (1984), *What do Unions do?* Basic Books, New York.

M. Goldfield (1987), *The Decline of Organised Labour in the United States*, University of Chicago Press.

Y. Haberfeld (1995), 'Why do workers join unions ? The case of Israel', *Industrial and Labor Relations Review*, 48(4).

A. Herod (1995), 'The Practice of Labour Solidarity and the geography of the global economy', *Economic Geography*, 71(4).

R. Hyman (1996), 'Institutional Transfer: Industrial Relations in Eastern Germany', *Work, Employment and Society*, 10(3).

S. M. Jacoby (1995), 'Recent Organizational Developments in Japan', *British Journal of Industrial Relations*, 33(4).

S. Jeffreys (1996), 'Down but not out: French trade unions under Chirac,' *Work, Employment and Society*, 10(3).

T. Kumar (1993), *From Uniformity to Divergence: Industrial Relations in Canada and the United States*, IRC Press, Kingston, Ontario.

S. Milne (1997), 'Union joins company chiefs in call for foreign investment', *Guardian*, 28 January.

M. W. Mitchell and J. Stone (1992), 'Union effects on productivity: evidence from western US sawmills', *Industrial and Labor Relations Review*, 46.

K. Moody (1997), 'Towards an International Social Movement Unionism', *New Left Review*, 225.

E. A. Ramaswamy (1995), 'The Power of Organized Labour' in *India Briefing*, The Asia Society, New York.

G. Standing (1992), 'Do Unions Impede structural adjustment?' *Cambridge Journal of Economics*, 16(3).

K. Thelen (1993), *Union of Parts: Labor Politics in Post-war Germany*, Cornell University Press, Ithaca, New York.

H. Thomas (ed.) (1995), *Globalization and Third World Trade Unions: the challenge of rapid economic change*, Zed Books, London.

R. Thomas (1997), 'The Coke driver and the Ruby Tuesday Bribe', *Guardian*, 17 March.

T. Tsuru and J. Rebitzer (1995), 'The Limits of Enterprise unionism: Prospects for continuing union decline in Japan', *British Journal of Industrial Relations*, 33(3).

Lowell Turner (1991), *Democracy at Work: changing world markets and the future of labour unions*, Cornell University Press, Ithaca, New York.

S. Webb and B. Webb (1894), *The History of Trade Unionism*, Longman Green, London.

References to Chapter 5

R. Adams (1991), 'North American Industrial Relations: divergent Trends in Canada and the USA', *International Labour Review*.

K. Ahlen (1989), 'Swedish Collective Bargaining Under Pressure: Inter-Union Rivalry and Incomes Policies', *British Journal of Industrial Relations*, 27(3).

J.-F. Amadieu (1995), 'Industrial Relations: Is France a Special Case?', *British Journal of Industrial Relations*, 33(3).

W. Brown (1993), 'The contraction of collective bargaining in Britain', *British Journal of Industrial Relations*, 31(2).

N. Chalmers (1987), *Industrial Relations in Japan: the peripheral workforce*, Routledge, London.

M. Cully and others (1998), 'The 1998 workplace Industrial Relations Survey: First Findings', Department of Trade and Industry, London.

L. Delsen and T. Van Veen (1992), 'The Swedish Model: Relevant for Other European Countries?' *British Journal of Industrial Relations*, 30(1).

R. Dore (1986), *Flexible Rigidities: Industrial Policy and Structural Adjustment in the Japanese Economy, 1970–80*, Athlone Press, London.

J. Due, J. Steen Madsen, C. Jansen and L. Petersen (1994), *The Survival of the Danish Model*, DJOF Publishing, Copenhagen.

J. Dunlop (1988), 'Have the 1980s changed US Industrial Relations?' *Monthly Labour Review*, 111(5).

P. K. Edwards (1986), *Conflict at Work*, Blackwell, Oxford.

C. L. Erickson and S. Kuruvilla (1998), 'Industrial System Transformation', *Industrial and Labor Relations Review*, 52(1).

D. Gallie (1985), 'Les lois Auroux: The Reform of French Industrial Relations?' in H. Machin and V. Wright (eds), *Economic Policy and Policy Making*, Frances Pinter, London.

J. Goddard (1997), 'Managerial Strategies, Labour and Employment Relations and the State: the Canadian Case and Beyond', *British Journal of Industrial Relations*, 35(2).

K. Hancock and D. Rawson (1993), 'The Metamorphosis of Australian Industrial Relations', *British Journal of Industrial Relations*, 31(4).

A. Hassel (1999), 'The Erosion of the German System of Industrial Relations', *British Journal of Industrial Relations*, 37(3).

S. Jeffreys (1996), 'Down but not out: French Unions after Chirac', *Work, Employment and Society*, 10(3).

D. John (1993), 'Election could deprive Australian Unions of their place in the sun', *Guardian*, 10 March.

H. Katz (1993), 'The Decentralization of Collective Bargaining: A Literature Review and Comparative Analysis', *Industrial and Labor Relations Review*, 47(1).

P. Lawrence and L. Barsoux (1990), *Management in France*, Cassell Educational, London.

R. M. Locke (1994), 'The Demise of the National Union in Italy – lessons for Comparative Industrial Relations theory', *Industrial and Labor Relations Review*, 45(2).

A. McElvoy (1998), 'Unions should recognize that a brighter future awaits them outside New Labor', *Independent*, 12 March.

K. Moody (1997), 'Towards an International Social Movement Unionism', *New Left Review*, 225.

M. Morishima (1991), 'Information Sharing and Collective Bargaining in Japan: Effects on Wage Negotiation', *Industrial and Labor Relations Review*.

G. Muller (1997), 'Institutional Resilience in a Changing World Economy? The Case of the German Banking and Chemical Industries', *British Journal of Industrial Relations*, 35(4).

A. D. Nagelkerke and W. F. de Nijs, (1999), 'Institutional Dynamics in European Industrial Relations', *Labour*, 12(4).

R. Nielsen (1996), *Employers' Prerogatives*, Handel Shojskolens Forlag, Copenhagen.

J. Pontusson and S. Kuruvilla (1992), 'Swedish Wage Earner Funds: An Experiment in Industrial Democracy', *Industrial and Labor Relations Review*, 45(4).

K. Rafferty (1994), 'Japan Locked in Pay Rise Battle', *Guardian*, 14 January.

J. Rees (1993), 'Australia Plans far-reaching Reforms in Industrial Relations', *Far Easter Economic Review*, 15 July.

D. Sadowski, M. Schneider and K. Wagner (1994), 'The Impact of European Integration and German Unification on Industrial Relations in Germany', *British Journal of Industrial Relations*, 32(4).

E. Savoie (1994), 'Rough Terrain for Collective Bargaining', in P. B. Voos (ed.) *Contemporary Collective Bargaining in the Private Sector*, IRRA,

University of Wisconsin, Madison.

S. Scheuer (1997), 'Collective Bargaining coverage under Trade Unionism', *British Journal of Industrial Relations*, 35(1).

K. Sisson (1987), *The Management of Collective Bargaining: An International Comparison*, Blackwell, Oxford.

W. Streeck (1982), in G. Lembruch and P. Schmitter (eds), *Patterns of Corporatist Policy Making*, Sage, London.

N. Tait (1998), 'Union Warms to Win–Win for Chrysler', *Financial Times*, 9 May.

M. Terry (1993), 'Workplace Unions and Workplace Industrial Relations: the Italian Experience', *Industrial Relations Journal*, 24(2).

K. Thelen (1993), *Union of Parts: Labor Politics in Post War Germany*, Cornell University Press, New York.

B. Townley (1987), 'Union Recognition: A Comparative Analysis of the Pros and Cons of a legal procedure', *British Journal of Industrial Relations*, 25(2).

L. Troy (1992), 'Convergence in Industrial Relations and Unionism: Canada and the USA', *British Journal of Industrial Relations*, 30(1).

P. B. Voos (ed.) (1994), *Contemporary Collective Bargaining in the Private Sector*, Industrial Relations Research Association, University of Wisconsin, Madison.

L. Ulman (1974), 'Connective and Competitive Bargaining', *Scottish Journal of Political Economy*, 21(2).

J. Walsh (1997), 'Employment Systems in Transition? A Comparative Analysis of Britain and Australia', *Work, Employment and Society*, 11(1).

References to Chapter 6

D. Ashton and F. Green (1996), *Education, Training and the Global Economy*, Edward Elgar, Cheltenham.

S. Beavis and S. Ryle (1996), 'Rifkind refbuffed by Firms over Social Chapter hypocrisy claim', *Guardian*, 1 February.

S. Brittan (1992), 'Save us all from the credentialist Fad', *Financial Times*, 13 August.

C. Buechtemann and D. Soloff (1994), 'Education, Training and the Economy', *Industrial Relations Journal*, 25(3).

R. Dore and M. Sako (1989), *How the Japanese learn to work*, Routledge, London.

Economist (1994), vol. 332, 24 July.

L. Elliott (1995), 'OECD damms British skills training', *Guardian*, 24 May.

A. Felstead and F. Green (1994), 'Training during the Recession', *Work, Employment and Society*, 8(2).

D. Finegold and K. Wagner (1998), 'The Search for Flexibility: Skills and Workplace Innovation in the German Pump Industry', *British Journal of Industrial Relations*, 36(3).

H. Gospel (1994), 'The Survival of Apprenticeship Training: A British, American and Australian Comparison', *British Journal of Industrial Relations*, 32(4).

C. Handy, C. Gordon, I. Gow and C. Randlesome (1988), *Making Managers*, Pitman, London.

S. Head (1996), 'The New Ruthless Economy', *New York Review of Books*, 29 February.

J. Heyes and M. Stuart (1998), 'Bargaining for Skills: Trade Unions and Training at the Workplace', *British Journal of Industrial Relations*, 36(3).

J. Hyman (1992), *Training at Work*. Routledge, London.

H. James (1985), 'The Disillusioned Apprentices', *The Times*, 13 December.

P. James (1996), 'Employee Development Programs: the US Auto Approach', *Personnel Review*, 25(2).

J. Jeong (1995), 'The Failure of Recent State Vocational Training Policies in Korea – from a comparative perspective', *British Journal of Industrial Relations*, 33(2).

B. Jones (1997), book review in *British Journal of Industrial Relations*, 35(3).

D. King (1997), 'Employers, Training Policy and the tenacity of Voluntarism in Britain', *Twentieth Century British History*, 8(3).

K. Koike (1994), 'Intellectual Skills and Long-Term Competition' in K. Imai and R. Komiya (eds) *Business Enterprise in Japan*, MIT Press, Cambridge, Mass.

C. Lane (1987), 'Capitalism or Culture? A Comparative Analysis of the Position in the Labour Market of Lower White Collar Workers in the Financial Services Sector of Britain and Germany', *Work, Employment and Society*, 1(1).

C. Lane (1990), 'Vocational Training, Employment Relations and New Production Concepts in Germany: Some Lessons for Britain', *Industrial Relations Journal*, 21(4).

B. Mahnkopf (1992), 'The Skill-oriented Strategies of German Trade Unions', *British Journal of Industrial Relations*, 30(1).

B. Maurice, J. Silvestre and F. Sellier (1986), *The Social Foundations of Industrial Power*, MIT Press, Cambridge, Mass.

McKinsey, Global Institute (1993), *Manufacturing Productivity*, McKinsey and Company, New York.

C. Noble (1997), 'International Comparisons of Training Policies', *Human Resource Management Journal*, 8(1).

S. Prais and K. Wagner (1988), 'Productivity and Management: the Training of Foremen in Britain and Germany', *National Institute Economic Review*, 123.

J. O'Reilly (1992), 'Where do you Draw the Line?' *Work, Employment and Society*, 6(3).

H. Rainbird (1995), 'The Changing Role of the Training Function', *Human Resource Management Journal*, 5 (1).

S. Ryle (1997), 'Skills Shortage Stifling Growth', *Guardian*, 27 January.

J. R. Shackleton (1992), *A Sceptical Look at the Economics of Skill Provision in the UK*, Institute of Economic Affairs, London.

D. Soskice (1994), 'Social Skills from Mass Education: Rethinking the

Company-based Initial Training Paradigm', *Oxford Review of Economic Policy*, 9.

H. Steedman (1993), 'Do Workforce Skills Matter?' *British Journal of Industrial Relations*, 31(2).

J. Storey and K. Sisson (1993), *Managing Human Resources and Industrial Relations*, Open University Press, Milton Keynes.

P. Thompson, T. Wallace, J. Flecker and R. Ahlstrand (1995), 'It ain't what you do, it's the way that you do it: production organization and skill utilization in commercial vehicles', *Work, Employment and Society*, 9(4).

D. Turnham (1996), book review of G. Rodgers, *Workers, Institutions and Economic Growth, Industrial and Labour Relations Review*, 49.

R. Walton (1985), 'From Control to Commitment in the Workplace', *Harvard Business Review*, March–April.

References to Chapter 7

A. Aldridge (1976), *Power, Authority and Restrictive Practices: A sociological essay on industrial relations*, Blackwell, Oxford.

Anon. (1992), 'Recent cases in labour law', *International Labour Review*, 131(2).

N. Bacon, P. Blyton and J. Morris (1996), 'Among the Ashes: Trade union strategies in the UK and German steel industries', *British Journal of Industrial Relations*, 34(1): 25–50.

M. Chandler (1964), *Management Rights and Union Interests*, McGraw-Hill, New York.

J. Clark (1993), 'Procedures and consistency versus flexibility and commitment in employee relations: A comment', *Human Resource Management Journal*, 4(1), 79.

R. H. Coase (1937), 'The Nature of the Firm', *Economica*, 10, 386–405.

L. Elliott (1996), 'Putting Trade in its place', *Guardian*, 28 May.

D. Fröhlich and U. Pekruhl (1996), *Direct Participation and Organizational Change: fashionable but misunderstood?*, European Foundation for the Improvement of Living and Working Conditions, Luxembourg

S. Head (1996), 'The New, Ruthless Economy', *New York Review of Books*, 29 February.

D. Ioannides and K. Debbage (1997), 'Post-Fordism and Flexibility: the Travel industry polyglot', *Tourism Management*, 18(4), 229–41.

T. Juravich (1985), *Chaos on the Shop Floor: A worker's view of quality, productivity and management*, Temple University Press, Philadelphia.

D. Marsden (1978), *Industrial Democracy and industrial Control in West Germany, France and Great Britain*, Research Paper 4, Department of Employment.

R. Nielsen (1996), *Employers' Prerogatives*, Handel Shojskolens Forlag, Copenhagen.

T. Ohta (1988), 'Works Rules in Japan', *International Labour Review*, 127(5).

A. H. Raskin (1986), 'Elysium Lost: the Wagner Act at Fifty', *Stanford Law Review*, 38(4).

R. Rideout (1998), 'Fairness at Work?' *Federation News*, 48(2).

M. Rosen and J. Baroudi (1992), 'Computer-based Technology and the Emergence of New Forms of Managerial Control' in A. Sturdy, D. Knights and H. Willmott, *Skill and Consent*, Routledge, London.

P. Selznick (1969, second edition 1980), *Law, Society and Industrial Justice*, Russell Sage Foundation, New York.

W. Streeck (1987) 'The Uncertainties of management and the management of uncertainty', *Work, Employment and Society*, 1(3).

M. Terry (1977), 'The Inevitable Growth of Informality', *British Journal of Industrial Relations*, 15.

K. W. (Lord) Wedderburn (1987), 'Labour Law: From Here to Autonomy?' *Industrial Law Journal*, 16.

B. Wootton (1920), 'Classical Principles and Modern Views of Labour', *Economic Journal*, 30.

References to Chapter 8

Anon (1992), 'Judicial Decisions in the Field of Labour Law: Dismissal for Refusing to Work Overtime', *International Labour Review*, 131(3).

M. E. Banderet (1986), 'Discipline at the Workplace', *International Labour Review*, 125(3).

W. Brown and D. Rea (1995), 'The Changing Nature of the Employment Contract', *Scottish Journal of Political Economy*.

C. F. Buechtemann (ed.) (1993), 'Employment Security and Labour Market Behaviour: Inter-disciplinary Approaches and International Evidence', *Cornell International Industrial and Labour Relations Report*, 23. ILR Press, Ithaca, New York.

B. Connell (1991), 'The Worker and Corporate Discipline: the Telecom Australia Experience', *International Labour Review*, 130(5).

D. Demekas (1995), 'Labour Market Institutions and Flexibility in Italy', *Labour*, 9(1).

L. Dickens et al. (1985), *Dismissed – A Study of Unfair Dismissal*, Blackwell, Oxford.

V. Di Martino and L. Wirth (1990), 'Telework: A Way of Working and Living', *International Labour Review*, 129(5).

L. Dolding (1994), 'Unfair Dismissal and Industrial Action', *Industrial Law Journal*, 23(3).

S. T. Hardy, N. Adnett and R. Painter, (1998). *TUPE and CCT Business Transfers: UK Labour Market Views*, Staffordshire University Press, Stoke-on-Trent.

B. Hepple (1986), 'Restructuring Employment Rights', *Industrial Law Journal*, 15.

B. Hepple (1992), 'Labour law and the New Labour force', in A. Gladstone et al. (eds), *Labour Relations in a Changing Environment*, W. de Gruyter, Berlin/New York.

S. Kuruvilla (1996), 'Linkages between Industrialization Strategies and Industrial Relations: Singapore, Malaysia, the Philippines and India', *Industrial and Labor Relations Review*, 49(4).

P. Leighton (1984), 'Observing Employment Contracts', *Industrial Law Journal*, 13.

R. L. Mathis and J. H. Jackson (1991), *Personnel/Human Resource Management* (6th edn), West Publishing, New York.

R. Milliken (1998), 'Legal Victory for Sacked Dockers', *Independent*, 5 May.

M. Morishima (1995), 'Embedding HRM in a Social Context', *British Journal of Industrial Relations*, 33(4).

T. Ohta (1988), 'Works Rules in Japan', *International Labour Review*, 127(5).

R. Rideout (1966), 'The Contract of Employment', *Current Legal Problems*, 19.

R. Rideout (1998), 'Fairness at Work', *Federation News*, 48(2).

R. Rogowski (1996), 'Individual Employment Rights in the European Union', *Industrial Law Journal*, 25(2).

K. W. (Lord) Wedderburn (1987), 'Labour Law: From Here to Autonomy?' *Industrial Law Journal*, 16.

D. Winkler-Buttner (1997), 'Differing Degrees of Labour Market Regulation in Europe', *Intereconomics*, 32.

References to Chapter 9

W. P. Anthony, P. L. Perrewe and K. M. Kacmar (1996), *Strategic Human Resource Management*, Dryden Press, Orlando, Florida.

C. Barnard, J. Clark and R. Lewis (1995), *The Exercise of Individual Employment Rights in the European Community*, Employment Department, Sheffield.

E. Batstone (1985), 'International Variations in Strike Activity', *European Sociological Review*, 1(1).

L. Betten (1995), *The Right to Strike in Community Law*, North-Holland, Amsterdam and New York.

D. Bird (1990), 'International Comparisons of Industrial Disputes in 1988 and 1989', *Employment Gazette*, December.

R. Blanpain and C. Engels (eds) (1993), *Comparative Labour Law and Industrial Relations in Industrialized Market Economies*, Kluwer, Deventer.

W. Brown and S. Wadhwani (1990), 'The Economic Effects of Industrial Relations Legislation since 1979', *National Institute Economic Review*, February.

K. Ewing (1998), 'Trade Unions and their "human rights" in Britain', *Federation News*, 48(1).

R. Franzosi (1989), 'One Hundred Years of Strike Statistics: Methodological and Theoretical Issues in Quantitative Strike Research', *Industrial and Labor Relations Review*, 42(3).

A. Gladstone (1993), 'The Settlement of Disputes over Rights' in R. Blanpain and C. Engels (eds), *Comparative Labour Law and Industrial Relations in*

Industrialized Market Economies, Kluwer Law International, The Hague, London, Boston.

J. Goetschy and P. Rozenblatt (1992), 'France: the Industrial Relations System at a Turning Point? in A. Ferner and R. Hyman (eds), *Industrial Relations in the New Europe*, Blackwell, Oxford.

T. J. M. Jacobs (1993), 'The Law of Strikes and Lock-outs' in R. Blanpain and C. Engels (eds), *Comparative Labour Law and Industrial Relations in Industrialized Market Economies*, Kluwer, Deventer.

A. Kjellberg (1998), 'Sweden: Restoring the Model?' in A. Ferner and R. Hyman (eds), *Changing Industrial Relations in Europe*, Blackwell, Oxford.

N. Kritsantonis (1998), 'Greece: The Maturing of the System' in A. Ferner and R. Hyman (eds), *Changing Industrial Relations in Europe*, Blackwell, Oxford.

R. Nielsen (1996), *Employers' Prerogatives*, Handel Shojskolens Forlag, Copenhagen.

T. Ohta (1988), 'Work Rules in Japan', *International Labour Review*, 127(5).

S. O'Keefe (1998), 'Industrial Action Ballots in Ireland: Nolan Transport v. Halligan and others', *Industrial Law Journal*, 27(4).

E. A. Ramaswamy and U. Ramaswamy (1981), *Industry and Labour*, Oxford University Press, Bombay and Calcutta.

P. Selznick (1969), *Law, Society and Industrial Justice*, Russell Sage Foundation, New York.

M. Shalev (1978), 'Lies, Dammed Lies and Strike Statistics: the Measurement of Trends in Industrial Conflict' in C. Crouch and A. Pizzarno (eds), *The Resurgence of Industrial Conflict since 1968*, Volume I, Macmillan, London.

M. Shalev (1980), 'Industrial Relations Theory and the Comparative Study of Industrial Relations and Industrial Conflict', *British Journal of Industrial Relations*, 18.

A. Simpson and C. Hines (1996), 'Banking on Failure?' *Guardian*, 13 May.

K. Sweeney and J. Davies (1997), 'International Comparisons of Labour Disputes in 1995', *Labour Market Trends*, April.

N. Tait (1993), 'Workers from the New World uptight', *Guardian*, 28 January.

M. Wasik and R. D. Taylor (1995), *Blackstone's Guide to the Criminal Justice and Public Order Act of 1994*, Blackstone, London.

References to Chapter 10

D. Campbell (ed.) (1992), *Is the Single Firm Vanishing?* ILO, Geneva.

P. J. Dowling and R. S. Schuler (1990), *International Dimensions of Human Resource Management*, PWS Publishing, Boston.

J. Eaton (1997), 'They Saw Us Coming', *The Professional Investor*, October.

P. K. Edwards (1998), *Multinational Companies and the Diffusion of Employment Practices*, Warwick University Papers in Industrial Relations, No. 61.

P. Evans (1980), 'The Context of Strategic Human Resource Management in

Complex Firms', *Management Forum*, 6.

A. Ferner (1994), 'Multinational Companies and Human Resource Management: An Overview of Research Issues', *Human Resource Management Journal*, 4(2).

A. Ferner (1996), book review, *Industrial and Labor Relations Review*, 50.

A. Ferner (1997), 'Country of Origin Effects and Human Resource Management in Multinational Companies', *Human Resource Management Journal*, 7(1).

M. Harrison (1998), 'Rolls threat to move work to US,' *Independent*, 25 November.

R. Higgott (1997), 'Taking the Global View', *Warwick Network*, Spring 1997.

P. Hirst and G. Thompson (1995), 'Globalization and the Future of the Nation State', *Economy and Society*, 24(3).

K. Hutchings (1996), 'Workplace Practices of Japanese and Australian Multinational Corporations Operating in Singapore, Malaysia and Indonesia', *Human Resource Management Journal*, 6(2).

D. Ioannides and K. Debbage (1997), 'Post-Fordism and Flexibility: the travel industry polyglot', *Tourism Management*, 18(4).

K. Legge (1995), *Human Resource Management: Rhetorics and Realities*, Macmillan Business, Basingstoke.

A. Mair (1994), *Honda's Global–Local Corporation*, St Martin's Press, New York.

D. Miles (1997), 'Globalization: the facts behind the myth', *Independent*, 22 December.

S. Milne and N. Bannister (1996), 'Union busting reputation a fear', *Guardian*, 6 November.

M. Milner (1997), 'The Shock of the New', *Guardian*, 23 September.

R. Pascale (1990), *Managing on the Edge*, Penguin Business Management, London.

H. V. Perlmutter (1992), 'The Transnational Corporation without boundaries', chapter two in D. Campbell (ed.), *Is the Single Firm Vanishing?* ILO, Geneva.

A. Price (1997), *Human Resource Management in a Business Context*, International Thomson, London.

H. Simonian (1998), 'Wheels in Motion', *Financial Times*, 9 May.

N. Tait (1998), 'Union warms to win–win for Chrysler', *Financial Times*, 9 May.

J. Warner (1998), 'Clash of views on global economy kicks off', *Independent*, 30 January.

A. Zeira and O. Shenkar (1990), 'Interactive and Specific parent characteristics: Implications for Management and Human Resources in International Joint Ventures', *Management International Review*, 30.

References to Chapter 11

J. T. Addison and S. Siebert (1994), 'Recent Developments in Social Policy in the New European Union', *Industrial and Labor Relations Review*, 48(1).

E. Balls (1995), 'Tread softly to stamp out child labour'. *Guardian*, 11 September.

A. Bellos (1996), 'Stores now back low pay fight?', *Guardian*, 28 October.

G. Chandler (1996), 'People and Profits', *Guardian*, 18 November.

W. Dawson (1999), 'Employees win 48-hour battle', *Independent*, 11 March.

S. Deakin and F. Wilkinson (1994), 'Rights v. Efficiency? The Economic Case for Transnational Standards', *Industrial Law Journal*, 23(4).

C. L. Erickson and S. Kuruvilla (1994), 'Labour Costs and the Social Dumping Debate in the European Union', *Industrial and Labor Relations Review*, 48(1).

G. Fields (1996), book review, *Industrial and Labor Relations Review*, 49.

R. Nielsen and E. Szyszczak (1996), *The Social Dimension of the European Community*, Handelshojskolens Forlag, Copenhagen.

J.-M. Servais (1989), 'The Social Clause in Trade: Wishful thinking or an instrument of social progress?' *International Labour Review*, 128(4).

R. Thomas (1996), 'Messy issues remain for new global solidarity', *Guardian*, 1 July.

S. Silvia (1991), 'The Social Charter of the European Community: A Defeat for European Labour', *Industrial and Labor Relations Review*, 44.

F. Williams (1994). 'US waves flag for workers' rights in WTO', *Financial Times*, 30 March.

D. Wyatt (1989), 'Enforcing EEC social rights in the UK', *Industrial Law Journal*, 18.

References to Chapter 12

N. Bacon, P. Blyton and J. Morris (1996), 'Among the Ashes: Trade Union Strategies in the UK and German Steel Industries', *British Journal of Industrial Relations*, 34(1).

A. Bar-Haim (1988), 'Workers' Participation in Israel', *International Labour Review*, 127(3).

H. Barkai (1977), 'Growth Patterns in the Kibbutz Economy', North Holland, Amsterdam.

B. Clement (1998), 'Plot to kill off extension to union rights', *Independent*, 17 March.

P. Cressey (1998), 'European Works Councils in practice', *Human Resource Management Journal*, 8(1).

I. Cunningham, J. Hyman and C. Baldry (1996), 'Employment: the power to do what?' *Industrial Relations Journal*, 27(3).

A. Danford (1998), 'Teamworking and Labour Regulation in the Auto components industry', *Work, Employment and Society*, 12(3).

Y. Delamotte (1988), 'Workers' Participation and Personnel Policies in France', *International Labour Review*, 127(2).

R. Donkin (1995), 'Happy Workers can Generate High Profits', *Financial Times*, 8 February.

C. Dorrenbacher and M. Wortmann (1994), 'Multinational Companies in the EU and European Works Councils', *Inter Economics*, 29.

A. Eaton and P. Voos (1992), 'Unions and Contemporary Innovations in Work Organization, Compensation and Employee Participation', in L. Mishel and P. Voos (eds), *Unions and Economic Competitiveness*, M. E. Sharpe, Armonk, New York.

P. K. Edwards (1987), *Managing the Factory*, Blackwell, Oxford.

S. Fernie and D. Metcalfe (1995), 'Works Councils are the Future but there is no need to be afraid', *Guardian*, 14 June.

D. Fröhlich and U. Pekruhl (1996), *Direct Participation and Organizational Change – Fashionable but misunderstood?* European Foundation for Improvement of Living and Working Conditions, Dublin.

D. Goodhart (1994), 'EEF prices works councils at £1 million', *Financial Times*, 28 April.

M. Gunderson (1995), 'Employee Buy-outs in Canada', *British Journal of Industrial Relations*, 33(3).

W. Hutton (1995), 'Call for World Works Councils to Counter Footloose Capitalism', *Guardian*, 2 February.

B. K. Keller (1995), 'Emerging Models of Worker Participation and Representation', *British Journal of Industrial Relations*, 33(3).

A. Kjellberg (1992), 'Sweden: Can the Model Survive?' (in A. Ferner and R. Hyman (eds), *Industrial Relations in the New Europe*, Blackwell, Oxford.

A. Kjellberg (1998), 'Sweden: Restoring the Model?' in A. Ferner and R. Hyman (eds), *Changing Industrial Relations in Europe*, Blackwell, Oxford.

H. Knudsen (1995), *Employee Participation in Europe*, Sage, London.

C. Lane (1989), *Management and Labour in Europe*, Edward Elgar, Cheltenham.

P. Lawrence and L. Barsoux (1990), *Management in France*, Cassell Educational, London.

C. McGlynn (1995), 'European Works Councils: Towards Industrial Democracy?' *Industrial Law Journal*, 24(1).

M. Morishima (1992), 'The Use of Joint Consultation by Japanese Firms', *British Journal of Industrial Relations*, 30(3).

G. Muller (1997), 'Institutional Resilience in a Changing World Economy? The Case of the German Banking and Chemical Industries', *British Journal of Industrial Relations*, 35(4).

T. Murakami (1997), 'The Autonomy of Teams in the Car Industry – A Cross-National Comparison', *Work, Employment and Society*, 11(4).

N. Parsons (1997), *Employee Participation in Europe*, Avebury, Aldershot.

R. Rogowski (1996), 'Individual Employment Rights in the European Union', *Industrial Law Journal*, 25(2).

J. Van Ruysseveldt, R. Huiskamp and J. Van Hoof (eds) (1995), *Comparative Industrial Relations*, Sage, London.

W. Streeck (1987), 'The Uncertainties of Management and the Management of Uncertainty: Employers, Labour Relations and Industrial Adjustment', *Work, Employment and Society*, 1(3).

N. Tait (1998), 'Union Warms to Win–Win for Chrysler', *Financial Times*, 9 May.

R. Taylor (1996), 'British Staff excluded from Works Council', *Financial Times*, 30 July.

L. Turner (1997), 'Participation, Democracy and Efficiency in the US Workplace', *Industrial Relations Journal*, 28(4).

J. Willcock and J. Eisenammer, (1994), 'Two-tier boards not the best way for investment banking', *The Times*, 30 October.

References for Chapter 13

Z. Bauman (1998), *Globalization: The Human Consequences*, Polity Press, Cambridge.

R. Bean (1994), *Comparative Industrial Relations*, Routledge, London.

P. Boxall (1996), 'Building the Theory of Comparative HRM', *Human Resource Management Journal*, 5(5).

C. Brewster (1997), 'The Business of Europe: convergence?', *Work, Employment and Society*, 10(3).

D. Campbell (1992), *Is the Single Firm Vanishing?* ILO, Geneva.

D. Coyle (1999), 'US employees top league in working hours', *Independent*, 6 September.

K. Ewing (1998), 'Trade Unions and their Human Rights in Britain', *Federation News*, 48(1).

J. Hatfield (1998), 'Multinationals', *Chartered Accountant Magazine*.

S. Head (1996), 'The New Ruthless Economy', *New York Review of Books*, 29 February.

P. Kane (1998), 'The Dark Side of the Global Dream', *Independent*, 12 August.

C. Kerr, J. Dunlop, F. Harbison and C. Meyers (1960), *Industrialism and Industrial Man*, Harvard University Press, Boston.

K. Legge (1995), *Human Resource Management: Rhetorics and Realities*, Macmillan Business, Basingstoke.

J. Lichfield (1999), 'France now Europe's tiger economy', *Independent*, 3 September.

L. Paterson (1998), 'Brown Calls for a Global Regulator', *Independent*, 1 October.

P. Pattullo (1998), 'Bitter Fruit', *Guardian*, 6 June.

H. V. Perlmutter (1992), 'The Transnational Corporation without Boundaries', Chapter Two in D. Campbell (ed.), *Is the Single Firm Vanishing?* ILO, Geneva.

J. Pilger (1998), 'Labour Renege on Open Government', *Independent*, 28 September.

S. Roach (1998), 'In Search of Productivity', *Harvard Business Review*, 76, September.

P. Scott (1997), 'What Next? Labour into Europe', *Work, Employment and Society*, 11(3).

S. Silvia (1991), 'The Social Charter: A Defeat for European Labour', *Industrial and Labor Relations Review*, 44(4).

H. Sjogren (1998), book review, *Business History*, 40(2).

R. Whittington (1993), *What is Strategy and does it matter?*, Routledge, London.

Index

Advisory Conciliation and
    Arbitration Service (ACAS),
    115, 117–19
Allied Industrial Workers' Union
    (USA), 136
Amalgamated Engineering and
    Electrical Union (AEEU) (UK),
    52, 60, 75, 83–4, 115–17, 121–2,
    126, 135
American Airlines, 151
arbitration, 119, 133, 135, 207
    compulsory arbitration, 5, 75,
    126, 135
Asea Brown Boveri, 153, 162
Australia, 12, 52, 75, 83–4, 115–17,
    121–2, 126, 135
Austria, 90, 115, 116, 119, 139
automation, 10

ballots (pre-strike), 137
BMW, 155, 157
Bridgestone/Firestone, 73
Britain, 4, 138
British Airways (BA), 144, 151, 154,
    194
British Steel, 27, 186, 195
British Telecom (BT), 145–7

CAMI (GM-Suzuki), 40, 44, 155

Canada, 12, 40, 70–4, 117–19, 131,
    134, 136, 139, 192, 207
Caterpillar, 157
China, 10, 13, 103, 158, 167
Chrysler, 156
Coca-Cola, 155
co-determination, 22, 54, 97, 104,
    116, 191, 194
collective bargaining, 4–6, 15–16,
    19, 21–2, 47, 49, 62–79, 100, 102,
    114, 120, 124–41, 155, 174, 178,
    189, 195–6, 204–5
    Denmark, 129
    Germany, 53, 67–9
    Japan, 27, 98–9, 116, 127
    UK, 76–7, 122
    USA, 70–4, 97–8, 100, 117–20,
    127–9, 156
Communication Workers of
    America (CWA), 146
Communications Workers Union
    (CWU) (UK), 146
conciliation, 119–20, 135
Confédération Générale de Travail
    (CGT), 106, 111
contract of employment, 108–11,
    116–17, 122, 131, 180, 199
convergence, 35, 42, 60, 72, 90, 198,
    202–5

corporatism, 5, 64, 68, 85
culture
    national, 8, 18, 25, 26, 87, 198
    organizational and corporate, 39,
        44, 87, 106

Daimler-Benz/Chrysler merger,
    156–7, 162, 193
Deming, W. Edwards, 42
Denmark, 12, 48, 50, 126, 129, 134,
    139, 180, 189
DGB (Deutscher
    Gewerkschaftsbund – German
    union federation), 54, 67
discrimination, 100, 112
    racial discrimination, 43, 100
    sex discrimination, 29, 100, 108,
        167, 173–4
Disney Corporation, 166
disputes of interest, 119, 134
disputes of right, 119, 134
down-sizing, 10

Employee Development
    Programmes (EDPs), 89
employment law, 105, 108–41
    France, 66, 100, 102, 110, 115–21
    Italy, 70, 100
    Japan, 98–9, 112–14
    Spain, 100, 112
    UK, 58, 76, 114
    USA, 127–9
European Union (EU), 13, 60, 65,
    76, 121, 129, 130, 137, 151, 159,
    165, 173, 194–6, 205
European Union social dimension,
    21, 60, 65, 106, 112, 130, 158,
    161, 164, 173–80

FIAT, 69–70
flexibility
    functional, 86, 91, 106
    numerical, 13, 18, 121, 199
flexible specialization, 7, 8
Ford (company), 25, 63, 72, 89, 145,
    153–4, 185

Fordism, 8, 151, 184
France, 12, 66–7, 84, 117, 133, 139,
    152, 159–61, 183, 190–1, 193,
    201
free trade, 13, 72, 149, 164
Fujitsu, 36, 154–5

General Motors (GM), 72, 78, 89,
    150, 153, 155, 185, 206
Germany, 10, 12, 14–15, 18, 50, 115,
    119, 121, 126, 131–2, 139, 180
globalization, 1, 6, 16, 19, 26, 45, 49,
    59–60, 94–5, 130, 142–63, 166,
    205
Greece, 48, 126, 135, 137, 141, 179

health and safety, 41–2, 100–1, 177,
    189, 207
Hitachi, 36, 113
homeworkers, 110
Honda, 9, 36, 88, 145, 156–7, 195
Hoover, 158
Human Resource Management
    (HRM), 6, 11, 16–18, 21–5, 35,
    38, 55, 77, 82, 87, 89–90, 101–2,
    104, 107–8, 121–2, 143–4, 147–9,
    162, 182, 186, 192–3, 197, 202–5
    in Japan, 30, 32, 43
    and unions, 163, 182
Hyundai, 58

ICL, 36
I G Metall (German trade union),
    51, 131
India, 2, 41, 109, 115–16, 137
industrial conflict *see* strikes
information, 3, 16, 21, 27, 43, 76, 111
International Confederation of Free
    Trade Unions (ICFTU), 166,
    168
International Covenant on
    Economic, Social and Cultural
    Rights (ICESCR), 130
International Federation of
    Chemical, Energy and General
    Workers' Unions (ICEF), 60

International Labour Organization (ILO), 50, 112, 129–30, 165, 168
International Trade Secretariats, 60
Internet, 153–4
Ireland, 121, 137, 202
Israel, 49, 191
Italy, 29, 50, 69–70

Japan, 7–9, 12, 19, 23–33, 38, 43, 74, 87, 95, 98–9, 112–15, 117, 126–7, 142, 144, 193, 198–9, 203
Japanese companies, 24, 29, 35
Japanese human resource management model, 184, 197–9
japanization, 24, 29, 35
job evaluation, 66, 91
JVC (company), 159–61

kaizen, 10, 25, 37, 39, 40–1, 157, 184
kanban, 8, 25, 42
Korea, 13, 18, 43, 58, 85, 93, 98, 103, 160, 167, 198

Labour Charter (in Versailles Peace Treaty, 1918), 95–7, 165
labour courts, 109, 112, 119–20, 134–5
labour standards, 29, 95–6
labour law *see* employment law
Labour Standards Act 1947 (Japan), 99, 114–15
LO (central union federation in Sweden), 64

Malaysia, 41, 109, 160, 198
managerial prerogatives, 97–8, 102, 108, 117, 125–6
minimum standards (labour), 11, 21, 95–7, 162, 164–80, 205, 207
minimum wages, 16, 111
Mitsubishi, 31, 44, 157
multinational companies, 21, 60, 142–63, 165, 193, 204, 206–7
see also transnational companies

NAFTA (North America Free Trade Agreement), 72
National Labor Relations Board (USA), 55, 73, 127–9
National Labour Court (Sweden), 64
Netherlands, 131–2, 139, 141, 150
New Zealand, 6, 141
Nike, 167–8, 171
Nissan, 9, 27, 37, 88, 156, 185
NUMMI (joint GM-Toyota plant), 39, 155

organization theory, 7
overtime, 113

participation, 6, 11, 22, 28, 35, 37, 41, 67, 99, 102–6, 174, 181–96, 206
part-time work, 110–12, 176
pay policy, 65
performance management, 30
performance related pay, 32, 189, 200
Prison Officers Association, 136
procedures, 4, 100–2, 110, 118–20, 141, 174
public sector, 55–8, 72, 76, 136–7, 139, 200

quality, 7, 38–9, 41, 47, 106, 150, 182, 192
and training, 85

Rail, Maritime and Transport Union (RMT) (UK), 162
Renault, 155, 185
Rover, 36, 145, 155, 185
rules, 3–4, 16, 94–107, 113–14, 116, 120, 125

Sainsbury's, 136
Scotland, 158, 161, 171
Sharp, 39
Shell, 171
Siemens, 155

Singapore, 41, 93
Social Charter (EU) *see* European
  Union social dimension
social dumping, 158, 164, 169, 180
South Africa, 6
Spain, 50, 111, 121, 134, 152, 179,
  188, 201
Staley (subsidiary of Tate & Lyle),
  136, 158
strikes, 57, 72–3, 78, 103, 105,
  114–15, 120, 124–41, 150, 157,
  161
Subaru-Isuzu Automotive (SIA),
  36, 41
sub-contracting, 13, 29, 62, 95,
  104–7, 110, 112, 121–2, 151, 158,
  168, 171, 199–200

Taft-Hartley Act (USA), 127, 133
Taiwan, 167
technology, 3–5, 7, 13, 37, 54, 60, 64,
  70, 81, 84, 86, 104, 111, 202, 207
Teamsters Union, 136
teamworking, 32, 36–7, 39, 88, 90–1,
  145, 182, 184–7, 192, 198
teleworkers, 110–11
Total Quality Management, 37, 182,
  186, 196
Toyota, 10, 35–6, 43, 145, 156, 185
trade unions, 3–4, 6, 10, 14, 17, 19,
  37, 45–61, 78, 94, 105, 111, 116,
  125, 132, 135, 137–8, 146, 158,
  162, 166, 170, 174, 181, 204
  Australia, 52–3, 74, 121–2
  Canada, 40, 48, 70–4
  Denmark, 48, 57, 126, 189
  France, 48, 50, 53, 57, 66–7, 130,
  160
  Germany, 50–1, 53–4, 67, 86, 126,
  156, 189
  Israel, 48–52, 57
  Italy, 50, 69, 126

Japan, 27–8, 32, 51–2, 60, 74,
  113–14
Netherlands, 48
Sweden, 54, 57, 126, 132
UK, 60, 76, 146, 186
USA, 39, 44, 47–8, 52, 54–6, 60,
  70–4, 89, 104, 128, 137, 156,
  182, 192
transnational companies, 2, 60, 93,
  142–63, 193–6, 204
  see also multinational companies

UK, 8, 76–7, 80–3, 92, 115, 118, 150,
  201–2
unemployment, 2, 15–16, 97, 111
United Auto Workers (Canada), 72
United Auto Workers (USA), 11,
  62–3, 72, 74, 137, 155–6, 162,
  193
United Paperworkers International
  Union (USA), 158
USA, 6, 8, 10–12, 25, 35–6, 70–4,
  117–20, 133, 139, 144, 153, 169,
  192, 198, 199–201

Volkswagen, 154, 202
Volvo, 91, 155

Wagner Act (USA), 127
Wales, 103, 159
Working Time Directive (European
  Union), 177–8
works councils, 105, 120
  European Union works councils,
  162, 178, 194–6, 206
  Germany, 47, 53–4, 60, 67–9, 104,
  116, 184, 187–9, 196
  Italy, 70
World Development Report
  (WDR), 2
World Trade Organization, 165–6,
  169